THE
JAMES SPRUNT STUDIES
IN HISTORY
AND POLITICAL SCIENCE

*Published under the Direction of
the Departments of History and Political Science
of The University of North Carolina at Chapel Hill*

VOLUME 51

———————— * ————————

Editors

HUGH TALMAGE LEFLER, CHAIRMAN
FEDERICO G. GIL
J. CARLYLE SITTERSON
KEENER C. FRAZER
GEORGE V. TAYLOR

6

PLACE, PROFIT, AND POWER

*A Study of the Servants of William Cecil,
Elizabethan Statesman*

By
Richard C. Barnett

CHAPEL HILL

*

THE UNIVERSITY OF NORTH CAROLINA PRESS

1969

Copyright © 1969 by
The University of North Carolina Press
All rights reserved
Library of Congress Catalog Card Number: 77-97023

Printed by the Seeman Printery, Durham, N.C.

PREFACE

Modern English government has evolved from the personal household of English kings. By the sixteenth century certain functions of government had become institutionalized, had emerged from the king's household, and were performed by elaborately organized departments of state serviced by an entrenched staff. Nonetheless, the bulk of government work, limited as it was, continued to be done in less formal ways by persons who, before the Reformation, came to their jobs by way of training and prior service in ecclesiastical households. After the reformation, when churchmen were out of fashion in Tudor government, the route to preferment lay through apprenticeship in the households of lay officials.

This is not to say that while employed in lay establishments they were in private employment. For the men who maintained large households were conspicuous precisely because they were themselves the leading executives in the slender Tudor bureaucracy. Since the Tudor state still regarded government as the responsibility of the monarch, resources were limited and the chief officers of the land received only nominal salaries for themselves and none at all for supporting personnel who were entirely the responsibility of the officer who employed them. So persons identified with the service of a Tudor office holder were in all likelihood busy about the Queen's business, encouraged to diligence by the hope of profit and eventual promotion into the diminutive royal service itself, with its correspondingly greater opportunities for reward.

William Cecil was the greatest of these Elizabethan statesmen and his household the best employment opportunity. By examining the personnel in detail, many problems and relationships of Tudor government are placed in sharper perspective. And by following the careers of Cecil's servants a better estimate emerges of the significance of the man himself as servant to the state. For Cecil's position depended upon information about the state which these servants, acting as his arms, ears and agents, supplied him. Thus the household in being and the scattered household functioned as parts of the apparatus which sustained Cecil at the right hand of the Queen for forty years.

TABLE OF CONTENTS

	Page
Preface	v
Summary of Findings	3
Sir John Abraham	23
Roger Alford	24
Hugh Allington	28
Thomas Bellot	32
George Blyth	40
Edward Browne	42
George Burden	43
William Cayworth	45
Henry and John Cheke	46
John Clapham	47
Robert Constable	49
William Cooke	50
Walter Cope	50
George Coppin	55
Richard Dane	58
Barnard Dewhurst	59
John Durninge	63
Henry Fades	64
John Floyde	65
Barnaby Gooch	65
Gabriel Goodman	68
Thomas Gresham	72
Ralph Grey	73
Arthur Hall	76
John Hart	79
Michael Hickes	80
Thomas Holcroft	87
Roger Houghton	89
Peter Kemp	91
Henry Lacy	94
Henry Maynard	94
Joseph Mayne	103
James Morrice	105
Robert Napper	106
Richard Neile	106
Thomas Ogle	108

John Parlor	109
Boniface Pickering	109
John Purvey	110
Robert Ramsden	112
Sir William Reede	113
Lawrence Robinson, alias Baker	114
Andrew Scarre	115
William Seres	116
Marmaduke Servant	120
Henry Sheffield	122
Richard Shute	123
Vincent Skinner	127
Quentin Sneynton	132
Thomas Speed, alias Lewkenor	135
Richard Spencer	136
John Stileman	138
Morris Thompson	139
Richard Troughton	140
Matthew Twiford	141
William Waad	142
Gilbert Wakering	143
Thomas Windebank	146
Francis Yaxley	154
Appendix	159
Index	173

PLACE, PROFIT, AND POWER

Summary of Findings

William Cecil was born in 1520, the only son of a wealthy Northamptonshire squire who had served Henry VIII as a Yeoman of the Wardrobe. The family fortunes had their origin in the decision of William's Welsh grandfather to follow Henry, Earl of Richmond. The choice was a good one. When Henry Tudor of Richmond became Henry VII of England, he relied more heavily upon such men as Cecil's grandfather than he did upon the great feudal lords, traditional advisers of the crown. To these "new men" went the usual rewards for loyal service.

By the time the third generation appeared, the family possessed wealth and access to the Court. William Cecil was well prepared to profit from any opportunity which might occur. Educated at St. John's College, Cambridge, and Gray's Inn, Cecil had the finest preparation which England could offer. Cambridge was at that time the most exciting intellectual center in the country. Cecil got caught up in the developments at Cambridge and soon found himself a member of the circle that included such men as John Cheke and Roger Ascham. It was the influence of the puritan John Cheke which gave Cecil his religious orientation. Cecil's first wife was John Cheke's sister, Mary.

Cecil's rash marriage to a girl whose family, while ably represented by a distinguished scholar, could not further his career in government service very nearly cost him both the prospects for such a career and his father's friendship. It was probably the only major personal strategic mistake Cecil ever made. He seldom again allowed emotion to dictate a course of action. Mary's early death corrected his error, but a very ordinary son was the reminder of an imprudent love. There were times when the son even appeared to the distraught father as a punishment.

Marriage in 1545 to Mildred Cooke, brilliant daughter of a scholarly father and dedicated puritan, brought Cecil distinguished connections whose value cannot be overestimated. Numbered among Mildred's kin were the Greys, Wottons, Stanhopes, Devereuxs, Shelleys, Copleys, Fitzwilliams, Dannets, Medleys, Copes, Bacons and Spencers. Most of these were courtier families. Two years after his second marriage, Cecil entered the household of Edward Seymour, Duke of Somerset.

By 1548 he had become Somerset's private secretary. Two years later he became Principal Secretary of State, an office he shared with Sir William Petre. At about the same time Cecil became surveyor to Princess Elizabeth. Knighthood followed in 1551, and by 1553, at the age of thirty-three, Cecil had already had a notable career.

Cecil negotiated the political rapids of these years, including the troubled transition to Mary's reign, without serious consequences for himself. During Mary's rule he withdrew from public service except for a term in parliament and for a special mission for the Queen. There was plenty of time to cultivate a deepening relationship with Princess Elizabeth, the heiress-apparent to the throne.

In November, 1558, Mary died and all eyes turned toward the young Princess at Hatfield. When the first courtiers arrived from the bedside of the dead Queen, they found William Cecil at the new Queen's side. Cecil was the first to be sworn a Privy Councillor. To him Elizabeth gave sole responsibility for the office of Secretary of State. His influence on the administration was immediately apparent. It was not to cease until Cecil's death.

Cecil's position was not instantly secured. There were many jealous barons who resented the displacement of the old nobility by Cecil and his ilk. Their disgust with the "Cecilian rule" was sharpened by religious differences which were sometimes coupled with economic discontent. In 1569 such a combination of issues led the princely Percy and Neville families to raise the Catholic north of England in revolt. Its failure in 1570 and the execution of the Duke of Norfolk in 1572 rid Cecil of chronic opposition from the ancient nobles.

The Queen demonstrated her confidence in Cecil as only a sovereign could. In 1571 he was created Baron of Burghley. With the death of the aged Marquess of Winchester, Lord Burghley became in 1572 Lord Treasurer of England. This was one of the great offices of state, ranking after the Archbishop of Canterbury and the Lord Chancellor. Induction into the ancient Order of the Garter preceded his promotion to the Treasurership. In all but name, Burghley had become first minister to the crown. Socially and politically secure, Burghley had been made financially independent by appointment as Master of the Court of Wards in 1561.

It was no little pleasure for Lord Burghley to be able to assure the Queen the same high level of service he himself was accustomed to rendering. He prepared his younger son, Robert, to continue the work he had begun. Yet in Elizabeth's eyes, Burghley himself was irreplaceable. It is said that when both Queen and Councillor were old, the Queen assured Burghley that even though he had brought up his son as much like himself as possible, "yet Burghley was to her in all things, and would be, Alpha and Omega."[1]

Such was the man who from 1558 until his death in 1598 devotedly served Queen Elizabeth I and England. It is amazing to us that the two of them made such a success of things. Everything essential to modern administration was either not present or severely limited in Elizabeth's

[1] John E. Neale, *The Elizabethan House of Commons* (New Haven, 1950), p. 244.

Summary of Findings

England. This study is an attempt to focus on one aspect of the problem of administration, the question of personnel.

The biographical technique has been employed and its results constitute the major portion of this study. By reconstructing the lives of as many of Burghley's associates as can be uncovered, numerous questions begin to have an answer. Their recruitment, employment, reward and subsequent careers, when they emerge, suggest a pattern of government service which bears only crude resemblance to the present. The quest then, as now, was for competence which, when discovered, had its reward and promotion. That this should be so ought not to surprise. Organization and regularity, characteristics of government service today, were lacking. Nor could they exist so long as the Queen's government was essentially personal, and service at least in part was domestic. Thus one spoke of the Queen's servants, or of Lord Burghley's servants, but not of civil servants. The consequence was a "civil service" characterized by all the uncertainties of personal relationships. This was especially true of all those who served in areas outside the medieval departments of state which had a kind of professional bureaucracy.

Just as there was no civil service, so there was no appointed Pentagon in which men worked. Burghley's staff operated largely at Burghley's side. This meant that they frequently found themselves toiling in the great houses Burghley built to reflect his station, wealth and probably his pride. No wonder these members of his household staff sometimes appear inextricably confused with wholly domestic servants. Indeed, upon occasion all members of Burghley's household waited table. It is to these monuments of stone and mortar, the Cecil palaces, that we first turn our attention. These were the workshops most familiar to the men described in succeeding pages.

William Cecil built three houses, each for a very good reason. The one in London, first called Cecil House, then Burghley House, was necessary for a nobleman with responsibilities at Court. A second was located near Stamford, Northamptonshire, the home of Cecil's father. Taking his title from the estate, Burghley constructed there a house which would be sufficient to support the dignity of a barony. The last was made necessary by the desire to provide for his second son. Built near Cheshunt, Hertfordshire, and called Theobalds, it grew far larger than Burghley originally intended. The enlargement, it is said, occurred to provide a hostelry ample for the Queen's visits and to give work to the unemployed.[2]

Burghley House was begun on the north side of the Strand by Sir Thomas Palmer who was executed in 1553. It was greatly embellished and completed by Sir William Cecil. Another residence, Cecil House, was subsequently built on the east side of Burghley House to ac-

[2] Francis Peck, editor, *Desiderata Curiosa Liber I* (London, 1732), p. 33.

commodate the household of Sir Robert Cecil.³ The Queen was entertained at supper in Burghley House for the first time on July 14, 1561, before the house was fully finished. Cecil complained that the building of it cost him lands worth £100 annually. Here the family lived during term times or whenever business required residence in London. It was here that the aged Lord Burghley died on August 4, 1598.⁴

Building operations at Burghley, near Stamford, Northamptonshire, were begun in the 1550's and continued until 1588. Seldom residing there, Burghley bore the cost of building and possibly of maintenance for his elder son, Thomas.⁵ Thomas wrote his father on August 27, 1587 as follows:

> Your lordship's buildings go on very fast this year, and I hope, by Michaelmas, they will be ready to cover with lead; the next year it will be some comfort if your lordship can get leave to see the perfection of your long and costly buildings, wherein your posterity I hope will be thankful unto your lordship for it, as myself must think myself most bound, who of all others receiveth the most use of it.⁶

Built to maintain the honor of his barony, Burghley emerged as one of the great houses of England, both then and now. Attended by good fortune, it survives to be enjoyed by Burghley's posterity in the twentieth century.

Probably the most important of Burghley's building projects was the construction of Theobalds. This was his most frequented residence outside London. He purchased the manor of Theobalds in 1564 for his younger son, Robert. It lay just off the main road from London to Ware, plete.⁷

The Queen's visit had a decisive effect on the building of Theobalds. Originally intended as the endownment of a younger son, it became a kind of offering to the Queen. Hence, the Queen expected lavish expenditure, even instigated it. The mansion therefore became less a nobleman's house than the Queen's occasional palace. In 1571-1572, £2,700 was spent on construction, the largest amount spent in any one year.⁸ The result was "a succession of state rooms dedicated entirely to the Queen and, in fact, rendering Theobalds as a whole comparable to the finest of her palaces."⁹ The house was completed in 1585 though the great gallery had to wait for its chimney piece until 1591.¹⁰ Summerson considers Theobalds

---

³ Sir George Gater and Walter G. Godfrey, editors, *Survey of London*, 30 volumes. (London, 1937), XVIII, the Strand, Part II of three parts, p. 125.

⁴ J. Alfred Gotch, *The Homes of the Cecils* (London, 1904), p. 55.

⁵ Peck, *Curiosa*, p. 29.

⁶ Cecil Papers, v. 165/95.

⁷ Sir John Summerson, "The Building of Theobalds, 1564-1585," *Archaeologia*, XCVII, MCMLIX, p. 108.

⁸ *Ibid.*, p. 111.

⁹ *Ibid.*, p. 112.

¹⁰ *Ibid.*, p. 114.

Summary of Findings

perhaps the most important architectural adventure of the whole of Elizabeth's reign, certainly the most influential.[11]

Though Sir Christopher Hatton's Holdenby was larger, Theobalds nonetheless pleased the Queen. Roger Manners, writing to his nephew, the Earl of Rutland, on June 2, 1583, reported the Queen's judgment of Theobalds. He said, "She was never in any place better pleased, and sure the house, garden and walks may compare with any delicate place in Italy."[12] The gardens were surrounded by water so that one could row between the shrubs. They contained elaborately contrived arrangements of materials. Especially significant was the summer house which contained white marble busts of the twelve Roman emperors. Paul Hentzner, the German traveler, described the splendors of these gardens but could not see the palace because the staff was in London attending Lord Burghley's funeral.[13]

Burghley House in the Strand and Theobalds in the country were the two homes most favored with Lord Burghley's presence. At neither place could he be free from the responsibilities of his high office. Probably the most vexing of these must have been the importunities of expectant suitors who would gladly drive down from London to haunt his antechamber in hope of gratification. Burghley nonetheless often sought the countryside, took great pleasure in his gardens at Theobalds, and escaped to them whenever he could get away from London. And well might he find satisfaction in his lovely gardens for the work was superintended by John Gerard, the great Elizabethan herbalist.

Our most specific references to household servants occur in connection with extraordinary entertainments given by Lord Burghley, usually the Queen's visits to Theobalds. Household servants' lists have survived for her visits of 1572, 1581 and possibly for 1591. There is some confusion about the latter list because several men who appear last, as if tacked on, were dead by 1591. As it is known that the Queen did visit in that year, the list is accepted with the exception of the names of men known to have been dead.

Probably the most sumptuous single entertainment ever offered by Burghley was the dinner on April 30, 1581, for the French Commissioners. At the Queen's insistence the French king sent a distinguished company which included the Dauphin, his brother, and a French Secretary of State. These persons were accompanied by a train of five hundred gentlemen. Their purpose was to treat for the marriage of the French King's brother, the Duke of Alencon, and Elizabeth, now in her late forties. England's reasons for negotiation were diplomatic. Elizabeth was fearful of Spain. Burghley did his part to accomplish his

[11] *Ibid.*, pp. 126-127.
[12] H.M.C., *Rutland MSS.* (London, 1880), Appendix, 12th report, part IV, v. I, pp. 150-151.
[13] Paul Hentzner, *Travels in England* (London, 1889), pp. 52-53.

mistress' purpose. The English prepared a mighty spectacle. The Commissioners were to confer with the Privy Council, on April 25th to dine with the Queen, on the 27th with Leicester and on the 30th with Burghley.[14]

The dinner provided by Lord Burghley was laid at Burghley House in the Strand. All the Privy Councillors were invited. At least a third of the peerage of England was present. Burghley selected forty-nine gentlemen and thirty-four yeomen to attend the diners. These included many who were normally employed in the Exchequer or the Court of Wards but who were probably dependents of Burghley. A few were relatives: his nephew, Francis Bacon; his son, Thomas; and his brother-in-law, Henry Killigrew. On no other occasion does a household list contain as many as eighty-three names. The principal guests sat in the great chamber, others were served in the garden. Those seated above the salt enjoyed the services of Henry Killigrew, Francis Bacon, and Thomas Cecil as interpreters. Burghley's secretaries assisted those nearer the salt.

The preparations were elaborate, the charges enormous. Special "turkey" carpet was purchased. The Queen's picture was secured, possibly especially painted for the occasion. The sum of £69.3.6 was spent either in preparing the house or in repairing it afterward. Fortunately, a part of the expense was shared by friends who sent Burghley presents valued at £69.2.3. Burghley nonetheless had to rent dishes at a charge of £11.12.4, the equivalent of a quarter of a year's wages for his entire household of twenty-two in 1556. He had to hire extra cooks at a charge of £25.10.4, exceeding the wages of his entire household for half a year in 1556.[15] The total cost of the single dinner, including the presents, was £362.19.11. This represented nearly twenty per cent of Burghley's annual household expenditure.[16] It was almost as much as he received annually from the crown as Lord Treasurer of England.[17] The Queen herself had been entertained at Theobalds for several days at less than the cost of this single dinner.

The Queen's visits were themselves quite burdensome. They could be ruinous for someone who had no access to revenues beyond his estates, someone without entree at Court. In 1575 Burghley lodged at least ten of England's great nobles, a number of untitled government officers, and unnumbered maids of honor, squires of the body, gentlemen ushers and lesser servants accompanying the Queen on her progress.[18] On that occasion the Queen was at Theobalds from May 24 until June 6, 1575.

[14] Conyers Read, *Lord Burghley and Queen Elizabeth* (London, 1960), pp. 257-258.
[15] B. M., *Landsdown MSS.*, v. 33, f. 70.
[16] Read, *Burghley*, p. 258.
[17] *Ibid.*, p. 83.
[18] Cecil Papers, v. 140, p. 21.

Summary of Findings 9

Burghley's economy must have been magnificent for his steward's accounts indicate an expenditure of only £340.17.4.[19] In 1572 Burghley had been able to manage the Queen's visit with only fifty-eight servants.[20] In May, 1591, Lord Burghley entertained the Queen for ten days at a cost of £1,011.2.7. It was on this occasion that the host spent £100 for a dress as a gift for the Queen.[21] Seventy-three servants were mobilized to handle this visit.[22]

One would like to speak definitively and authoritatively about the size of Burghley's household. Unfortunately, the evidence on its face value may not, indeed, does not tell the whole truth. We can discount the surviving household lists from the reign of Elizabeth for they contain too many names of persons known to have been otherwise regularly engaged except on those extraordinary occasions when Lord Burghley requisitioned their services. As a record of persons related to Burghley as clients or servants, the lists are invaluable. We should not expect to determine either the size or the personnel of the household from them.

There are indications that households generally decreased in size after the death of Henry VIII. Early in Henry's reign the Earl of Northumberland had 166 persons in his household.[23] His grandson, the ninth Earl, maintained fifty-eight servants in 1586. Even though he had seventy servants by 1603, he never approximated the princely magnificence of his grandsire.[24] William Cecil's father, Richard, a wealthy knight and Yeoman of the Robes to Henry VIII, in the 1540's had as many as forty-seven household servants.[25] Ten years later Sir William Cecil had a household not quite half that of his father.[26]

Cecil wrote a list of the persons in his household in the mid-1550's. He named thirty-five persons, including his son, sister-in-law and a ward, referring to them all as servants. However, not more than twenty-two appear to have been salaried.[27] The quarterly summaries of wages paid indicate that the annual expenditure on salaries did not exceed £60 before Elizabeth's accession.[28]

While Cecil's own records of his staff end with the advent of Elizabeth and his own preoccupation with affairs of state, his steward's accounts provide some index of size. In 1567, Cecil paid £93.7.8 in wages; in 1568, £100. By 1570, the figure dropped to £80. Apparently Lord

[19] *Ibid.*, Box G 16.
[20] Cecil Papers, v. 140, p. 20.
[21] P. R. O., S. P. 15, v. CCXXXVIII, ff. 306-308.
[22] Cecil Papers, v. 140, p. 37.
[23] Richard G. Batho, "The Household Accounts of Henry Percy, Ninth Earl of Northumberland, 1564-1632" (London M.A. thesis, 1959), p. 330.
[24] *Ibid.*, p. 73.
[25] P. R. O., S. P. 1/184/f. 159a.
[26] B. M., *Lansdowne MSS.*, v. 118, p. 42.
[27] *Ibid.*, p. 44.
[28] *Ibid.*

Burghley, after receiving his barony in 1571, kept a household comparable to his new dignity. In 1573-1574, £166.9.2 was paid in wages. In 1574-1575, £172.7; 1575-1576, £166, 1576-1577, £183.3.9; 1577-1578, £190.10.5.[29] In the years 1593, 1594, and 1595 the average annual wage bill was about £200.[30] The significant increase can certainly be attributed to Cecil's advancement. It probably indicates an actual enlargement of his household. The subsequent gradual increase may be due in part to inflation.

Burghley's anonymous biographer related after Burghley's death that he kept eighty servants in his household in London, excluding those who attended Burghley at Court.[31] At the same time between twenty-six and thirty persons were left at Theobalds.[32] The household accounts indicate that Burghley normally had about ten persons with him at Court.[33] Based on materials extant, the number 120 probably represents the largest number of servants Burghley ever maintained at one time. Even this figure possibly represents a bit of padding by the biographer. It was his concern to show that Burghley maintained a state equal to his rank and responsibility. This was a point of honor, a matter of face.

At Theobalds during the years 1575-1578, Burghley, when absent, normally maintained a staff of thirty-four to thirty-eight. When the family was present the staff usually swelled to sixty-five or seventy. If both Lord and Lady Burghley, ordinarily accompanied by the Countess of Oxford, came from London to Theobalds, they normally brought about thirty servants with them. When they slipped away separately to Theobalds they might travel with as few as seven servants. Lady Burghley more frequently came from London with ten or eleven. Lord Burghley usually travelled with about fifteen.[34]

Comparison of Burghley's household with other notable establishments offers some perspective in which to view his. As a knight during the reigns of Edward VI and Mary, the Cecil household of twenty-two salaried servants compares favorably with the household of twelve wage earning servants maintained by Sir Robert Kempe in 1585.[35] Sir Nicholas L'Estrange, steward of the manors of the Duchess of Richmond, maintained fifteen servants in 1575.[36] Sir William Petre, senior Principal Secretary of State, in 1550 paid £51 in wages to his servants, indicating an establishment about the size of Cecil's.[37] By 1556 the amount

[29] Cecil Papers, Bills, Box G 16.
[30] Cecil Papers, Accounts 27/26,27,28.
[31] Peck, *Curiosa*, p. 29.
[32] *Ibid.*, p. 30.
[33] Cecil Papers, v. 226, March, 1577.
[34] Cecil Papers, v. 226, Accounts for 1575-1577.
[35] B. M., *Additional MSS.*, 19,208, pp. 42-43.
[36] *Ibid.*, 23,449, f. 41.
[37] F. G. Emmison, *Tudor Secretary: Sir William Petre at Court and Home* (London, 1961), p. 152.

Summary of Findings

paid to servants rose to £107. There were about sixty persons on the payroll.[38] Cecil had by this time left public office while Petre flourished under Mary. Sir William Cecil, Knight, was not the least well served of his class.

One of the important barons of Elizabethan England, Lord North, regularly employed forty servants between 1576 and 1589. Their service cost North about £80 annually. North's servants and retainers included thirteen gentlemen and sixty-two yeomen.[39] We have no comparable figures for Lord Burghley's retainers.

Among earls of the realm, the Earl of Derby had 118 servants in 1587 and 145 in 1590.[40] The Earl of Northumberland did not have as many as seventy until the last year of Elizabeth.[41] The Earl of Huntingdon, a relative of the Queen, kept seventy-five servants in 1564.[42] If we allow Lord Burghley a maximum of 120, it would seem that he maintained a household larger than was customary for a baron yet in keeping with his exalted rank as an officer of state. It did not exceed the household of at least one of the greatest nobles. It is even possible that it was actually shorthanded. Certainly this was the case if Burghley followed his own advice. Writing for Robert Cecil's benefit, Burghley counselled against keeping one too many servants. Better to keep two too few, he warned.[43] Lord Burghley's household, like his building program, represents his moderation and, probably, his good sense. To have excited the envy of greater nobles would have impaired Burghley's service to the state, to say nothing of its consequences on his purse.

The household of a Tudor minister of state, while incontestably private, was simultaneously the refuge of employees whom we would call civil servants. In fact, there was no sharp demarcation of duty so that domestic and official functions often overlapped. Such persons functioned as secretaries, deputies, clerks and messengers, working primarily on the business of the government. Yet their sole responsibility was to their employer, Lord Burghley. None of the security attached to such a position today was available to them. Their security was the health, success and gratitude of their master. The story of these times is the tale of endless maneuver by people anxious to get what they could while they could from whomever they could. The successful fellow found a powerful patron, became his dependent or even his servant, and hoped for the best for him and from him.

In this fashion many of those subsequently listed or described undoubtedly became associated with Lord Burghley. By far the largest

[38] *Ibid.*, pp. 153-154.
[39] B. M., *Stowe MSS.*, 774.
[40] Batho, "Accounts," p. 330.
[41] *Ibid.*, p. 73.
[42] H. M. C. Hastings MSS. (London, 1928), p. 354.
[43] Peck, *Curiosa*, p. 65.

single group is that of household and estate personnel, to which fifty-nine belong. Nine probable secretaries, eight chaplains and fifteen clerks complete the total of ninety-one.[44] By no means is it possible to maintain that all of Burghley's circle appear here. Doubtless further exhaustive research would uncover others.

Only eight of this number qualify as esquires. Seventy-six were gentlemen and nine were yeomen. Quite naturally the yeomen leave little behind of use to the historian whose detective work is therefore frustrated. The official records, if at all concerned with them, preserve only their births, marriages, deaths and possibly their misbehavior. Their lives do not become a part of the public memory. Without clues to place of origin, even these fragments elude the student. Gentlemen, on the other hand, usually have recorded pedigrees. County histories record their possession, occupation and exchange of estates as well as note their dignities. Wills contain a wealth of information. Often government dispatches cite them for meritorious service in war or record their petitions for favors. Frequently legal records bring to life some long past slander or hurt. Country house muniment rooms sometimes conceal material of great biographical interest. Gentlemen were, by and large, the principle body of participants in public life. They may sometimes be conjured back to life in shadow or in substance. Unfortunately, twenty-five of Burghley's personnel cannot with confidence be assigned to any social group.

There is no pattern evident in their election to Lord Burghley's service. Only thirty-six of the group can be traced to their county of origin. Five, probably more, clearly came from Wales. Eleven were born in Northamptonshire, Lincolnshire or Hertfordshire where Burghley's estates were concentrated. Another eleven were drawn from the home counties. Durham supplied two. Each of the others was born in a different county. Virtually all of them passed their last days in or near London. Where country estates have been discovered, none were further from London than Wiltshire. The Northamptonshire-Lincolnshire area was another focal point and the usual place of service for a few who lived and died there.

One must either conclude that the university records are incomplete in regard to certain of Burghley's personnel or else assume that petty schools and private education account for the evident excellence of their preparation. Of the eighty-four gentlemen and esquires, only sixteen had definitely established university records. A mere twelve were members of an inn of court. In only four instances did a person attend both a university and an inn. Without exception these university men received Cambridge degrees. Burghley demonstrated marked partiality for the university from which he graduated and of which he was Chancellor

[44] See appendix for identification of all names.

Summary of Findings 13

from 1559 until 1598. His old college, St. John's, did not, however, have a monopoly on the supply of his household. Two men received an additional degree from Oxford. Burghley's own Gray's Inn received six of the twelve introduced to the inns of court. Lincoln's Inn, noted for its puritanism, received four while the Middle Temple accepted two.

It cannot be said, for lack of positive confirmation, that Burghley gathered around himself a group of puritans. The religious position of twenty-three of his household can be ascertained with some assurance. Especially useful for this purpose are the religious preambles of wills. Ordinarily brief, perhaps only a few phrases, in one case the preamble occupied four finely written pages, half the total will. All of these are couched in clear, protestant terms which exclude the possibility of Catholicism, even if they do not establish dissatisfaction with the Elizabethan settlement and so qualify as puritan. It is worth noting that those closest to Burghley, men like Maynard, Hickes, Skinner, and Bellot, were the most outspoken protestants. In fact, the four-page proclamation was the work of Thomas Bellot, steward of Lord Burghley and executor of his will. It may be said that whenever religion is ascertainable, it is decidedly protestant.

Two members of Burghley's household, Vincent Skinner and Walter Travers, actually engaged in religious polemics for which they would certainly have won the admiration and approval of Lady Burghley if not literary immortality. Only six persons associated with Lord Burghley seem to have been engaged in literary pursuits of any kind.[45] No one of these attained unusual distinction. Lord Burghley was not primarily noted as a patron of poets, playwrights, or artists. His interest was the state. This consumed his energy and that of those around him.

It is not surprising, therefore, to find that seventeen servants, probably even more, sat in parliament. While they did not all owe their seats to Burghley's direct patronage, his endorsement may be considered their mainstay. How consistently their support in parliament repaid their obligation to Burghley is not known. Aylmer suggests that the idea of government solidarity in or outside parliament was almost unknown in Jacobean times.[46] It is probably too much to expect a tight little circle of Burghleymen during Elizabeth's reign. Among the seventeen who sat were Burghley's three principal secretaries, Maynard, Hickes and Skinner, as well as at least eight relatives.[47]

Burghley's attitude toward the employment of kinsmen was made clear in advice he prepared for his son, Robert. Burghley warned Robert against being served by kinsmen, friends, or men who intreat to stay, for

[45] Clapham, Gooch, Goodman, Hall, Neile, Travers.
[46] G. E. Aylmer, *The King's Servants* (New York, 1961), p. 353.
[47] R. Alford, G. Blyth (R), H. Cheke (R), W. Cope (R), G. Coppin, J. Durninge (R), A. Hall, M. Hickes, T. Holcroft, H. Maynard, J. Morrice (R), J. Purvey (R), R. Shute, V. Skinner (R), R. Spencer (R), W. Waad, F. Yaxley.

they expect much and do little.[48] Clearly there is merit in this admonition. Yet Burghley himself was unable to observe the letter of the law he laid down. There were at least fourteen relatives in Burghley's service during his lifetime, possibly more.[49] Five of these were nephews-by-marriage from the Cheke connection. Only one of them, Barnard Dewhurst, served him for a long period. The others were promoted to the Queen's service. It cannot, however, be maintained that Burghley practiced nepotism on a very large scale. Indeed, there is the contravening evidence of two very dissatisfied nephews, the Bacon brothers, who sought favor and advancement in the opposing faction, the Essex circle.

Instead of favoring puritans, Welshmen, relatives or any special interest group as such, it is apparent that Burghley picked those whom he knew to be competent. Too much was at stake to indulge in a fancy or a preference. His judgment must have been sound for there is record of only one dismissal. Toward the end of Burghley's life, Richard Shute was deprived of his feodaryship and of the Cecils' favor. Nor is there evidence of voluntary removal from Burghley's employ except by promotion at Burghley's own hand.

Servants so fortunately placed remained and served well. We cannot imagine that their lot was easy. If the staff was deliberately smaller than necessary, there must have been work for all. Burghley's philosophy, expressed in his advice to Robert Cecil, was as follows: "Feed them well, and pay them with the most; and then thou mayest boldly require service at their hands."[50] It was the reward which made hard work tolerable. And any sensible man knew that few were better placed than Burghley to reward well.

Here we encounter one of the most frustrating and elusive problems of the sixteenth century, the problem of reward. In our day most of the benefits of place are apparent, even contractual, and include an adequate salary as well as certain ascertainable fringe benefits. Aside from intangibles, such as prestige, influence and authority, arrangements beyond the contract approach impropriety, maybe even peculation, and often result in legal prosecution. Not so in the sixteenth century. Just as the Queen distributed offices to those whose aid was essential to good government, so also did her subordinates, carrying the logic of the arrangement forward. These men, whatever the level of their service, extracted from their offices all that could be got from them. No one condemned them for so doing for such was the character of public life.[51] If the unfortunate fall of Francis Bacon comes to mind, let it serve to illustrate the perils, not the invalidity, of the system. Certainly the exaction of sums beyond

[48] Peck, *Curiosa*, p. 65.
[49] H. Allington, G. Blyth, J. and H. Cheke, W. Cooke, W. Cope, B. Dewhurst, J. Durninge, B. Gooch, J. Morrice, T. Ogle, J. Purvey, V. Skinner, R. Spencer.
[50] Peck, *Curiosa*, p. 65.
[51] Arthur J. Slavin, *Politics and Profit* (Cambridge, 1966), p. 158.

the fixed fees was a routine of Tudor administration.[52] Nonetheless the student is baffled and deceived not only by the informality which characterized all offices of government,[53] and we may add household, but by the extent and sometimes by the exact nature of reward. Assumptions must therefore be made from implicit evidence. This is to say that given our understanding of the mechanics of the system, the opportunity for profit may be taken in itself as substantial reward. If one considers Lawrence Stone's guess that the ratio of aspirants to suitable jobs under Elizabeth was about five to one for the 500 leading county families and perhaps thirty to one for the remaining gentry,[54] then the great value of the places at Burghley's disposal within his household cannot be doubted.

Those who came earliest, in 1544 when Cecil first established a household, could not have foreseen the wisdom of their choice.[55] They could not have known how far Cecil would go nor how long he would continue to serve the state. Nor could they have imagined the extent of their own opportunities which Cecil's success opened to them. Three who chose wisely before 1548 were rewarded by their master with promotion into the royal service.[56] Once Cecil had established himself as Elizabeth's right arm there was no lack of fresh material with which to fill his household. The candidates knew that Cecil could help them, and probably also their families. Aylmer, in fact, asserts that rare was the fellow who sought advancement for himself alone and not also for his family.[57] In most cases they were not disappointed. As Fuller quaintly put it, when describing Lord Burghley's success: "His harvest lasted every day for above thirty years together, wherein he allowed some of his servants the same courtesy Boaz granted to Ruth, to glean even among the sheaves, and to suffer some handfalls also to fall on purpose for them, whereby they raised great estates."[58]

How well Burghley paid his salaried servants after Elizabeth's accession is not known. Nor do we know how many were salaried. Probably the ordinary household servants, many of whom lodged in, were paid wages. These Burghley remembered richly in his will, offering them four years' wages and their bedding. Most of the gentlemen probably were not salaried. Burghley left each of them a handsome piece of plate.[59] A bequest by Thomas Bellot states that he was among

---
[52] *Ibid.*, p. 160.
[53] Wallace T. MacCaffrey, "Place and Patronage in Elizabethan Politics," *Elizabethan Government and Society*, ed. S. T. Bindoff, J. Hurstfield and C. H. Williams (London, 1961), p. 105.
[54] Lawrence Stone, *The Crisis of the Aristocracy* (Oxford, 1965), p. 467.
[55] B. M., *Lansdown MSS.*, v. 118, p. 35.
[56] Roger Alford, Francis Yaxley, Richard Troughton.
[57] Aylmer, *King's Servants*, p. 82.
[58] Thomas Fuller, *The Holy State*. Second Edition (Cambridge, 1648), p. 258.
[59] Arthur Collins, *The Life of William Cecil, Lord Burghley* (London, 1732), p. 96.

those unsalaried servants.[60] Ordinarily stewards received a salary. And, indeed, Bellot received a £20 annuity after Burghley's death. This very sum was the stated salary paid a steward at that time in the household of the Earl of Northumberland.[61]

Possibly the single most important source of income for all the higher servants, and for some others as well, was the gratuity. Informal as it was, it is a difficult source to trace. Occasionally a note survives disclosing its payment. Henry Maynard is known to have received a gratuity of £100 on one occasion.[62] Barnard Dewhurst got £3 for assisting a suitor for a ward.[63] An excellent example is the case of Richard Bradshaw, Lady Burghley's chamberlain. A suitor for a wardship first gave Bradshaw £10 as an inducement to approach Lady Burghley who was in turn expected to intercede with her husband. As the matter progressed too slowly, £3 more was given to speed up Bradshaw. Ultimately Lady Burghley obtained the desired wardship for the suitor who paid Lady Burghley £250 for her pains while paying the Queen only £233.6.8 for the wardship.[64] While these men were gentlemen, even a yeoman might benefit from this source. By decision of the steward, one yeoman of the household, Thomas Canfield, was paid the sum offered to Burghley by Robert Middleton to obtain a wardship.[65] This seems to be a conscious attempt to spread the favors more widely. At the same time it gave the steward a means by which excellence might be rewarded and control maintained.

In the Burghley household there must have been a steady flow of gratuities from the guests who dined and lodged there. Batho tells us that the Earl of Northumberland customarily gave £3 for distribution when he paid a short visit to another nobleman's home.[66] Visitors came almost daily to the Cecils'. The household had also to receive a steady stream of suitors who expected favors or aid from Burghley and who gratified innumerable servants in order to have their turn with the great man. The profits of such transactions are incalculable. The public position of Lord Burghley, however, warrants a rather generous estimate of their value. For Burghley, provided he could bear the strain and nuisance accompanying this traffic, the burden of rewarding his own servants must have been greatly reduced.

We tread on firmer ground when discussing the ascertainable sources of reward. Even here there are imponderables. Whether or not a grant or office constitutes a reward for service depands upon the purchase price,

[60] P. C. C., 81 Wood.
[61] Batho, "Accounts," p. 45.
[62] See Maynard biography.
[63] See Dewhurst biography.
[64] Joel Hurstfield, *The Queen's Wards* (London, 1958), p. 265.
[65] Cecil Papers, M. 485, v. 84, petition 9.
[66] Batho, "Accounts," p. 294.

Summary of Findings 17

tenure and other conditions not usually known. Since stated salaries, whether paid by the crown or by a noble employer, were notoriously low, wards, leases, feodaryships, stewardships, annuities and the like were in great demand. Hence the fact that one of these goes to an individual is here regarded as sufficient evidence of some reward. In the instance of offices, they may have been valuable not only for the small fee but also as a means of establishing the recipient's local pre-eminence.[67]

This said, it is perhaps significant that Lord Burghley granted fifty-four wardships to thirty-three of his servants.[68] Except for two yeomen, all the recipients were at least gentlemen. No scandal is suggested in Burghley's accounting of his responsibility for a government office. Most of the recipients would today be employed directly by the government. Only a few appear to have worked for Burghley largely in a private capacity. Even this distinction is ours, not theirs.

Burghley possessed extensive means of reward as both Master of the Court of Wards and as Lord Treasurer. As Treasurer at his command lay scores of crown offices to which were attached attractive fees or stipends. Fortunately most could be handled by deputy so that Burghley, by granting them to the deserving faithful, did not lose their service.[69] Included here are gentlemen pensioners, bailiffs and stewards of royal manors, royal woodwards, keepers of forests, collectors of tolls, escheators and feodaries, surveyors, receivers and, most important, certain clerkships. Approximately thirty-four persons obtained fifty-one such offices. Most were worth from £2 to £20 annually in stated salary, probably more in fees, and of intangible value as a source of prestige. A few, the clerkships, were known to be worth several hundred pounds.

There is some evidence in the Cecil circle to support Aylmer's contention that most who sought advancement had the welfare of their families also in mind.[70] Three families appear especially to have benefited by having a member placed in Burghley's service. Roger Alford, who came in the 1540's, immediately secured for his brother, Lancelot, appointment as Clerk of the Hanaper in Dublin. Later Roger persuaded Burghley to arrange an Irish Tellership for his brother. Roger's brother Francis may also have profited from the connection although evidence for this assumption is not incontestable. Thomas Windebank, Burghley's dedicated secretary, had only one brother. Well rewarded himself, his brother, Richard, settled into the captaincy of a Kentish castle which was passed on to his son, Aaron.

The finest example of family benefits is that offered by the Bellots. Thomas became Burghley's steward in 1566 and obtained, in the course

[67] MacCaffrey, *Elizabethan Government and Society*, p. 123.
[68] See appendix.
[69] Aylmer, *King's Servants*, p. 127.
[70] *Ibid.*, p. 82.

of forty year's service to the Cecils, numerous plums of his own. His brother, Owen, became a royal woodward in Denbigh and secured a stewardship in a noble house related to the Cecils. John, another brother, was made collector of crown rents in Chester and also secured a stewardship with the Earl of Rutland, who had been a ward in Burghley's custody. Still another brother, David, became steward to Sir Raynald Mohun. Robert Bellot, sometime servant in the Cecil household, succeeded to the woodwardship in Denbigh, became feodary of Denbigh and farmer of the tolls of the village of Wrexham. Two brothers obtained ecclesiastical preferment. Three of them also obtained employment or grants from Dean Gabriel Goodman of Westminster.

Burghley was able to obtain favorable grants and valuable offices outside his own official bailiwick for several servants. Dean Gabriel Goodman proved a most obliging associate. In addition to the Bellots, so generously dealt with, four other servants assisted the Dean and Chapter of Westminster as officers. Two others were Westminster borough bailiffs, chosen by the Dean. Four individuals obtained leases of property from the Dean and Chapter, excluding Lord Burghley himself who enjoyed the lease of St. Alban's House on the south side of the Henry VII chapel.[71] This residence, located directly across from the Court of Wards, possibly served as an office. At least ten of Burghley's servants, in one way or another, had gainful connections with Westminster.[72]

Some of these well placed and generously rewarded servants quite obviously founded fortunes and families. Others, like Vincent Skinner, experienced misfortune and failed despite their opportunities. Notable among the successes were two secretaries, Henry Maynard and Michael Hickes. Both established reputations for wealth and profited as money lenders. Both bought country estates and left them, intact and debt-free, to male heirs. Hickes, whose brother became a Viscount and fabulously rich, left £2,200 in cash. Maynard, at his death worth £4,500 in cash, left the largest sum of any in the Cecil entourage. Hickes' son, William, eventually became a baronet, probably by purchase. Just as Michael Hickes was associated with Robert Cecil at the changing of sovereigns in 1603, so in 1901 were their descendants similarly joined together. At that time Sir Michael Hicks-Beach served under Robert Cecil, Marquess of Salisbury and Prime Minister. Maynard's children attained distinction as well. His eldest son became a baron, the second a leading courtier and the third, auditor of the Exchequer. Each secretary honored his master by naming a son William.

Barnard Dewhurst's cash estate was £3,655, to be left at interest for his sons. They did not apparently build very significantly upon the foundations laid by their father. Walter Cope had the dubious distinction

[71] Westminster Abbey Library, Register Book III, f. 169; Register Book VII, f. 56.
[72] See appendix.

Summary of Findings

of leaving a debt of £27,000. Even so, his wife salvaged a goodly sum and his only child, a daughter, married well. George Coppin, a business associate of Cope, also prospered. His estate was sufficient to establish an elder son on landed property and to provide £2,000 as a stake for a younger son. Gilbert Wakering is reputed to have raised a considerable fortune. Thomas Windebank, while leaving only £850 in cash, left a landed estate and a son established in the succession to his office, a Signet Clerkship. The boy improved upon his father's record and became Secretary of State to Charles I.

On the whole, James was kind to those of Burghley's household who were still active at his accession. Of the eleven who were knighted, all but two received the honor during the reign of James I.[73] This was doubtless due to the influence of Robert Cecil who retained a good number of his father's servants and clients. Thomas Bellot's will indicates the extent of the friendship that survived among the personnel who once served together under Burghley. Henry Maynard, Michael Hickes, George Coppin, Gilbert Wakering, John Clapham, Roger Houghton, a Pickering of Westminster, and Marmaduke Servant each received a bequest from the old steward who knew them so well and remembered them twelve years after Lord Burghley's death.[74] Surely the death of Burghley the patron was not a catastrophe for many of his retainers and servants. Possibly the regular household servants fared worst of all. Burghley seems to have anticipated this when he left each of them four year's wages.[75] Robert Cecil could only employ a few of these because his own household was already complete while his resources were not extensive immediately after his father's death.

What of the influence theoretically available to Lord Burghley through the agency of his variously placed former servants? First, and most important, as Lord Treasurer Burghley had immense authority. Busy as he was, it must have been useful to possess devoted and unquestionably loyal subordinates like Roger Alford, a Teller, and Vincent Skinner, Writer of the Tallies. The latter had a very broad picture of the whole state of the finances. Especially was the office "serviceable," to quote Skinner, ". . . in the matter of issues, no way being so open for overture of the actions of princes, or for discovering of their secret intentions, as by the issues of treasure."[76] Both the Exchequer and the Court of Wards were naturally of enormous significance by virtue of the patronage each represented.

Just as the Queen could not spend without Burghley's knowledge,

---

[73] The exceptions were Abraham, Burghley's steward in the 1550's, and Reede, knighted before 1591. Those knighted in 1603 or after were: Cope, Coppin, Hickes, Holcroft, Skinner, Spencer, Waad, Wakering and Windebank.

[74] P. C. C., 81 Wood.

[75] Collins, *Burghley*, p. 96.

[76] See Skinner biography.

neither was she likely to correspond very privately unless she took pen in hand herself. After 1567 Thomas Windebank, Clerk of the Signet, hovered near. He was even spoken of as the Queen's private secretary. This is not to suggest he played the role of spy. It is only to emphasize the fact that always close to the Queen's person was a Burghley appointee, obligated and loyal to his master. In the beginning of the reign, and earlier, the well-served Cecil had Francis Yaxley in the same capacity. Though the point appears of little significance, it is appropriate here to mention that even at the Queen's gates one of the Yeomen Porters, Richard Troughton, was advanced to the post from Burghley's service. And if we may assume that William Day, mentioned in Windebank's biography, did indeed serve Burghley as suggested, then even in the Chapel Royal might the Queen find a member of the Cecil faction, at least in 1572.[77]

Little of strategic consequence can be seen in Hugh Allington's service as a Clerk of the Privy Seal after 1572, especially as the office was ordinarily performed by deputy. Nor can anything sinister or particularly valuable be detected in the appointment of a nephew and friend, both former inmates of Burghley's household, as Clerks of the Privy Council. Conceivably their records and their corresponding function might prove useful. The nephew, Henry Cheke, served only briefly whereas William Waad's tenure was unusually long.

After 1560 Lord Burghley was free to operate in the confidence that his backyard was secure. In that year, one of the most constant and faithful of his friends and servants, Gabriel Goodman, became Dean of Westminster. As such he had responsibility for the borough of Westminster. This remained true after the incorporation in 1586. Here lived the Queen, Lord Burghley, and many of the great officers of state. Most important, here sat the government of the land. Responsibility for this unique borough lay safely in the hands of this stalwart friend of the Cecils.

The importance of Burghley's various connections with Wales is not measureable. Simple Welshmen must have rejoiced in their Welsh Queen and her Welsh first minister. The more pragmatic Welshmen probably had cause to be thankful for the channels opening government patronage to them. Certainly Gabriel Goodman provided the most valuable link between Wales and the Court both because of his extraordinarily durable and strong relationship to Lord Burghley and because of his keen sense of obligation and attachment to Wales. Thomas Bellot was another who opened a way for Welshmen to glimpse the promised land. No doubt pedigree-proud Welsh gentry searched their family trees for evidence of family ties with either the Goodmans or the Bellots.[78]

[77] Sir Sidney Lee, ed., *The Concise Dictionary of National Biography,* To 1900 (London, 1953), p. 328.
[78] G. Dyfnallt Owen, *Elizabethan Wales* (Cardiff, 1962), p. 13.

Summary of Findings

Those fortunate enough to possess such natural claims upon these well-placed Welsh expatriates would have had ample reason for activating them since there were so few Welshmen in the Council in the Marches of Wales to serve their interests.[79] Unhappily this study has not revealed how much Goodman and Bellot meant to the gratification and contentment of the influential men of Wales. It has only established a clear picture of the influence and place Goodman and Bellot enjoyed with Lord Burghley. These were the trusted men whom Burghley made executors of his will. It is but consistent with their opportunity to assume that they served to draw peripheral Wales more closely into the web of government influence, serving both England and Wales in doing so.

Another difficult question is the extent of Burghley's influence north of the Trent, ". . . where men knew no other prince but a Percy or a Neville . . ." until the sixteenth century was well advanced.[80] Certainly the Percy and Neville families occupied the primary seats of authority until their failure in the rising of 1569-1570. Their elimination left on the scene a number of families of secondary importance, as the Greys, Selbys, Forsters, Whartons and Woodringtons. These families fell heir to the government favor heretofore largely monopolized by the great feudal magnates. As early as Cardinal Wolsey's time, however, a crown party was beginning to emerge. The heads of the leading border gentry families were provided with annual pensions in return for service. The result was that dependence upon the Percy and Neville estate and household organizations ceased as careers and incomes became available from the crown.[81]

Linked together by kinship and well represented in the administration of the border, they acquired a vested interest in the new order when the estates of the fallen nobles were dismembered in 1570. It was necessary to be assured of support in an area which had risen behind its natural leaders against the economic, religious and political policies of Elizabeth. At the same time such men as Cecil and Leicester were deeply resented.

Burghley may have used the Court of Wards as a means of acquiring personal partisans on the border. At least he took advantage of the death in 1564 of Sir Ralph Grey of Chillingham, Northumberland, to admit his two minor sons into his own household. Fully aware of their extensive family connections, Burghley maintained a permanent relationship at least with Ralph who was regularly referred to as Burghley's servant. Burghley was godfather to Ralph's son, William, who became first Lord Grey of Wark. And Ralph acquired the reputation as the strongest man in the Middle Marches. This was a sturdy and strategic connection.

[79] Penry Wiliams, *The Council in the Marches of Wales* (Cardiff, 1958), p. 145.
[80] Rachel R. Reid, *The King's Council in the North* (London, 1921), p. 21.
[81] M. E. James, ed., *Estate Accounts of the Earls of Northumberland, 1562-1637*, Surtees Society Publications, CLXIII (1955), p. XIV.

From 1574 until 1586 Burghley possessed a direct voice in the Council in the North.[82] George Blythe, a nephew, was first a deputy secretary and later secretary of the Council and Keeper of the Signet. He was succeeded by another nephew, Henry Cheke, in 1581. Each died while in office. Theirs was a key position in the government of the north. Burghley personally suggested each appointment.

Burghley also singled out a professional soldier, on the northern border, Sir William Reede. As early as 1560, Burghley had taken note of him. Thereafter he saw that Reede was promoted, knighted and that he secured desired leases. Reede admitted his obligations to Burghley, served as Burghley's personal representative on occasion, and ultimately persuaded Burghley to accept the services of his son. Clearly Burghley felt better served if, in addition to a crown party, loyal and dependent, he had also certain persons obligated and faithful to himself.

Perhaps the same explanation serves to justify the usefulness to Burghley of John Cheke, whose military career in Ireland lasted only from 1578 until his death in 1580. Similarly Barnaby Gooch's Irish duty in the 1570's and 1580's must have provided his relative, Lord Burghley, with useful reports of an unofficial nature. Robert Constable, in the late 1590's, probably continued the tradition of a man on the scene. Certainly Burghley manifested an open interest in the welfare of each of these men while they were in Ireland.

A curious and unlikely influence derived from Burghley's espousal of the person and career of William Seres, Stationer. He was a personal servant for whom Burghley secured reward in his chosen profession. Twice, as he was able, Burghley obtained grants of monopoly for Seres. The second, a patent issued in 1559, was the more valuable because guaranteed by the long reign of the Queen. It authorized Seres to print all books of private prayers. One of the three largest patents granted to any member of the Company of Stationers in Elizabeth's reign, it made Seres correspondingly influential among stationers. In fact, Seres served longer than any other Elizabethan stationer as Master of the Company.

The Company of Stationers, by its 1557 charter of incorporation, obtained an almost complete monopoly on the printing and distribution of books. Nine years later the Corporation acquired the authority to search and seize books violating the laws. A portion of the executive function of the government had been passed to the Company of Stationers. It is significant, in this light, to note the prominence of Seres in the trade and, at the same time, his close collaboration with Burghley. Here, too, Burghley had a representative, either by design or by chance.

Only the university printers were excluded from the monopoly given the Company of Stationers. Even here, Burghley had great influence. Cambridge might be described, with numerous reservations, as a Cecil

[82] Reid, *King's Council*, p. 488.

preserve. Burghley's immense authority derived in large part from his position as Chancellor of the University from 1559 until his death. That he was an active figure in the administration can be seen in the surviving correspondence. From the University he drew all of his university-trained staff, including his chaplains. And to the University he frequently returned his chaplains as fellows, masters, or as occupants of special chairs.[83]

The amassing of biographical details reveals how ubiquitous Burghley's influence was. No small part of his usefulness can be ascribed to his lines of communication extending, often, into unlikely areas of activity and into every geographic center of domestic importance. If Burghley's success as foreign policy advisor to the crown lay partly in his superior intelligence service, similarly must his national administration have profited from the eyes and ears scattered so adroitly about sensitive areas of national life.

By patient skill Burghley established a foundation from which to render service to the nation such as no meteoric Essex could hope to match. In time it meant that Burghley became almost indispensable. As a single administrator and advisor, he could always be replaced. But Burghley was a great deal more. He was the focus of a functioning machine, orderly, stable and responsible to his direction. If there was not the tradition of loyalty which bound people to a Percy, there was the sense of obligation which was ordinarily sufficient bond in the kind of men Burghley chose. They were, in the main, men of principle strengthened by strong religious conviction. And if we can conclude from their lack of distinguished attainment that they were in fact second-rate men, then perhaps Hurstfield is right when he joins with Edmund Spenser, Thomas Wilson and Francis Bacon to suggest that the Cecils deliberately surrounded themselves with second-rate men who could never seriously threaten the Cecil hegemony.[84] Whatever the reasons behind their selection, the evident result was a closeknit body of followers whose loyalty and faithfulness extended for decades. Their master was well-served, and so served well his country and his Queen.

Sir John Abraham

Sir John Abraham, Cecil's steward at Burghley House in Stamford, and likely of his estates in the area, is one of the more shadowy figures crossing Cecil's path.[1] Unfortunately, no information has been found outside the few surviving papers relating directly to his responsibilities in

[83] See appendix for list of chaplains.

[84] Joel Hurstfield, "Political Corruption in Modern England: The Historian's Problem," *History*, LII, (February, 1967), p. 27.

[1] B. M., *Lansdown MSS.*, v. 3, f. 56, p. 118.

Cecil's service. His birth, the occasion of his knighthood and his death are facts long buried in the past. Only his poorly written letters to Cecil really assure us that such a man lived.

The earliest reference to him is found in his accounts, preserved among the Cecil Papers at Hatfield, covering the period from April 27, 1555 to April 29, 1556. These are endorsed in Cecil's hand and written in Abraham's own tedious scrawl.[2] During the year only £143.6.5 was disbursed. Yet Abraham carefully noted each expenditure, indicating to Cecil in this way how £90.14.2 was spent on the building operation which would eventually transform Burghley House into the great baronial seat it is today.

The transformation was to be great. When Abraham sent his accounts, he reported to Cecil that £3.15.8 had been paid out to household servants in wages. The establishment over which he presided must have been small. In a list of servants and wages paid at Lady Day, 1556, compiled by Cecil himself, it is noted that Abraham paid four servants at Burghley.[3] At Midsummer, 1556, the number under his charge had increased to five while by Michaelmas the number had grown to eleven, including Hicks the joiner and Cordall the mason.[4]

The three extant letters from Abraham to Cecil come from the same period and reflect Cecil's concern for the building operations which were moving too slowly and for estate affairs.[5] They do nothing to rescue Abraham himself from virtual anonymity. Scattered accounts in the *State Papers* reveal Abraham collecting rents for Cecil both directly from tenants and from other collectors.[6] After 1557 Abraham drops from sight.

It is possible that Abraham was a part of Cecil's inheritance from his father, Richard Cecil, who died in March 1553, leaving Cecil the family estate at Stamford.[7] It is also likely that Abraham was a tenant of the Cecils for he recorded in his accounts receipt from himself of one quarter of malt.[8]

Roger Alford

We have Cecil's own testimony that Roger Alford entered his service in 1547, one of the earliest appointees.[1] In a household list drawn up by

[2] Cecil Papers, Box G1 (M.485/97).
[3] B. M., *Lansdowne MSS.*, v. 118, p. 42.
[4] *Ibid.*, p. 45.
[5] H. M. C., *Salisbury MSS.*, I, 136; P. R. O., State Papers 11/8; B. M., *Lansdowne MSS.*, v. 3, f. 75, pp. 153, 153r.
[6] P. R. O., S. P. 11/28, 30, 31, 93.
[7] Conyers Read, *Mr. Secretary Cecil and Queen Elizabeth* (London, 1955), p. 42.
[8] Cecil Papers, Box G1 (M. 485/97).

[1] B. M., *Lansdowne MSS.*, v. 118, p. 35.

Cecil in 1555 when at Wimbledon, Alford is described as a clerk, and mentioned immediately following the priest and steward.[2] His salary at this time was £5 a year, only one other receiving a salary as high, none higher.[3] His position was essentially that of secretary, the duties differing only in quality and quantity from those of Henry Maynard and Michael Hickes who served the very eminent and busy William Cecil, Baron of Burghley and Lord Treasurer of England.

Possibly Alford undertook a broader scope of duties after the death of Edward VI made Cecil once more a private citizen. Often confidential, they suggest the trust placed in Alford. In April, 1553, Alford was sent up to Stamford to inquire about the recently deceased Richard Cecil's will, about which Cecil felt some anxiety, and to assure the immediate collection of rents and orderly management of the estates. Alford's letter to Cecil reveals how completely he understood the latter's mind in the matters committed to his care.[4]

Alford's recapitulation of events occurring in 1553 at the request of Cecil in October, 1573 is another indication of the nature of Alford's service. At the attempted usurpation of the English throne by Northumberland for Lady Jane Grey, Cecil balked and would not assist. Fearful for his life, Cecil made disposition of his property and devised elaborate plans to escape. In all of this Alford was an active participant, a confidant, himself providing one of the proposed hideaways.[5]

It is not surprising that so intimate and valuable a servant should have his reward. Before the last year of the reign of Edward VI, Cecil procured the reversion of the office of teller of the receipt of the exchequer which Alford occupied in January, 1555, surrendering it in June 1562.[6] On March 3, 1552, Alford received a twenty-one year lease of property in Lincolnshire for the yearly rent of £22.13.4. The reversion of which was later granted by the crown to Cecil himself.[7]

After 1560 Cecil was able to augment Alford's reward from the Court of Wards. Alford received the wardship of Giles Sewster which in 15 Elizabeth paid him £40 although the regular annual exhibition seems to have been £10.[8] At his death the residue of this wardship became the property of his daughter Anne Alford.[9] In addition to the annual exhibition, Alford received valuable leases of his ward's lands.[10] He also succeeded in causing his annual exhibition to be doubled in 1574.[11] In

[2] *Ibid.*, p. 36.
[3] *Ibid.*
[4] H. M. C., *Salisbury MSS.*, I, 116.
[5] B. M., *Cotton MSS.*, Titus B. II., No. 175, f. 374.
[6] Great Britain, *Cal. of Pat. Rolls,* Elizabeth, II (London, 1948), p. 340.
[7] *Ibid.*, p. 165.
[8] P. R. O., Wards 9/380.
[9] P. C. C., 38 Arundel.
[10] P. R. O., Wards 9/373.
[11] P. R. O., Wards 9/380.

justification for his added generosity, Cecil might recall not only yeoman service as secretary, but Alford's service in the parliaments of 1558 and 1559 in which he undoubtedly acted as a Cecil man.[12]

Little is heard from Alford after he surrendered his teller's office in 1562, nor is the reason for this known. He is referred to in 1564 as earnest in religion and fit to be trusted, whereupon he was appointed a justice of the peace for Buckinghamshire in the same year.[13] In 1575 he wrote Burghley on behalf of another from whom he doubtless collected a fee, concluding his letter by professing himself unwell.[14] By 1580 he was dead.

His will, after bequeathing his soul and body to "the almighty God" and professing his faith, disposed of his major property outside his lands which had been devised in 1570. To his son Alford gave the house and household stuff in Whitefriars by Fleet Street, continuing his wife in possession until his son's marriage. Daughter Anne got the ward and £120 with which to pay the Queen for the ward and certain other charges. Alford proposed that his son, already at Oxford, should study at Lincoln's Inn under his good friend Mr. Lambart. "Also my meaning is," said Alford, "when he shall grow towards twenty years that he shall serve my lord treasurer my old master, who I trust will accept him and notwithstanding permit him to continue his study at law."[15]

Minor bequests went to William Walter of Wimbledon, who got a black gown; to Lord Burghley and Sir Thomas Cecil, each of whom received a horse; and to Lambart who was given two gilt standing cups and a cow. Son Edward, a minor, was designated sole executor. Edward's administrators included his mother, his godfather, Sir Thomas Cecil; Lambart, and James Dalton of Lincoln's Inn; Philip Scudamore and George Burden, the latter, another secretary in Burghley's service.[16]

As Cecil and Alford continued on good terms until the latter's death, Alford's withdrawal from a lucrative court post is curious. It was a difficult and responsible job and it is possible that he found it too demanding. The chance survival of his accounts for 636 days, submitted in 1560, suggest the difficulty of the work. In the period of the account £13.6.8 was spent for boat hire to Greenwich, Westminster, the Tower or wherever the Queen was in residence for the purpose of declaring the state of receipts and payments. And at a *per diem* rate for travel and diet of 26s.8d., during the period he drew £848. He directed a staff of five clerks "for the speedy execution and dispatch of the affairs aforesaid" which supervised the paying out of £157,948.10.6.[17]

[12] History of Parliament Trust, unpublished biography.
[13] *Ibid.*
[14] H. M. C., *Salisbury MSS.*, II, p. 124.
[15] P. C. C., 38 Arundel.
[16] *Ibid.*
[17] P. R. O., E. 101/429/11.

Alford's removal from court may also have been accomplished by his marriage to a wealthy widow, Elizabeth, daughter of Thomas Ramsey, esquire, and widow of John Clarke, esquire, of Hitcham, Buckinghamshire. Elizabeth's inviting country estate at Hitcham may have lured the tired administrator away from court. To it he retired and became a country squire.[18]

Alford represents a frequent sixteenth century social phenomenon, the attraction to London of impoverished gentry from the further provinces, their enrichment through court or business, and their subsequent return to the land as refurbished squires. His family home was Aldford Castle in Cheshire where Alfords had long been lords of the manor.[19] Roger's grandfather of Holt, Denbighshire, married Jane, daughter of John Salisbury, a well-known Welsh family. Roger's father Robert, while apparently the first to make the trek to London, retained a residence at Erbistock, near Holt. Robert's marriage to Anne, daughter of Edmund Brydges of Sudley, Gloucestershire, was, like his father's, a good marriage. The Brydges, recipients of a barony in 1554, graduated to ducal ranks in 1719. Roger was eldest child of Robert and Anne Alford. His three brothers deserve notice for they rose in part through Roger's tie with the Cecils.[20]

Francis, the second son of Robert, was a student at both Cambridge and Oxford and sat in the parliaments of 1563, 1571, 1572, 1584, 1586 and 1588. Conservative in religion, he opposed puritan demands in parliament. Francis actually married a Catholic, yet one who received an annuity of £20 from the exchequer.[21] In 1569 the nineteen-year-old brother of Thomas Bellot, Cecil's steward, was employed in Francis Alford's household although by 1571 he had entered Cecil's domestic service.[22] In October, 1588 Francis wrote Burghley relating the offer of John Alford of Yorkshire, a kinsman, of 400 marks for the wardship of Sir William Fairfax's son as Sir William seemed near death. In the same letter Francis asked for the collectorship of the late monastery of St. Mary's, Yorkshire, then in hands of Fairfax.[23] Francis's home, Salisbury Court, Fleet Street, was not far from his brother Roger's home.[24]

Of Edward, the third son, nothing is known beyond his place of residence, Aston-sub-Edge, Gloucestershire.[25]

Launcelot, the fourth and youngest son, was appointed Clerk of the

[18] Josiah George Alford, *Alford Family Notes* (London, 1908), p. 25.
[19] *Ibid.*, p. 10.
[20] *Ibid.*, p. 24.
[21] Richard C. Gabriel, "Members of the House of Commons, 1586-1587" (London M.A. thesis, 1954), pp. 194-195.
[22] P. R. O., S. P. 15/209.
[23] P. R. O., S. P. 12/34.
[24] Nora Minnie Fuidge, "The Personnel of the House of Commons, 1563-1567" (London M.A. thesis, 1950), Section III, p. 3.
[25] Alford, *Family Notes,* p. 25.

Hanaper in Dublin in 1548, just one year after Roger entered Cecil's service. When in 1573 the Irish tellership, a very lucrative sinecure in the gift of Lord Burghley, became vacant, Robert wrote Burghley, suggesting Launcelot for the job. He got it. In 1582 Launcelot obtained a twenty-one year lease of York House, Twickenham, Surrey, on the Thames, a home later occupied by James II while Duke of York.[26]

Hugh Allington

Hugh Allington was one of those men fortunately placed to catch the eye of the great statesman whose servant he became. He was the son of George Allington of Rushforth, Norfolk, who died in 1558, and Anne Cheke, who died in 1557. Anne was a sister of Cecil's first wife. Hugh's grandfather was Sir Giles Allington of Horseheath, Cambridgeshire, once Sheriff of Cambridge and Huntingdon. His great-great grandmother was a Howard, thus giving him slight claim to kinship with the Dukes of Norfolk and with the Queen herself. More important for his future was the fact that he was Cecil's nephew by marriage.[1]

Born about 1537 at Hanbury, Worcester, Hugh was sent to Eton, then to Cambridge, being admitted to King's College in August, 1554 at the age of 17. By the time he received his B.A. in 1559 he was an orphan.[2] Possibly he had already become a regular visitor at the Cecil homes when his employment began.

The first positive evidence we have of Allington's service under Cecil is a letter of February 5, 1562, written by Allington from Westminster to Cecil's secretary, Thomas Windebank, who had been sent to the continent with young Thomas Cecil. The tone of the letter bespeaks some experience on the part of the writer as well as intimacy with Windebank. Allington's principal news was that Windebank's predecessor, Mr. Day, had been advanced to the provostship of Eton.[3]

On February 10, 1562, Allington wrote again to Windebank requesting a signed note from him for the £90 paid to Windebank before he and Thomas Cecil left for the continent, on May 30, 1561. Allington, probably still a little inexperienced, was called to account and "somewhat blamed" for delivering the money without taking a receipt.[4] The last letter from Allington to Windebank, written from the Strand on December 14, 1562, recommended in very obscure language that Windebank return

[26] *Ibid.*, p. 32.

[1] A. R. Maddison, ed., *Lincolnshire Pedigrees*, Harleian Society Publications, L (1902), pp. 5-6.

[2] John Venn and J. A. Venn, editors, *Alumni Cantabrigiensis*, Part I, 4 volumes (Cambridge, 1922-1927), I, p. 23.

[3] P. R. O., S. P. 12/84.

[4] P. R. O., S. P. 12/96.

home with young Thomas.[5] This correspondence, written either from the court or from Burghley's house in the Strand, is interesting because it places Allington in the Cecil service as early as May 1561.

Cecil, in his own careful way, documented the next step in Allington's career. In one of his numerous memoranda he recorded that Windebank left his service in 1563 and was replaced by Hugh Allington.[6]

Without the letter from Nicholas White to Sir William Cecil, written from Ireland on February 26, 1569, we would not know exactly how Allington, Windebank and presumably Day served Cecil. White reported that:

> Edward Waterhouse, Secretary to the Lord Deputy, arrived here, furnished with all instructions as well concerning his master's private causes as also touching the whole state of that realm. And as he is wise, so the writer knows him to be an inward man with his master, and the same in effect that Mr. Allington is to Cecil in the affairs of his office. The Deputy uses him also as a 'Register' of all his proceedings, and entrusts him with as much as any master could commit to a servant.[7]

Since White and Cecil wrote to one another in unusually frank terms, it may safely be assumed that White accurately described Allington's role of confidential secretary to Cecil.

A letter from John Wod, the secretary of the Scottish regent, Murray, to Cecil in 1568 suggests that Allington was accustomed to dealing with Cecil's Scottish correspondence.[8]

On July 8, 1562 the twenty-five year-old Allington received what was likely his first valuable gift from Cecil, a grant of the wardship and marriage of Thomas Barne, son and heir of William Barne, with an annuity of £16 from January 17, 1562, when William died.[9] To this was added another wardship on June 1, 1565, that of Francis Minsterchamber[10] Three years later Allington was given the reversion of the Clerkship of the Court of Requests for life, after Richard Oseley, who unfortunately held the office for a very long time.[11]

While the value of the Requests' office would long be denied him, compensation came on July 29, 1572 when Allington accepted appointment as one of the Clerks of the Privy Seal, also a lifetime appointment.[12] And in the very next year his stock of wards was replenished by the grant of the wardship of Anne Baynton for which Allington

---

[5] P. R. O., S. P. 12/21.
[6] H. M. C., *Salisbury MSS.*, V, 69.
[7] H. M. C., *Salisbury MSS.*, I, 9.
[8] Great Britain, *C. S. P., Scotland* II (Edinburgh, 1900), p. 490.
[9] Great Britain, *Cal. of Pat. Rolls,* Elizabeth II, (London, 1948), p. 269.
[10] P. R. O., MSS. Cal. Pat. Rolls, 1-16 Elizabeth, p. 150.
[11] *Ibid.*, p. 234r.
[12] P. R. O., MSS. Cal. Pat. Rolls, 1-16 Elizabeth, p. 298.

paid £6.13.4.[13] Much later, on August 30, 1586, the crown was again the agent providing a valuable grant, this time a patent for the lease of Spalding rectory in Lincolnshire for twenty-one years.[14]

Allington appeared in the Docquet Book as a Clerk of the Privy Seal for the first time in April, 1572. Thereafter he was represented by a deputy, William Parker, who signed his own name in the place of Allington after June, 1577.[15] Parker continued to deputize for Allington and was succeeded in 1603 by his son, Thomas Parker who had already served fourteen years under his father.[16] In 1615 Allington's fellow clerks cited the difficulties they encountered in persuading the aged Allington to sign certain indentures prepared for the reformation of abuses in their office. At the same time they complained of the pertinacity of Thomas Parker who insisted on signing as if he were a clerk rather than a deputy.[17]

The Clerkship of the Court of Requests, which had been granted to Richard Oseley and Hugh Allington in 1568, was enjoyed by Oseley until his death in 1598-1599. Francis Mills, upon learning of Oseley's death, wrote immediately to Sir Robert Cecil with the request that his late master's (Lord Burghley's) promise might be kept that Mr. Allington make him his deputy in the office.[18] Cecil obliged by writing Allington who explained that arrangements had long been made for the office, presumably not including Mills. Allington hoped that for the short time left him there the arrangements might stand and:

> I may quietly make my profit of it, having had, by my said lord's means, the grant thereof from her Majesty ever since the tenth year of her reign, trusting that as Her Majesty dispensed with my ordinary attendance in respect of my sickly state, so now at these years I may quietly enjoy these small things it pleased her so long ago to bestow on me.[19]

That the office just described, though an official one, was intended as a reward for services rendered to Lord Burghley is made clear by Allington himself in a plaintive cry to Sir Robert Cecil in February, 1600. Having just received a letter from the Privy Council bidding him contribute £10 for the forces in Ireland, directed to him as Clerk of Whitehall, a place he had had only one year, Allington declared that "unless the Council give credit to the Masters of that Court against such

[13] P. R. O., Wards 9/380.
[14] P. R. O., MSS. Cal. Pat. Rolls, 17-30 Elizabeth, p. 24r.
[15] P. R. O., Privy Seal Office, Index 6743, Docquet Bk., 1571-1580.
[16] H. M. C., *Salisbury MSS.*, XV, p. 87.
[17] Great Britain, C. S. P. D., IX (London, 1858), p. 272.
[18] H. M. C., *Salisbury MSS.*, IX, p. 85.
[19] *Ibid.*, p. 94.

as impugn their authority . . . the reward I have for my services under your father will be but slender."[20]

The most eloquent testimonial of his success in Cecil's service is the marriage of Allington in 1580 to Lord Burghley's sister Elizabeth, widow of Robert Wingfield.[21] Until his marriage at the age of forty-three, he must have devoted himself completely to the service of the Cecils, too busy to seek the diversions of family and home.

In 1587 Allington was designated one of the gentlemen in gowns to celebrate the passing of the Queen of Scotland. Mrs. Allington was one of the female mourners.[22] In the following year Allington morned again, on this occasion less regally but more profitably. His mother-in-law, Jane Cecil, died leaving him £20 and making him one of the trustees of a fund she left for the poor workers of Stamford. Mrs. Allington was designated the sole executor of the will.[23] In 1590 Magdalene Purvey, a sister of Allington's mother, died. From her Allington received a small inheritance, a 40s ring.[24]

By 1591 Allington's health had begun to fail. In this year he wrote to Barnard Dewhurst asking for the loan of certain books belonging to Lord Burghley, "to pass the time, he not having a body fit to travel abroad." He continued to serve Burghley; for in the same letter he requested the return of certain papers which he had sent that he might rewrite them.[25] All his later letters were sent from Tynwell, Rutland, a manor owned by Cecil. They suggest his retirement there. It was to Tynwell that Thomas Cecil, having become Earl of Exeter, wrote in 1605 requesting Allington to search among Exeter's evidences at Burghley House for proof of his grandfather's gentility.[26]

It is likely that Allington spent his remaining years quietly at Tynwell. It was there that he died and was buried in 1618, at the age of eighty-one.[27]

His will opens with a profession of faith strongly protestant if not puritan in character. He requested to be buried without ceremony. To the poor of several parishes he left £100. To one nephew, his namesake Hugh, he bequeathed a £30 annuity. The total sum of his bequests, excluding the annuity, exceeds £2100, a clear indication that he had prospered. Having no direct heirs, his wife's family, his brothers and their children were the principal beneficiaries. The descendants of Lord

[20] H. M. C., *Salisbury MSS.*, X, p. 42.
[21] Maddison, *Lincolnshire Pedigrees*, p. 7.
[22] Great Britain, *C. S. P., Scotland*, IX (Glasgow, 1915), pp. 458-459.
[23] P. C. C., 23 Rutland.
[24] P. C. C., 73 Drury.
[25] H. M. C., *Salisbury MSS.*, XIII, p. 455.
[26] B. M., *Harleian MSS.*, I, No. 374, Article 24.
[27] P. C. C., 94 Meade.

Burghley were remembered as were his associates in the Court of Requests.[28]

Thomas Bellot

Thomas Bellot, steward of the Cecil household, was born about 1534, one of the nine sons and three daughters of Thomas and Alice Bellot of Great Moreton, Cheshire. Alice was the daughter of William Roydon of Burton, Denbigh. Eventually the family removed to Denbigh and settled in Gresford where the parents are buried.[1] Bellots had inhabited the manor of Great Moreton since early in the fifteenth century when a John Bellot married the heiress of the house of Moreton. Members of the family fulfilled their role as minor gentry by serving from time to time as collectors of subsidies in the hundred of Northwich in which they lived. They were people of local consequence only, and possessed of but small means.[2] It is therefore not surprising to note the exodus from the district of most of the twelve children born to Thomas and Alice.

It is not clear how Thomas Bellot, the second son, at the age of thirty-two found employment as steward of Cecil's household. However, we have Cecil's own statement that he employed Bellot in 1566.[3] Very likely Bellot and Cecil were brought together by Gabriel Goodman, a Welshman who moved from Cecil's employ into the deanery of Westminster. During his forty years at Westminster, Goodman employed numerous fellow countrymen, including several of Thomas Bellot's brothers. Perhaps both Bellot and Goodman were brought to Cecil's attention by Roger Alford, another Welshman in Cecil's employ in 1547. However introduced, Bellot served the Cecils for forty-seven years, virtually becoming one of the family. So completely did Bellot identify himself with his master's service that he never married.[4]

As steward, Bellot ran the splendid Cecil establishments, the mansion in the Strand and the country estate at Cheshunt, Hertfordshire. The latter was the great Theobalds which one day James I would take for his own pleasure. According to a contemporary writer, a sixteenth-century steward was expected to purchase provisions, supervise all offices, receive money from bailiffs and the receiver-general, pay the servants, keep the lord informed as to the state of his household, sit in judgment

---

[28] *Ibid.*

[1] George John Armytage and J. Paul Rylands, editors, *The Visitation of Cheshire*, 1613, Harleian Society Publications, LIX (London, 1909).

[2] George Ormerod, *The History of the County Palatine and City of Chester*, 3 volumes (London, 1882), III, p. 45.

[3] H. M. C., *Salisbury MSS.*, V, p. 70.

[4] Ormerod, *Chester*, III, 45.

over other servants, marshall the lord's hall with a white staff and "to countenance the meat from the surveying place, or dress, to the lord's table."[5]

A very basic responsibility, which made many of the other duties possible, was the keeping of careful records. Many of those kept by Bellot survive, telling in their own way a very interesting story. The basic menu of each meal was set down with its cost, the numbers fed and frequently the names of distinguished guests. Records were also kept of the purchases of household departments, with weekly, quarterly and annual summaries.[6]

Bellot's duties extended beyond the conventional. In personal and family matters, he was frequently Cecil's deputy. The exchequer records reveal that Bellot occasionally colected Cecil's official salaries.[7] After Lady Burghley's death, Bellot very largely handled the details of her bequest of a loan fund for certain men of Romford.[8] In the case of a wardship secured by Robert Middleton shortly before Burghley's death, Bellot acted as the dispensing agent. The transaction was undoubtedly profitable both to him and to another servant to whom the composition for the wardship was granted.[9]

In 1582 it fell to Bellot to relate to Burghley the cheerless news of the rapid decline of the health of his son-in-law, Thomas Wentworth, who soon died.[10] Probably among his most pleasant duties was the distribution of his master's charities, to which he frequently added his own contribution, "to the re-edifying of churches, founding of Hospitals, and succouring wonderful numbers of Poor. . . ."[11] Bellot had ample opportunity to bestow Burghley's charities when he undertook his last sad duty, itself a mark of the esteem and confidence in which Burghley held Bellot. Burghley named him, together with his other old Welsh friend, Dean Gabriel Goodman, as an executor of his will.[12]

Bellot did not consider his duty done with the settlement of Burghley's affairs. Rather he devoted himself to the welfare of Burghley's heirs. According to Strype, Burghley had charged Bellot with the care of his three granddaughters whose delinquent father, the Earl of Oxford, might attempt to steal them away. Bellot had been instructed to

[5] Sir Joseph Banks, ed., "A Breviate Touching the Order and Government of a Nobleman's House . . . ," *Archaeologia,* XIII (1800), pp. 316-317.
[6] Cecil Papers, v. 226, M. 485/58.
[7] P. R. O., E. 403/2259.
[8] H. M. C., *Salisbury MSS.,* IV, p. 495.
[9] Cecil Papers, v. 84.
[10] Great Britain, *C. S. P. S.,* II (London, 1865), p. 74.
[11] Sir Henry Chauncy, *The Historical Antiquities of Hertfordshire,* 2 volumes (Bishops Stortford), I, p. 589.
[12] The will is published in Collins, *Burghley,* p. 97.

thwart such a move, reminding the Earl of the terms by which Burghley agreed to provide dowers for the girls.[13]

That the Cecil family regarded Bellot's services as invaluable is illustrated by the request of the Countess of Bedford to Sir Robert Cecil in 1599 desiring the assistance of Bellot for the marriage of Sir Robert's niece.[14] Later Bellot concerned himself on behalf of Lady Bridget Vere, Oxford's daughter, when her husband, Lord Norris, drew up an indenture for a jointure which Bellot felt inadequate on the basis of her marriage portion. Bellot therefore warned her uncle, Sir Robert Cecil, suggesting a fair figure in the place of the proposed one.[15] When another Oxford daughter, Lady Susan Vere, prepared to meet the Queen in 1603, her charges exceeded her ready cash and Bellot was willing to supply her with money provided Sir Robert approved.[16]

The terms of Bellot's will make abundantly clear the expression which the Cecil family's gradituide took. Bequest after bequest is simply restoration to the donor of some choice gift. For instance, to William Cecil, Sir Robert's son, went a chain of gold; to William's sister Frances, a little gilt bowl which Sir Robert's wife had given Bellot; to the eldest daughter of Elizabeth Vere, then Countess of Derby, went a gilt bowl given by her mother; to Lady Susan Vere a jug with gilt given by Lady Burghley to Bellot. The list, far longer, stands as eloquent tribute to the relationship between the aged steward and his master's brood.[17]

To some degree these gifts may have been the normal and expected manner of reward. Bellot described one bequest he made as "a cup with a cover which my Lord bequeathed to such servants as had no wages," thereby suggesting that this sixteen-ounce cup was in part merited.[18] The statement at the same time reveals that there was a body of men in Cecil's employ who depended for their livelihood upon an informal method of reward. It must be assumed that these persons relied upon the informal fees which the suitors of Cecil were willing to pay for the furtherance of their causes. And those closest to the master were in a position to profit most.

While there is no documentation for this informal salary, there is ample evidence that Bellot profited in other ways from his employment. Four years after he became Cecil's steward, Bellot was given the wardship of Elizabeth Charleton, at a cost to himself of only £11.[19] In 1575 he became the Court of Wards' feodary or agent for the Welsh county

---

[13] John Strype, *Annals of the Reformation*, 3 volumes (Oxford, 1824), III, part 1, pp. 84-85.
[14] Great Britain, *C. S. P. D.*, V (London, 1869), p. 186.
[15] H. M. C., *Salisbury MSS.*, XII, p. 61.
[16] H. M. C., *Salisbury MSS.*, XV, p. 391.
[17] P. C. C., 81 Wood.
[18] *Ibid.*
[19] P. R. O., Cal. Pat. Rolls, 1-16 Elizabeth; Wards 9/373.

of Denbigh, his family's home. The position was necessarily filled by a deputy, likely his brother John who succeeded to the office in 1578.[20]

In the year preceding his appointment as feodary, Bellot had been granted a twenty-one year lease of the tolls of the village of Wrexham, Denbigh, and of Mylcombe wood in Cornwall.[21] From an exchequer record of 1587 recording the payment of fees, we learn that Bellot was bailiff of the royal manor of Edmonton, receivng an annual fee of £6.[22] These awards all accrued to Bellot during the lifetime of Burghley. Burghley's final reward was contained in his will, of which Bellot was one of two executors. Bellot was left two horses with their furniture, the piece of plate already mentioned, and an annuity of £20 for life.[23]

After Burghley's death, Bellot joined with a John Budden to purchase two Dorset manors, Wanborough and Cranborne, of the yearly value of £73.19. for which they paid £2,015.4.2. though they were almost certainly acting as trustees for Sir Robert Cecil who subsequently took his title from the Cranborne estate.[24]

One suspects a similar responsibility in what appears to be a very significant award, the grant of the customs of all silks and other materials made to Thomas Bellot and Roger Houghton, Sir Robert Cecil's steward, soon after Burghley's death, at an annual rent of £9,382.[25] There is nonetheless the possibility that this was a genuine reward arranged by Sir Robert Cecil for his father's old steward and his own. Walter Cope, writing to Cecil in 1601, stated that as Cecil had the customs of all "tufftaffetayes" and satins wrought with gold and silver, there was no need to trouble the Queen for a more specific enumeration.[26] On the other hand, the materials included in Bellot's grant were definitely stated and gold and silver cloth was excepted.

Roger Houghton, in a note to Cecil in 1601, just when the customs grant was becoming operative, declared that he had received £500 from Bellot, which sum Houghton promptly paid into the exchequer as a part of Cecil's rent, making the total paid to that point £2,500.[27] If these figures refer to the customs grant, there is a very great likelihood that Bellot was superintending a joint collecting agency.

In a transaction of 1602 Bellot admittedly acted as Sir Robert's trustee.[28] It is not clear in another case whether the parties involved

[20] Unpublished list of officers of Court of Wards, compiled by Professor Joel Hurstfield.
[21] P. R. O., Cal. Pat. Rolls, 1-16, Elizabeth, pp. 338, 328.
[22] P. R. O., E. 315/309.
[23] Collins, *Burghley*, pp. 97-98.
[24] Great Britain, *C. S. P. D.*, V (London, 1869), p. 355; P. R. O., Calendar and Index of Patent Rolls, 38-43 Eliz., p. 39r.
[25] H. M. C., *Salisbury MSS.*, XII, pp. 77-78.
[26] H. M. C., *Salisbury MSS.*, XI, p. 396.
[27] *Ibid.*, p. 404.
[28] Great Britain, *C. S. P. D.*, VI (London, 1870), p. 162.

were acting on behalf of Cecil or for themselves. In August, 1604 Sir Thomas Windebank, Thomas Bellot and William Blake were granted, in fee farm, the purchase of the manors of Stamford and Dunston, with the castle of Dunstaburgh, Northumberland.[29]

We have a much clearer picture of what undoubtedly was a reward to Bellot, when the Bishop of St. Asaph wrote Lord Salisbury in 1605 disclosing how he proposed to repay Salisbury's favor to him. The Bishop said: "Because I would show my readiness to do you service for your undeserved favour showed to me, poor wretch, I have likewise sealed and delivered a patent of the Registership to Mr. Bellot, your servant. . . ."[30] The undeserved favor may well have been translation to the see of St. Asaph, a favor which could be improved upon as St. Asaph was not the most desirable episcopal seat.

While we cannot form an accurate picture of Bellot's income from his many gifts, grants or awards, his benefactions provide some measure of his capabilty. Bellot's tomb to this day proclaims his generosity without revealing when, where or how much.[31] During his last illness, Lord Salisbury asked to see the great church in Bath where Bellot had bestowed some of his father's money, committed to his trust, and a great part of Bellot's own. When he saw the church, Lord Salisbury noted that old Mr. Bellot had spent all upon charitable objects and left nothing for his kinsman.[32]

Certainly the records of Bellot's gifts to Bath Abbey are generous in their praise of him. He began his donations in the reign of Elizabeth and continued to deal generously with the Abbey until his death in 1611[33] Bellot's giving exceeded £300. It was variously used to repair the south isle, restore the bells, purchase chairs, to provide the choir seats for the gentry, for the repair of the great east window and for the purchase of the ornaments and implements for the service.[34] While no ostentatious memorial proclaims his munificence, it is forever enshrined in poetry.

An anonymous admirer of the church, writing to coax money for further improvements from a new bishop in the early seventeenth century, had this to say of Bellot:

... So far that BELLOT'S Star outshined
Whoever hath to Church been kind,
As doth Full-Moon, in Starry night,
Exceed the lesser torches Light.

[29] Great Britain, *C. S. P. D.*, VIII (London, 1857), p. 146.
[30] H. M. C., *Salisbury MSS.*, XVII, p. 374.
[31] Robert Clutterbuck, *The History and Antiquities of the County of Hertford*, 3 volumes (London, 1815-1827), II, p. 113.
[32] Edward Nares, *Memoirs of Lord Burghley*, 3 volumes (London, 1828-1831), III, p. 495.
[33] *The History and Antiquities of the Cathedral Church of Salisbury and the Abbey Church of Bath* (London, 1723), p. 163.
[34] *Ibid.*, pp. 165-166, 177.

The Chapel Ornaments, the Floor,
The Benches, Windows, Seats and Door,
Call BELLOT Father; and the Bell
Rings BELLOT, though it ring a knell.
Hospitals, Baths, Streets, and Highways,
Sound out the noble BELLOT'S praise,
'Cause he was pious, and hath given
Much,—whose Reward shall be in Heaven.

The poet continued in another section to compare "bounteous BELLOT" with a James whose gifts were solicited by the poet.[35] It is interesting to note that Dr. James Montague, the new bishop, responded with £1000 and the church was completed.

W. K. Jordan has found among the charity commissioners' reports evidence of further generosity to the city of Bath. To establish a place where the diseased poor might come to benefit from the waters Bellot purchased a large house and converted it, at a cost of £200, into a hospital. To provide for its perpetuation along the lines he stipulated, he conveyed to the municipal authorities an estate of £300 as an endowment.[36]

Bellot's philanthropy was not confined to churches or to Bath. He caused a market house to be erected in Westminster Manor, belonging to the Abbey, which was to be devoted to such charitable purposes as Bellot, in conjunction with the Dean and Chapter of Westminster, should decide.[37]

One other benefaction has been located, a gift of sentiment, illustrating the strength of the bond between Burghley and his steward. In 1609, just over ten years after Burghley's death, Bellot, himself an old man of seventy-five, made a final gesture to the memory of his master. He gave a house, bought for £50, to the school-masters of Stamford School to be enjoyed forever. This was Lord Burghley's old school.[38]

Only in Bellot's will do we find any further trace of charitable works. Out of about £350 in ready money left for the use of various persons, nearly £100 was designated for the relief of the poor in several parishes.[39]

As we continue our examination of Bellot's will, Sir Robert Cecil's comment on how little Bellot left his relatives comes to mind. Actually he left as much as £40 to one brother, £30 to another, £20 to others and £30 to his namesake nephew.[40] While these sums are not small, it must be assumed that they appeared so beside Bellot's total worth. There-

[35] *An Historical Description of the Church Dedicated to St. Peter and St. Paul, in Bath, Designed as a Guide to Strangers* (Bath, 1778), p. 13.
[36] W. K. Jordan, *The Forming of the Charitable Institutions of the West of England*, American Philosophical Society Transactions, New Series, L, Part 8 (1960), p. 60.
[37] Westminster Abbey Library, General Catalogue, No. 17215.
[38] B. L. Deed, *A History of Stamford School* (Cambridge, 1954), p. 19.
[39] P. C. C., 81 Wood.
[40] *Ibid.*

fore he must have been far more generous than we have discovered and far richer than his will indicates.

The Cecil family was remembered primarily by the return of valuable plate which had been gifts to him. It is amusing to note how Bellot anticipated the critics of his obviously handsome gift to Sir Robert. Bellot said: "And because there will be some ready for to judge I give but as it were a feather of his own [,] that is a piece of plate that was my lords [,] for the same Mr. Roger Goldsmith in Lumber Street will acknowledge that I bought if of him."[41]

Many members of the Cecil household were remembered by Bellot. To Henry Maynard went several books, to Mrs. Maynard a square cabinet with black leather, partly gilt, together with its contents. Michael Hickes received 70s. and a hope ring; George Coppin, 70s.; Gilbert Wakering, 30s.; John Clapham, 30s.; Roger Houghton, a Flanders desk with the contents, and a Flanders gilt bowl; Mrs. Houghton, seven gold 30s. pieces and a little cyprus chest with the contents; Pickering of Westminster, 15s.; and Marmaduke Servant, 30s. Several other friends outside the service of Burghley were likewise left small legacies. Bellot made his brother George and Roger Houghton, "my special friend," his executors. Bellot omitted the appointment of the usual overseers because of the trust and confidence he had in the integrity and wise-dealing of Houghton, who very likely was his understudy as Burghley's steward before becoming steward to Sir Robert Cecil.[42]

Perhaps the most interesting aspect of the will is the unusually lengthy religious preamble, consisting of half the four-page document. It is a comprehensive statement of faith and at the same time an agonized confession, the whole couched in a pronounced protestant tone. Full of pious phraseology, it is the reflection of just such a man as might have felt at home with the sober Lady Burghley and in an almost puritan household.[43]

The same fervent religious expression was used by Thomas Bellot's brother George, the sixth son, who died in 1627, a bachelor like Thomas.[44] He served as Receiver General of Westminster Abbey from 1593 until 1608, receiving his appointment from Burghley's old servant, Dean Gabriel Goodman, who made George Bellot one of his executors.[45] It is necessary to consider most of these brothers whose way appears to have been made in part by the success enjoyed by Thomas Bellot, the second brother, under Lord Burghley. Only the firstborn remained on the family lands.

[41] *Ibid.*
[42] *Ibid.*
[43] *Ibid.*
[44] P. C. C., 100 Skynner.
[45] Westminster Abbey Library, Unpublished List of Officers; General Catalogue, No. 25379.

The third son, Hugh, born in 1542 and eight years younger than Thomas, chose religion rather than administration. After taking a B.A. at Christ's College, Cambridge, Hugh became in succession a fellow of Jesus College, Cambridge; a proctor of the university; in 1571, rector of Gresford, Denbigh; in 1585, Bishop of Bangor, being in 1595 translated to the Bishropic of Chester where he died the following year, aged fifty-four. He was primarily noted as a great persecutor of the Catholics and as an assistant in translating the Bible into Welsh. It is said that his intimacy with Gabriel Goodman, Dean of Westminster, probably helped him procure some of his preferments.[46] It is even more likely that his brother's connection with the Cecils brought him to the attention of the authorities.

Associated with his brother, Bishop Hugh, was the ninth and youngest brother, Cuthbert, who was a prebend at Chester Cathedral at the time of his brother's death. Afterward, Gabriel Goodman brought him to Westminster as prebend where he joined his brother George, already Receiver General, and probably his brother Owen.[47]

Owen, the eighth brother, had become sacrist or keeper of the monuments in the Abbey in 1579.[48] In 1581 he became clerk of the second kitchen in the Abbey household.[49] Eventually he became steward to Lord Norris, probably the Lord Norris of Rycote who married Burghley's granddaughter, Bridget Vere.[50] Owen also succeeded his brother Robert as a royal woodward and custodian of forests in Denbigh, a position paying £8.0.10d. annually.[51]

Four of the brothers, including Thomas and Owen, served as stewards in noble households. It seems logical to assume that Thomas taught them in the service of Burghley. There is no evidence of this beyond the rather strong circumstantial indicators in the careers of each of the four. Each seems to have found a master somehow connected with the Cecils, often a man who had himself at one time resided in the Cecil household. John, the fourth brother, found employment with Edward, Earl of Rutland, who grew up in the Cecil household. By 1586, John was serving the Earl as clerk of the kitchen, eventually becoming the Rutland steward.[52] In 1599 John was made a collector of rents by the crown for royal property in Chester, the fee of which was £8.13.3. annually.[53] David, the seventh brother, was steward to Sir Raynald Mohun, a great

---

[46] James Mew, "Hugh Bellot," *DNB*, 21 volumes. Edited by Leslie Stephen and Sidney Lee (London, 1885-1890), II, p. 195.

[47] Ormerod, *Chester*, p. 45.

[48] Westminster Abbey Library, Unpublished List of Officers.

[49] B. M., *Lansdowne MSS.*, v. 33, f. 70, p. 175.

[50] Ormerod, *Chester*, p. 45.

[51] P. R. O., E. 315/309.

[52] Great Britain, *C. S. P., Scotland*, I (London, 1858), 453; Ormerod, *Chester*, p. 45.

[53] P. R. O., E. 315/309.

Devonshire knight who married Mary Killigrew, Burghley's niece by marriage.⁵⁴

Robert, the fifth brother, appeared in 1568, at the age of seventeen, in the service of Francis Alford, a younger brother of Roger Alford, Burghley's secretary. By 1571 he had become gentleman servant to Lord Burghley.⁵⁵ On the occasion of the Queen's vist to Theobalds in 1572, Robert's special assignment was cupboard keeper for beer.⁵⁶ Eventually he was assigned to Burghley's daughter, the Countess of Oxford, who spent much of her time in her father's household. Robert served the Countess as a gentleman usher.⁵⁷

It is possible that this Robert, though only fifteen at the time, may have been the Robert Bellot who assisted the feodary of the Court of Wards in the East Riding of Yorkshire as early as 1566.⁵⁸ In 1574 Robert receved the grant of a valuable lease in Denbigh for twenty-one years.⁵⁹ Elizabeth made him royal woodward of Denbigh in 1576, for which he received a fee of £8.0.10 annually.⁶⁰ In the last year of Elizabeth's reign, Robert inherited what had virtually become the family feodaryship of Denbigh.⁶¹ By 1595 he had succeeded his brother Thomas in the farm of the tolls of Wrexham in Denbigh.⁶² Bishop Hugh Bellot employed his brother Robert as his sole executor and bequeathed him most of his goods.⁶³

Robert likely inherited the estate of his brother Hugh because he was one of the two brothers who married, the other being Edward, the eldest brother. However, it seems likely that only Edward had children. The most distinguished descendant of this house was Sir John Bellot, Baronet, Sheriff of Staffordshire, 1661-1662. The family had become extinct by 1714.

George Blyth

Cecil never allowed himself to forget Mary Cheke, his first wife, who died a few years after their marriage. During the rest of his life, Cecil employed and promoted members of her family. George Blyth was such a person. Son of John Blyth, a Cambridge Regius Professor of Physic,

⁵⁴ Ormerod, *Chester*, p. 45.
⁵⁵ P. R. O. State Papers 15/f.209.
⁵⁶ Cecil Papers, v. 140, p. 20.
⁵⁷ Ormerod, *Chester*, p. 45.
⁵⁸ P. R. O., Wards 9/373.
⁵⁹ P. R. O., Cal. and Index, Pat. Rolls, 1-16 Eliz., p. 336.
⁶⁰ P. R. O., E. 315/309.
⁶¹ List of Court of Wards Officers, Unpublished, Compiled by Professor Joel Hurstfield.
⁶² P. R. O., Cal. and Index, Pat. Rolls, 31-37 Eliz.
⁶³ P. C. C., 72 Drake.

and Alice Cheke, sister of Mary, George quite naturally caught the eye of his uncle, Sir William Cecil. Educated at Trinity College, Cambridge, where in 1554 he received the B.A. and in 1558 the M.A., George remained to become a fellow of the college in 1560, and Deputy Regius Professor of Greek in the University in 1562.[1] In March, 1563, Blyth was admitted to Lincoln's Inn for training in law.[2]

The date at which Blyth entered his uncle's service is unknown. In 1568 he was traveling in France, perhaps to further his education, possibly on Cecil's behalf. Writing to Michael Hickes from Orleans, Blyth said he was using the French tongue because he had lost the use of his own. He had returned to England by 1571 when an exchequer warrant described him as a servant of Lord Burghley.[3] Blyth appeared in 1572 in a list of gentleman servitors, immediately below Bellot the steward, on the occasion of the Queen's visit to Theobalds.[4]

Blyth's reward or promotion came rapidly. In August, 1572, he was granted the office of secretary and custodian of the signet of the Council of the North for life, apparently in reversion for the office was then held by another.[5] Provided with the prospect of security, Blyth married Anne Egerton in London in 1573.[6] He had obviously reached the top in Burghley's service for in the conduct of exchequer business in June, 1574, he was described as secretary to the Lord Treasurer.[7] Blyth must have been almost immediately added to the Council of the North, for in August the Lord President wrote in appreciation of his service to Burghley who had proposed Blyth for the job.[8] Four years later, upon the death of Thomas Eynns, Blyth became secretary, an office he held until his death in 1581. He resided in the Cathedral Close of York.[9]

While not a wealthy man, Blyth held several manors of the crown, had a lease of sixty years on certain Devon tithes, and received at least one wardship, that of William Wyntershall in 1572.[10] He was also able to join with his cousin, Peter Osborne, and another in standing surety for the payment of £50 for another wardship, one presumably reserved for Osborne.[11] Such goods as he possessed, not enumerated in the brief will, he left to his wife Anne.[12]

[1] *Alumni Cantabrigiensis*, I, 171.
[2] History of Parliament Trust, unpublished biography.
[3] *Ibid.*
[4] Cecil Papers, v. 140, p. 20.
[5] P. R. O., Cal. Pat. Rolls, 1-16 Eliz., p. 329r.
[6] History of Parliament Trust, unpublished biography.
[7] P. R. O., E. 315/202.
[8] History of Parliament Trust, unpublished biography.
[9] *Ibid.*
[10] History of Parliament Trust, unpublished biography; P. R. O., Cal. Pat. Rolls, 1-16 Eliz., pp. 318, 343r.
[11] P. R. O., Wards 9/221.
[12] P. C. C., 29 Darcy.

Blyth had a short career in parliament when he sat for Maldon in 1571. It happened that another Burghley partisan, Peter Osborne, had been returned for Maldon and Guilford but chose to sit for Guilford. It is not surprising that Cecil should instigate the return of Blyth in a place vacated by his nephew-by-marriage and Blyth's cousin, Osborne, who also was an exchequer official.[13]

Edward Browne

Little can be said about many of the persons surrounding Cecil, for the keys which would unlock obscure deposits of information are lacking. In only three places can the name Browne be found. The earliest reference is the very useful list of servants prepared in 1572 for the Queen's visit to Theobalds. A Mr. Browne was detailed to do something in the hall.[1] The fact that he does not appear on subsequent lists suggests only that he was not among those assigned responsibilites on the occasions mentioned. In 1580 a Mr. Browne conducted exchequer business as a gentleman usher to Lord Burghley.[2]

This is very likely the Edward Browne, gentleman, whose will was made in 1588 and who lived in the parish of St. Clement Danes, London where a Cecil servant might logically have a residence. His request that he be buried in the ordinary church without any pomp or great ceremony may be evidence of extreme protestant convictions. After several small bequests to members of his family, he designated £5 for the poor. To Mr. Steward he left an "olde riall that olde Mrs. Cecil bequeathed me." This is undoubtedly Thomas Bellot who also witnessed the will. Browne requested his wife to provide £100 for his brothers and sisters if she should die before re-marrying. A servant, his "man," received some clothing.[3]

The will suggests that Browne, whose father was living, faced death while still comparatively young. This must be the same Edward, son of Anthony Browne, to whom Jane Cecil, Burghley's mother, had left 15s. in the same year. The father, Anthony, also received 15s. and was asked to serve as a trustee of Mrs. Cecil's foundation for the poor workers of Stamford.[4] The Brownes, likely neighbors of the Cecils in Lincolnshire or Northamptonshire, must have been highly esteemed friends to be asked to administer a trust jointly with relatives of Mrs. Cecil.

In August, 1598, after Burghley's death, a Thomas Browne, possibly

---

[13] History of Parliament Trust, unpublished biography.

[1] Cecil Papers, v. 140, p. 20.
[2] P. R. O., E. 315/203.
[3] P. C. C., 5 Leicester.
[4] P. C. C., 23 Rutland.

of this same family, wrote to Sir Robert Cecil, asking that he be allowed ". . . your cloth to shadow me now, as naked and destitute of my late most honourable Lord. He always affected my poor name and family. . . ."[5]

George Burden

Born of a Kentish family, educated at Rochester Grammar School, Magdalen Hall, Oxford, then Trinity College, Cambridge, Burden entered the service of William Cecil in 1549, only two years after Roger Alford, whose friend he was.[1] In a list of servants compiled after 1553, when a priest entered his household, Cecil described Burden as his schoolmaster.[2] Precisely what other work he performed while in the Cecil household is not known. However, Burden's participation in large land transactons suggests that the scope of his employment exceeded the duties of a schoolmaster.[3]

Burden very probably acted as the agent of Secretary Cecil when he spent £58.15s. for the exchange of £9,400 from silver to gold, this being a part of the £16,000 delivered to Valentine Browne for the Queen's affairs in 1560.[4]

In 1564 Burden received appointment as deputy receiver-general to the Dean and Chapter of Westminster and possibly moved out of the immediate Cecil household. The dean who offered the appointment was another former Cecil schoolmaster, Gabriel Goodman.

In spite of his new employment, Burden appeared in December, 1575 as a receiver of rents for "young" Hoby's lands from John, Lord Russell who married the widowed Lady Hoby, William Cecil's sister.[5] Perhaps Cecil, as Master of the Court of Wards, had assigned his servant as supervisor of the Hoby lands. In any case, Burden's relations with the Hobys were warm as his numerous bequests to them indicate.

In April, 1573, Burden married Elizabeth Philippes, a widow, of Bridewell.[6] Three years later, on July 7, 1576, he was joined with Godfrey Goodman, a brother of Dean Goodman, in a grant of the offices of receiver and solicitor to the Dean and Chapter of Westminster, posts to be held for life and to be performed by themselves or their deputies.

[5] H. M. C., *Salisbury MSS.,* VIII, p. 325.

[1] B. M., *Lansdowne MSS.,* v. 118, p. 35.
[2] *Ibid.,* p. 36.
[3] History of Parliament Trust, unpublished biography.
[4] P. R. O., E. 101/429/11, f. 10r.
[5] P. R. O., Wards 9/381.
[6] George John Armytage, ed., *Marriage Licenses Issued by the Bishop of London, 1520-1610,* Harleian Society Publications, XXV (London, 1887), p. 56.

Burden himself was specifically gven the right to hold both offices for his life, "without interference of Godfrey Goodman," and to enjoy the £40 annual fee.[7] When Burden undertook the office, surety for his good performance of the same was provided by Thomas Cecil, eldest son of Lord Burghley, and by William Seres, stationer, an old servant of Burghley's. The bond was for £1000.[8]

The new position meant closer ties to Westminster Abbey. Burden was given a lease of a dwelling within the Abbey precincts. For 40s. a year Burden enjoyed the use of a house in the outer court of the "College," with a little garden within the quadrant of the college, plus an orchard, garden plot and stable.[9] In 1589 Burden received the leases of two other Westminster Abbey tenements for forty years, at 26s.8d. annually.[10]

Nor had Burden's old master, Lord Burghley, forgotten him. During these years Burden received at least one wardship, that of Richard Turner, for which he gave £73.4d. in ready money.[11] Perhaps this was in part an eloquent thanks for Burden's support in the parliaments of 1572, 1576 and 1581, in all of which he represented Aylesbury whose patron was Dame Dorothy Packington.[12] Though Burden's role in parliament cannot be accurately reconstructed, it is inconceivable that he should have done otherwise than support Lord Burghley whose great responsibility was the program of the government.

Burden's financial manipulations included an agreement, made jointly with William Walter of Wimbledon in 1570, to construct a house as a resort for Westminster School during onslaughts of the plague. Eventually he became too deeply committed financially to be certain of the integrity of his own property in case of his death.[13] To safeguard his lands against forfeiture, he transferred them to Elizabeth, wife of Roger Alford, with reversion to his own wife within ten days of his death.[14]

At his death in 1593 he owed the Dean and Chapter a considerable sum of money. Nonetheless his numerous legacies, whether paid or not, reflect his good intentions toward Westminster School, the Cecils and the Hobys. A bequest, likely honored, was the gift of several volumes of Cicero to his great friend and associate, William Camden. Dean Goodman was an overseer of the will.[15]

[7] Westminster Abbey Library, Register Book VI, 1570-1586, p. 27, f. 155.
[8] *Ibid.*, ff. 159-160.
[9] *Ibid.*, f. 210.
[10] *Ibid.*, Register Book VII, 1587-1597, p. 15, f. 89.
[11] P. R. O., Wards 9/221.
[12] History of Parliament Trust, unpublished biography.
[13] Westminster Abbey Library, Register Book VI, f. 53.
[14] History of Parliament Trust, unpublished biography.
[15] *Ibid.*

William Cayworth

In 1544, at the age of twenty-four, William Cecil presumably established his first household. Only two servants joined him that year, the first being William Cayewood, followed by Audrey Ogle, Mildred Cecil's cousin.[1] How Cayworth, or Cayewood as he was alternately called, served in the 1540's is not known. By 1555 he had become the steward of Cecil's ever-growing household, entitled to three yards of cloth for his livery and 10s. per quarter as his wage.[2] Sir John Abraham, steward at Burghley House in Northamptonshire, in his accounts for 1555-1556, referred to the sealing of the chamber where "Cayworthe leys."[3] In January, 1557, Cayworth was galloping to Hatfield, possibly with messages from Cecil to the Princess Elizabeth.[4]

Other records provide glimpses of Cayworth receiving funds, making payments, handling the Cecil payroll, recording the journey of his master from Wimbledon to Burghley in 1557, and keeping track of household charges. In a fairly busy week in May, 1557, during which Cayworth made another trip to Hatfield where his dinner cost 6d., Cayworth fed the Cannon Row establishment for 13s.7d. when there were at least forty persons there. With extraordinary charges, including transportation, clothes, nails and books, running to 19s. 8d., the total for the week just described amounted to but 33s.3d.[5]

No other evidence is available to indicate active service in Cecil's employ beyond 1557 until 1562 when a William Cayworth wrote to Cecil from Stamford about deer for his park.[6] The final reference to any William Cayworth is a letter from Cayworth to Cecil, dated November 25, 1566, written from Cliff Park. He informed Cecil that certain rents, due at Michaelmas, were being sent by John Clement, a servant of Sir Walter Mildmay.[7] It may be significant that 1566 was the year in which Thomas Bellot became steward to Cecil, indicating the possible death or replacement of Cayworth at that time.

Nothing was discovered about this person outside the facts contained in the extant accounts and letters. He remains personally obscure.

[1] B. M., *Lansdowne MSS.*, v. 118, p. 35.
[2] *Ibid.*, p. 45.
[3] Cecil Papers, Box G 1, f. 13.
[4] Cecil Papers, General 139, f. 7.
[5] Cecil Papers, v. 143, pp. 80-81.
[6] Great Britain, *C. S. P. D.*, I (London, 1856), p. 198.
[7] P. R. O., State Papers 12/f. 65.

Henry and John Cheke

Henry and John Cheke were the sons of Cecil's brother-in-law, Sir John Cheke, the distinguished Greek professor at Cambridge, who died at the age of forty-three in 1557, when Henry was only nine and John about seven. Henry, at least, was educated by a tutor, William Ireland, appointed by Sir John, and possibly also by Peter Osborne, Sir John's friend and relative, from whom Henry later received financial help.[1] Lady Cheke, the boy's mother, married Henry MacWilliams, a gentleman of the court. Her own considerable fortune went to her children by MacWilliams.[2]

John Cheke attended Peterhouse, Cambridge, from which he likely entered Lord Burghley's service. He left in 1578 to follow a military career.[3] Strype described John as a youth of great hope who was noted by his uncle, Lord Burghley, and taken into his family where for at least six years he served in the retinue of his uncle, after which he left for the wars in Ireland. He was killed there in 1580.[4]

Henry attended Trinity College, Cambridge, and took an M.A. at King's College, Cambridge in 1568.[5] He sat for Bedford in the parliament of 1571, again in 1572, and for Boroughbridge in 1584. He had estates at Elstow, Bedfordshire; Wintney, Hampshire; and the manor of Yearley in the North Riding of Yorkshire.[6] By 1574 he was troubled with illness and debts. He naturally turned to his uncle, asking Burghley for an office or the reversion of one.[7] On July 18, 1576, he was duly sworn a clerk of the Privy Council.[8] Within a week of his cousin George Blyth's death in 1581, he had replaced Blyth as Secretary of the Council of the North, installed upon the recommendation of his uncle, Lord Burghley.[9]

His letters to Cecil in Greek in 1566 and in Latin in 1568 proclaim him an able linguist. During travels abroad from 1577 to the end of 1578, he studied both Italian and French. He died in 1586, clearly a protestant. The wardship of Thomas, Henry's son by Frances, sister of

---

[1] History of Parliament Trust, unpublished biography.

[2] John Strype, *The Life of Sir John Cheke* (Oxford, 1821), p. 133.

[3] Thomas Alfred Walker, ed., *A Biographical Register of Peterhouse Men, 1284-1574* (Cambridge, 1927), pp. 242-243.

[4] Strype, *Cheke*, pp. 138-139.

[5] Hazel Matthews, "Personnel of the Parliament of 1584-1585" (London M.A. thesis, 1948), Section III, p. 41.

[6] Matthews, "Personnel," p. 41.

[7] History of Parliament Trust, unpublished biography.

[8] Great Britain, *Acts of the Privy Council*, IX (London, 1894), 166.

[9] History of Parliament Trust, unpublished biography.

the Earl of Sussex, appears to have been granted to Peter Osborne, the old family friend and cousin.[10]

John Clapham

John Clapham was born in London in 1566. He was the son of Luke Clapham, a north country man born in Firby, a small hamlet of the parish of Bedale in the North Riding, Yorkshire. Luke, an educated man, was admitted a sizar at Pembroke College, Cambridge, in 1559 and transferred to Caius College, Cambridge in May, 1565.[1] John's life is obscure from his birth until his first publication in 1590, a translation from the French of Bishop Amyot's version of Plutarch's *De Tranquilitate Animi*.[2]

Clapham himself tells us he entered Burghley's household " 'even from my tender age,' " owed much of his education to Burghley's generosity and spent more than seven years in attendance on his person.[3] By that reckoning, Clapham must have been present among the Cecils by 1591. Clapham, writing from Theobalds to Sir Robert Cecil on April 29, 1595 on the theme of Burghley's health, provides our first glimpse of him in service.[4] In 1596, Clapham, then at the Court, was addressed by a William Partheriche who sent a plan for a sea coast fortification he wished Burghley to see.[5] Clapham's position must have been that of clerk or secretary.

The last sight of Clapham fulfilling his duty to Burghley is found in the letter Clapham wrote from Burghley House in the Strand to Sir Robert Cecil, September 3, 1598, shortly after Burghley's death. Clapham desired permission to accompany the corpse to Stamford, at the same time requesting Cecil to present him with one of Burghley's horses and its furniture. At the same time he admitted being unable to find a patent which the Lord Chamberlain thought to be in his custody, having seen it in Mr. Barnard's time. Clapham explained that although, by Burghley's special appointment, he occasionally had access to the evidence house, the greatest part of Burghley's evidences were unknown to him, not having been delivered to him by any note after Mr. Barnard's death. Besides, Clapham insisted, he had no leisure in which to acquaint himself

[10] P. R. O., Wards 9/221.

[1] John Clapham, *Elizabeth of England*. Edited by Evelyn Plummer Read and Conyers Read (Philadelphia, 1951), pp. 4-5.
[2] History of Parliament Trust, unpublished biography.
[3] Clapham, *Elizabeth*, p. 8.
[4] H. M. C., *Salisbury MSS.*, V, p. 191.
[5] Great Britain, *C. S. P. D.*, IV (London, 1869), p. 331.

with the evidence house because of continual attendance upon Burghley.⁶

There is more specific reference to Clapham's responsibility in a petition from Robert Middleton, seeking after Burghley's death to assert his claims to a wardship. The composition or fee for obtaining the wardship was granted to one of Burghley's servants in the presence of Thomas Bellot and the petition describing the transaction was said by Middleton to remain "with Mr. Clapham, keeper of the book of wards to the late Lord Treasurer. . . ."⁷ That Clapham was indeed privy to wardship transactions is confirmed by a letter written in 1600 by George Freville to Sir Robert's secretary, Percival, in which Freville discussed a wardship, stating that Burghley's clerk, Clapham, would know best about it.⁸

Though only thirty-two years old when Burghley died in 1598, Clapham had become a highly valued servant. Burghley, who left only two life-time annuities, directed that one go to Thomas Bellot and the other, for £6.13.4., to John Clapham.⁹ Though relatively small, it was a mark of high favor and an acknowledgment that Burghley felt some responsibility for his future. Bellot himself left Clapham a small legacy when he died in 1611.¹⁰

Clapham, who had begun his public career the year before Burghley's death by representing Sudbury in the parliament of 1597, was admitted to Gray's Inn in 1602.¹¹ His career reached its climax with his appointment as one of the six clerks of Chancery.¹² We know little about the job except that it was a lucrative opportunity. John Chamberlain, writing to Dudley Carleton a few days after Clapham's death, reported that the person who had the reversion of the next clerkship to fall vacant had sold his right for £6,000.¹³ Very likely Clapham's reversion had been arranged for him by Lord Burghley.

In 1608 the prosperous John Clapham built a hospital at Firby, his father's Yorkshire home, providing for a master and six brethren. The endowment consisted or property worth £30 annually. To this hospital were given pictures of himself and his wife, Anne, daughter of Edmund Kidderminster.¹⁴

Only from his father's will do we learn that John died on December 6, 1618, at the age of fifty-two. Luke Clapham, who died four years later, composed an epitaph for himself to be used if buried in Christ Church,

⁶ H. M. C., *Salisbury MSS.*, VIII, pp. 328-329.
⁷ H. M. C., *Salisbury MSS.*, XIV, p. 90.
⁸ H. M. C., *Salisbury MSS.*, X, p. 83.
⁹ Collins, *Burghley*, p. 97.
¹⁰ P. C. C., 81 Wood.
¹¹ History of Parliament Trust, unpublished biography.
¹² *Ibid.*
¹³ Norman Egbert McClure, ed., *The Letters of John Chamberlain*, 2 volumes (Philadelphia, 1939), II, p. 193.
¹⁴ Clapham, *Elizabeth*, p. 8.

Newgate Market, where his son was buried. It reflected the father's pride in his son that he wished to be identified simply and solely as the father of John Clapham, one of the six clerks of Chancery.[15]

Clapham's literary production, begun in 1590 with a translation, became more ambitious as he grew older. A Latin poem on the subject of Narcissus followed in 1591. After Burghley's death he started his *History of England,* a work based on the chronicles which he digested and reduced. The first volume, dealing with the Roman period, was published in 1602. Later the work was brought down to Saxon times. In the spring of 1603 his *Certain Observations Concerning the Life and Reign of Elizabeth* was issued. The £5 which he gave to the foundation of the Bodleian Library was used to purchase books, among them his own *History.*[16]

Robert Constable

A Robert Constable is first found associated with Lord Burghley in January 1577, when particulars of a lease are given to Roger Rast for Robert Constable, gentleman servant to the Lord Treasurer.[1] In the same year a Robert Constable was granted an office with a fee of 6s.8d.[2] On September 16, 1578, William Heydon wrote Lord Burghley about the suspicious arrival in Snetsham, "a haven of small resort," of a ship called the "Robert of Flamborough," belonging to Robert Constable, esquire. The ship contained two packets of wool and two salt hides, covered with coals, apparently intended for transport to Flanders. Heydon had arrested the ship and asked for directions.[3] Clearly the owner of the ship belonged to the Yorkshire Constables whose estate was called Flamborough. Possibly Burghley's servant was the owner of the ship and a Yorkshire man.

In any case, Burghley's old servant joined the English forces in Ireland and became a captain. As such he was captured by the Irish rebels in late 1597. On January 4, 1598, the Earl of Ormonde wrote to Burghley about Constable, enclosing a letter from him, referred to as Burghley's old servant.[4] From another letter sent from Ormonde to Burghley in which Ormonde promised to aid Constable, we may deduce that Burghley wrote effectively on his behalf.[5] He was not released before Burghley's death in August. However, he was apparently free in

---
[15] P. C. C., 25 Savile.
[16] History of Parliament Trust, unpublished biography.

[1] P. R. O., E. 315/203.
[2] P. R. O., E. 315/309.
[3] H. M. C., *Salisbury MSS.,* II, p. 202.
[4] Great Britain, C. S. P., *Ireland,* VII (London, 1895), p. 9.
[5] *Ibid.,* p. 85.

February, 1599, when a complaint was lodged against him and another for "spoil committed" on a French ship.⁶ Constable was dead by September 6, 1599.

Aside from the evidence cited, there is none connecting him with Burghley's service. He does not appear on any of the lists of servants. These brief references give but slight substance to an otherwise unknown man.

William Cooke

The case for William Cooke can be succinctly put. Though not included in the chronological list of the admittance of servants to his service, Cecil included his brother-in-law William Cooke in a list of those to be provided with liveries in 1554, Cooke's to cost 5s.¹ Perhaps he served in the character of a retainer rather than as a servant, though in either case he must have been a part of the household. His service thereafter is wrapped in silence.

Only when he received a promotion, perhaps by way of reward, in October, 1561, does he emerge again. Shortly after Cecil became Master of the Court of Wards and Liveries in 1561, William Cooke was granted the office of Clerk of the Liveries for life.² This is the extent of our information except a bit from an unpublished genealogical chart which records that Sir William Cooke of Higham, Gloucester, a son of Sir Anthony Cooke, married Frances, daughter of John, Lord Grey, youngest son of Thomas Grey, second Marquis of Dorset. The couple had six children.³

Walter Cope

Walter Cope was born sometime during the years 1551-1558, the second son of Edward Cope of Hanwell, Oxfordshire, and Elizabeth, daughter and heir of Walter Mohun of Wollaton, Northamptonshire. He was a member of a rather distinguished puritan family and second cousin of Mildred, Lady Burghley. He married Dorothy, daughter of Richard Greville of Wootton.¹ His grandfather, Sir Anthony Cope of

⁶ *Ibid.,* p. 477.

¹ B. M., *Lansdowne MSS.,* v. 118, f. 41r.
² Great Britain, *Cal. Pat. Rolls,* Elizabeth, II (London, 1948), p. 250.
³ "Robert Cecil's Relations," an unpublished series of genealogical charts compiles by Howard Vallance Jones, Chart II.

¹ Margaret K. Mort, "Personnel of the House of Commons in 1601" (London M. A. thesis, 1952), Section III, p. 59.

Hanwell, had been Chamberlain to Queen Catherine Parr and had served as sheriff of Oxfordshire. While Walter's father, Edward, did not live long enough to maintain the family honors, his eldest son, Sir Anthony, became sheriff of Oxfordshire, an M. P. from 1586-1604, and was imprisoned as a puritan in 1587, a factor which did not prevent his being knighted in 1590.[2]

By his own statement, made after Robert Cecil's death in 1612, Walter admitted to having been trained for thirty-eight years under Burghley and Cecil.[3] If this is correct, Cope must have entered Burghley's service as a very young man in about 1574. In the list of servants at Theobalds prepared for the Queen's visit in October, 1581, Cope appears prominently as an usher, a gentleman usher no doubt, who was himself served by a man.[4] In only one letter does Burghley speak directly of Cope. Writing to Walsingham from Hertford Castle, in November, 1582, Burghley said he was sending his servant Walter Cope with the £5 in gold, "which you signified her Majesty's pleasure to have. . . ."[5] In September, 1585, he received particulars for an Essex manor, just as many of Burghley's servants did.[6]

Cope's service under Burghley appears to have been well rewarded. In 1579 he was made surveyor of the Queen's possessions in Kent during good conduct, an exchequer appointment, the fee for which was £20.[7] Cope was also made feodary of Oxfordshire in 1584, although the work was done by the same deputy his predecessor had used.[8] During the last few years of his exercise of the office, he was also feodary for the Duchy of Lancaster, beginning in 1598.[9] The Duchy of Lancaster normally did not employ Ward's feodaries. The exception to this rule seems to have been Walter Cope. In 43 Elizabeth Cope ceased to be feodary for the Court of Wards in Oxfordshire, becoming instead feodary in London and Middlesex, the gift of the new Master of Wards, Sir Robert Cecil.[10]

In 1586 Cope was granted an unusually long lease, a fifty-year lease of the manor of Aswick in Lincolnshire.[11] The last gift which can reasonably be attributed to Lord Burghley was the wardship of Henry Conny in 1592 and even this may have come through the intercession of Robert Cecil.[12] Cope's absence from the list of servants at Theobalds for the

[2] *Concise D. N. B.*, p. 277.
[3] John Gutch, *Collectanea Curiosa*, 2 volumes (Oxford, 1781), I, p. 122.
[4] Cecil Papers, v. 140, p. 25.
[5] P. R. O., S. P. 12/f. 237.
[6] P. R. O., E. 315/203.
[7] P. R. O., E. 315/309.
[8] Unpublished list of officers of the Court of Wards, compiled by Professor Joel Hurstfield.
[9] Robert Somerville, *History of the Duchy of Lancaster* (London, 1953), p. 627.
[10] Unpublished list, Wards Officers, compiled by J. Hurstfield.
[11] P. R. O., Cal. Pat. Rolls, 17-30 Elizabeth, p. 11r.
[12] P. R. O., Wards 9/221.

Queen's visit in 1591 lends a shadow of credibility to the assumption that Cope had already passed into the employ of Robert Cecil who by this date was acting Secretary of State and had his own establishment, and who was a very great friend of Walter Cope.

Although Cope received what were probably fairly lucrative gifts from Lord Burghley, no office of state fell his way during the reign of Elizabeth. By 1602, when Cope could afford the luxury of a gift of several early English volumes to the Bodleian Library, it is apparent that Robert Cecil had become his zealous advocate.[13] In 1602, John Chamberlain spoke of Cope's daily expectation of becoming a gentleman of the Privy Chamber.[14] Cecil, according to Chamberlain, did Cope the extraordinary favor of making him a partner in his entertainment of the Queen, when Cope had the opportunity of presenting the Queen with some "toys," for which he had many fair words but not the expected Privy Chamber place.[15]

Chamberlain's remarkable letters provide a clue to Cope's character at this time. Cope, avid in the study of genealogies as was his late master, had sought to have Dudley Carleton work on the families of France while residing in France but met with little success. Chamberlain, gently chiding Carleton for his failure to gratify Cope, said: "Though I hold him [Cope] neither apt nor greatly able to do any friend he hath good, yet must we sometimes hold a candle before the devil, and do as the people of Calicut, that worship him not so much for any help they look for at his hands, as because he should do them no harm."[16]

Promotion, beginning with knighthood in 1603, came more rapidly in the spacious days of James I.[17] The anticipated Privy Chamber appointment finally fell upon Cope and with it, like manna from heaven, came a grant of the third part of all the fines payable to the king upon suit of debt, and actions for damage commenced in the Court of King's Bench, when the debt or damage amounted to £40. This was Cope's for twenty-one years at a rent of £22.4.5½. and the third part of a farthing.[18] In 1603 Cope also became an auditor of the Duchy of Lancaster, a position he purchased from Richard Connock who had paid Sir Francis Godolphin £200 for it.[19]

Honor mingled with an accumulation of lucrative positions. Cope accompanied the Lord Admiral to Spain in 1605 for the signing of the

---

[13] William D. Macray, *Annals of the Bodleian Library, 1598-1867* (London, 1868), p. 22.

[14] Mort, "Commons," p. 59.

[15] McClure, *Chamberlain*, I, p. 177.

[16] McClure, *Chamberlain*, I, pp. 162-163.

[17] History of Parliament Trust, unpublished biography.

[18] Thomas Faulkner, *History and Antiquities of Kensington* (London, 1820), p. 59.

[19] Great Britain, *C. S. P. D., James I*, 1603-1610, p. 60.

treaty of peace on June 9, 1605.[20] Perhaps as a reward for this and other services, certainly for a substantial purchase price, James in 1606 granted Cope chantry lands and parsonages worth £100 annually.[21] In June, 1608, Cope became a chamberlain of the Exchequer, just a few months after receiving two-thirds of the King's interest in the manors of Elworthy and Bradney, forfeited for recusancy.[22]

Actually Cope had become a speculator in real estate and the full story of his business ventures would doubtless make fascinating reading. The evidence makes clear his ability to think big. When the alum business was in crisis in 1612, the holders of the monopoly sought the King's protection for their privileges. A rival bidder, thought to have been Sir Walter Cope, offered to buy all the interests with £180,000 to be provided by the King. The scheme involved repayment to the King over a period of ten years, with a clear gain to the Crown of £296,000. In this venture Cope was an unsuccessful bidder.[23]

When Chamberlain and his brother encountered Cope in his coach in Paul's church-yard one December day in 1608, Cope willingly paused to discuss money matters. His interest is not surprising as he and others, called contractors, had shortly before entered into a great bargain with the King for £5,000 a year in parsonages besides £2,000 a year Cope had himself got from the King. Chamberlain, reporting the episode to Carleton, concluded his remarks by saying that even so they were not expected by the "world" to be great gainers.[24]

It was not long until Cope began to live like a man of wealth. In 1607 he moved from London into his newly built mansion in Kensington, called Cope Castle.[25] In 1609 Chamberlain reported to Carleton the rumor that Cope was being considered for secretary.[26] Further favor came, as in 1611 Cope and Arthur Gorges were given a patent for a public register for general commerce to be kept for the entire kingdom. The venture never materialized.[27] In 1612 the significance of Cope's palatial residence and social status appeared in concrete form. In that year Cope Castle was the scene of a magnificent celebration in honor of the marriage of Cope's only child, a daughter, to Sir Henry Rich, son of the Earl of Warwick.[28] The castle would one day become famous as Holland House, its name taken from Sir Henry's subsequent title, first Earl of Holland.

[20] McClure, *Chamberlain,* I, p. 205.
[21] McClure, *Chamberlain,* I, p. 229.
[22] Great Britain, *C. S. P. D.,* VIII (London, 1857), pp. 403, 436.
[23] William H. Price, *The English Patents of Monopoly* (Boston, 1906), p. 87
[24] McClure, *Chamberlain,* I, p. 277.
[25] Mort, "Commons," p. 59.
[26] McClure, *Chamberlain,* I, p. 280.
[27] Mort, "Commons," p. 59.
[28] McClure, *Chamberlain,* I, p. 346.

Almost immediately after the wedding, Cope set out to join Lord Salisbury who had gone to Bath in hope of recovering his health. Salisbury died before Cope arrived. Cope, one of Salisbury's executors, later wrote an ineffective apology for Lord Salisbury which he presented to the King with the insinuation that he possessed secrets useful for the King's service.[29]

The King must have been either impressed or intimidated by what he heard, for in November, 1612, James visited Cope at Kensington whereupon it was announced that Cope had been made Master of the Court of Wards and Liveries.[30] Chamberlain thought that if the two late Lord Treasurers, Cope's predecessors in the office, could look out of their graves "they would be out of countenance with themselves and say to the world quantum mutatus."[31]

Perhaps Chamberlain's low estimate of Cope was correct. On July 21, 1614 Chamberlain reported the rumor that Cope would likely be transferred to some office of less importance.[32] Soon after, Chamberlain wrote that Cope had died suddenly while preparing to attend his brother's funeral. It was thought that the loss of Sir Anthony Cope and the talk of losing his place had broken Cope's heart, especially as his brother was undergirding him financially.[33] Indeed, so tangled was Cope's estate that Lady Cope had to compound for her income of £500 left her, accepting instead £3,500 in cash, in order to help clear the estate.[34]

Cope made his fellow contractors his executors and heirs, provided they cleared up his debts and paid certain sums to his wife and daughter.[35] With debts of £27,000, all the executors declined the business except his son-in-law and a nephew who had to sell some of their own lands to clear the debts.[36] Sir George Coppin, a fellow of Cope's in Burghley's service, a Kensington neighbor, and a contractor, denied the claims of all these ties in refusing.

At his death, Cope owned the manor of Earl's Court in Kensington, the manor of Abbots' Kensington, the capital messuage of West Town or the Old House in Kensington, and two hundred acres of meadow or pasture as well as Nottingwood.[37] He had acquired other manors during his lifetime and disposed of them. One such, Knotting Barns, had passed from the Marquis of Winchester to Lord Burghley, then was sold by Thomas, second Lord Burghley to Cope in 1599, for £2,000. Cope found

[29] *Ibid.*, p. 369.
[30] McClure, Chamberlain, I, p. 390.
[31] *Ibid.*, p. 392.
[32] *Ibid.*, p. 550.
[33] *Ibid.*, p. 554.
[34] *Ibid.*, p. 560.
[35] P. C. C., 66 Rudd.
[36] McClure, *Chamberlain,* I, pp. 560, 575.
[37] Faulkner, *Kensington,* p. 59.

a buyer in 1601, Henry Anderson, a London merchant, willing to pay £3,400.[38]

Cope also had a career in parliament. He represented St. Mawes in the parliament of 1588, Weymouth in that of 1601, Westminster in 1604, and Stockbridge in 1614. He also served as a justice of the peace in 1601 for Middlesex, serving as a part of the quorum.[39]

George Coppin

George Coppin was a member of a well-to-do family resident in Dunwich, Suffolk where a senior George, who died in 1578, had a fishmonger's shop.[1] A Robert Coppin, likely the brother of George, senior, owned three fishing vessels. Both incorporated firm protestant statements in their wills and both were prosperous.[2] Unfortunately the genealogical evidence is not sound enough to establish beyond doubt satisfactory relationships. A contemporary herald's visitation provides a descent from a Robert to George, and to our George who married Anne, daughter of Thomas Norton of Bedford, and had four sons, only the youngest of whom had issue.[3] The family had produced members of parliament and bailiffs of Dunwich since the latter years of the reign of Henry VIII.[4] Very likely the George we meet in Burghley's employ was a younger son, sent away to seek his fortune.

We meet him first in Burghley's service, possibly as a page, during the Queen's visit to Theobalds in 1581.[5] More we know not until in 1597 Coppin was elected to parliament for New Romney through the influence of Sir Robert Cecil, to whom the nomination of one burgess had been transferred by the Lord Warden.[6] Only during the last few months of Burghley's life can Coppin be related to the Cecil household, and then he was apparently in continuous attendance. Five letters from Coppin to Sir Robert Cecil survive, all written during July, 1598. In them Coppin described the state of his master's health. Each letter records a further step in the great statesman's physical decline. By July 26th, the doctors had been sent for in haste, presumably to watch over the last remaining days.[7] Though not mentioned by name in Burghley's will, he very

---

[38] *Ibid.*, pp. 426-427.
[39] Mort, "Commons," p. 59.

[1] P. C. C., 35 Langley.
[2] P. C. C., 15 Pyckering.
[3] Walter C. Metcalfe, ed., *The Visitations of Hertfordshire*, Harleian Society Publications, XX (1886), pp. 45-46.
[4] Fuidge, "Commons," Section III, p. 95.
[5] Cecil Papers, v. 140, p. 25.
[6] History of Parliament Trust, unpublished biography.
[7] Cecil Papers, v. 62, pp. 43, 85, 87, 88; v. 63, p. 4.

likely benefited from the provison which set aside a piece of plate of the value of from £3 to £4 for each gentleman servant who served without wages.[8]

Burghley had in other ways provided for Coppin, an apparently valued younger clerk. In 1592 Coppin was permitted to buy the wardship and marriage of one Thomas Sturge of Norfolk, for which he paid either £16 or £33.6.8. and was to receive annually either £6.13.4. or £10, all depending upon another transaction.[9] At the same time Coppin got the lease of Sturge's messuages in Norfolk, worth £16.10.0. a year, for a fine or payment of £16 in cash.[10] As the ward was not over four years of age, the grant was a good one. The Sturge manor of Calveley was in Coppin's possession in 1607, after which he soon sold it to one Thomas Bateman.[11] How Coppin secured it is not known.

Burghley was without question responsible for the office of clerk of the Crown in Chancery which was given to Coppin for life on January 31, 1597.[12] Certainly Burghley had discussed with Sir Thomas Egerton, Lord Keeper and Master of the Rolls, ways of eliminating the chaos that existed in certain Chancery departments.[13] Whether or not Burghley was serving the interest of Chancery or Coppin, or perhaps both, it is certain that Coppin was put on the high road to wealth. Chamberlain reported, when Coppin died, that the office was worth seven or eight hundred pounds a year.[14] Coppin's subsequent history bears out our assumption of growing wealth.

Even before his promotion to Chancery, in 1596 Coppin was involved, and litttle more than this can be ascertained from the evidence, in a major financial matter. While it would appear from the entry in the Lord Chamberlain's records that he was either lending money or standing bond, as the conditions of the contract were not copied, no conclusion can safely be drawn.[15] There are three similar entries for 1598 and 1599 in which sums of several thousand pounds are mentioned.[16] It can only

[8] Collins, *Burghley*, p. 96.
[9] P. R. O., Wards 9/158.
[10] P. R. O., Wards 9/188.
[11] Charles Parkin, *History of the County of Norfolk*, 11 volumes (London, 1805-1810), X, p. 241.
[12] P. R. O., Cal. and Index, Pat. Rolls, 38-43, Eliz., p. 80.
[13] History of Parliament Trust, unpublished biography.
[14] McClure, *Chamberlain*, II, p. 293.
[15] P. R. O., Lord Chamberlain 4/193, Entry Book, Recognizances for Debt, f. 165.
[16] P. R. O., Lord Chamberlain 4/194, Entry Book, Recognizances for Debt, ff. 29-30, 69, 171. For a discussion of the problem of recognizances, see the following: H. R. Trevor-Roper, "The Elizabethan Aristocracy: an Anatomy Anatomized," *Economic History Review*, Second Series, III (No. 3, 1951), pp. 279-298; also Richard T. Spence, "The Cliffords, Earls of Cumberland, 1579-1646," (London Ph.D. thesis, 1959), pp. XXIV-XLVI.

be said with certainty that Coppin became a man of considerable business activity.

With the advent of James I in 1603 Coppin, in company with many others, received a knighthood. In 1607 he became a commissioner for the sale of crown lands, along with Sir Walter Cope and others. In the 1607 grant, they bought, at fifteen years purchase, lands of the annual value of £2,133 for a purchase price of £32,000.[17] Coppin bought and sold other lands as an individual. The lordship or manor of Camois in the town of Hardingham, Norfolk, worth £20 annually in 1554, came into Coppin's hands and was sold by him in 1609 to Thomas Bateman.[18]

Coppin also possessed and passed to his heirs a messuage called the White Hart, in the parish of St. Margaret's, Westminster; another adjoining, thirty-six and a half acres of land in St. Margaret's, Westminster, Kensington, and Paddington; and other property in the area valued at £30. Much of this land passed to the Finch Family and eventually to William III.[19] Coppin built a fine mansion house in the early year of the reign of James I on the site now occupied by Kensington Palace. A part of the Coppin mansion was incorporated in the early palace, having been called Nottingham House while owned by the Finches.[20]

By 1610, Coppin had become a justice of the peace in Middlesex.[21] He continued in close association with Thomas Bellot, Burghley's steward, who died in 1611. The esteem in which Bellot held Coppin is indicated by the size of the legacy Bellot left him. While only 70s., it was almost as much as that left Sir Michael Hickes, a secretary to Lord Burghley.[22]

Coppin was a faithful supporter of the Church of St. Martins-in-the-Fields. It was here that his son George was baptized on August 9, 1601 and buried September 13, 1602, the latter at a cost of 14s. for the ground, cloth, "afternoones knell and peales."[23] To this church Coppin contributed on different occasions 26s. as poor rate and 20s. as benevolence.[24] Furthermore, "Sir George Coppin was a very prominent vestryman from 1606 till his death in March, 1620."[25]

Coppin's will proclaims his eager and devout protestantism. The poor of Dunwich received £20, those of St. Martin's, £10. The home in St.

[17] Great Britain, C. S. P. D., XII (London, 1872), p. 497.
[18] Parkin, *Norfolk*, p. 224.
[19] Faulkner, *Kensington*, p. 407.
[20] Information obtained from an historical marker located in one of the principal state rooms of Kensington Palace.
[21] History of Parliament Trust, unpublished biography.
[22] P. C. C., 81 Wood.
[23] John V. Kitto, ed. and transcriber, *The Accounts of the Churchwardens of St. Martin's-in-the-Fields*, 1525-1603 (London, 1901), p. 556.
[24] *Ibid.*, p. 577.
[25] *Ibid.*, p. 556.

Martin's parish and the house "late built" in the parish of St. Margaret's, Westminster, together with lands in Middlesex, were left to his wife and then to their son Robert. They were requested to divide equally between them Coppin's plate, jewelry and household stuff. Thomas, the only other surviving son, received the rectory of Clanton, in Devon, and £2,000 to be employed for his use by the executors until he reached twenty-one.[26]

Other bequests, exceeding £305, were made. Among them was £40 to be set aside for a small monument in St. Martin's. Each household servant was to receive £10 above his wages. The residue of the estate was left to Coppin's executors, his wife and son, Robert. Overseers of the will were Coppin's brother-in-law, Dr. John Bowle, subsequently bishop of Rochester, and John Wright, a friend from Gray's Inn.[27]

Richard Dane

Three undated letters, addressed to Lord Burghley, in the *Lansdowne Manuscripts,* constitute the whole of our evidence relating to this troublesome servant. A quarrel arose between Dane and Edward Bowker, a footman to Lord Burghley. According to Dane, Bowker had grown extraordinarily insolent by virtue of Burghley's good treatment of him. During the recent progress of the Queen, Bowker used Dane badly. In fact, all the servants were willing to testify that Bowker "became a common quarreller and too troublesome a person to serve any honorable man." Yet Dane put up with a great deal of ill-usage for the sake of quiet and because of Bowker's age.[1]

While the Court was at Oatlands during the time of contagion, on July 21, being asked to keep the door, Bowker quarrelled with Dane, reviled him and challenged him to fight. They left the chamber and began the descent of the stairs leading to the court when Bowker struck Dane from behind and threw him down the stairs. Dane believed his neck would have been broken had not a gentleman of Burghley's chamber been there by chance to catch him. The two men thereupon exchanged some twenty blows. Dane protested that his cousin, Mr. Thomas Bodley, esquire, "never knew me a quarreller in twelve years I was with Mr. Secretary."[2]

Dane therefore asked Burghley to take some order with Bowker so that the others might honor Burghley by their service. Dane concluded each of the letters as he did this one: "And your poor servant will as

[26] P. C. C., 30 Soame.
[27] P. C. C., 30 Soame.

[1] B. M., *Lansdowne MSS.,* v. 99, item 76, f. 191.
[2] *Ibid.*

he is nevertheless bounden to pray unto God for preservation of your honorable estate all the days of his life."³

The other two letters, each offering prayers for Burghley, contain requests. In the first, Dane asked for a certain Martin's place at Bayone or Saint John de Luze which was then void.⁴ In the second he requested Burghley to grant a John Cloke the office of escheator of Kent and Middlesex.⁵ In neither case is there any evidence of success or failure. We hear no more of Richard Dane, nor can anything be gleaned from other records. He must have been well-connected for the Thomas Bodley, described as his cousin, is presumably the same person who served the Queen as usher and as diplomat and who subsequently collected and endowed the Oxford library which bears his name.⁶

Barnard Dewhurst

Barnard Dewhurst, born about 1533, was from a Lancashire family. How Dewhurst found his way into Burghley's service is not known. He married an Anne, said to have been a daughter of a Mr. Warde.¹ It seems likely that Anne Dewhurst was the niece of Burghley through his first marriage. The evidence for this assumption is by no means conclusive. Magdalene Purvey, Mary Cheke Cecil's sister, thus Burghley's sister-in-law, in her will of 1590 referred "to my niece Anne Dewhurst, the wife of Barnarde Dewhurst, gentleman," and then made her nephew Barnard Dewhurst one of her executors.² This relationship would be sufficient to explain how Burghley and Dewhurst met.

That Dewhurst was prominently used by Burghley as one of a group of guarantors of the marriage settlement between the Cecils and the Cobhams in 1589, all of whom were related to one or the other of the contracting families, also suggests there was an acknowledged kinship between Burghley and Dewhurst. The contract was sealed and delivered to Dewhurst on behalf of all the guarantors in the presence of witnesses among whom were Michael Hickes and Henry Maynard, Burghley's secretaries. Dewhurst very likely filed the contract away among the other family papers in the evidence house of which he seems to have been the custodian.³

Dewhurst first appeared in the Cecil household as a servant who was

³ B. M., *Landsdowne MSS.*, v. 99, item 76, f. 191.
⁴ *Ibid.*, item 78, f. 195.
⁵ *Ibid.*, v. 110, item 12, f. 44.
⁶ *Concise D. N. B.*, p. 118.

---

¹ Cecil Family Papers, "Marriage Settlement of Earl of Salisbury with Daughter of Lord Cobham," 1589, pp. 34-35.
² P. C. C., 73 Drury.
³ *Marriage Settlement*, p. 23.

designated clerk of the kitchen on the occasion of the Queen's visit to Theobalds in 1572, though the assignment to this position was cancelled.[4] The Latin inscription on his tomb describes Dewhurst as a secretary to Burghley.[5] Evidence for this assertion is not decisive, or perhaps the term secretary had itself a rather general meaning. Certainly the bulk of the evidence suggests that during the height of Burghley's career Vincent Skynner, Michael Hickes and Henry Maynard were the important secretaries, assisted by younger men such as John Clapham, George Coppin and Gilbert Wakering. Yet in an era as conscious of status and position as was the sixteenth century, surely it would have been improper to employ Dewhurst as a guarantor of the marriage settlement of 1589 while reserving Hickes and Maynard for witnesses unless, in fact, the older Dewhurst was senior in rank as well as in age.

Certainly we may safely assume that Dewhurst's position in the Cecil establishment was on a par with that of Burghley's secretaries. In 1574, and again in 1579, Dewhurst picked up particulars of leases from an exchequer office "for the Lord Treasurer of England" just as did George Blyth when he was termed secretary to the Lord Treasurer.[6] When Hugh Allington, Burghley's brother-in-law and former secretary, wrote Dewhurst in November, 1591, for the loan of certain of Lord Burghley's books, at the same time asking that certain papers sent to Burghley be returned, it seems possible to attribute secretarial responsbilities to Dewhurst.[7] No simlar construction can be placed on Dewhurst's duties on the occasion of the dinner for the French Commissioners in 1581 when, with another, he had charge of the silver vessels.[8]

In 1580, when Thomas Fermor of Somerton, Oxfordshire died, leaving a five-year-old minor who became the ward of the crown, George Shirley, one of Fermor's executors, purchased the wardship, possibly on behalf of the mother. Shirley left in the audited accounts of the executors, a list of sums paid to agents who assisted in pressng the suit for the wardship. Among the sums mentioned was £3 given Mr. Barnard, "one of my lord's secretaries."[9] Again, in the matter of wardships, another case of itemized sums paid to secure a wardship in 1595 included two references to money either offered or paid to Lord Burghley, "as Mr. Barnard knoweth."[10] As there is no trace of a Mr. Barnard in Burghley's employ at any time and as John Clapham, keeper of Lord Burghley's book of wards, obviously succeeded Mr. Barnard just at the time of Barnard Dewhurst's death, it can reasonably be suggested that Dew-

[4] Cecil Papers, v. 140, p. 20.
[5] Chauncy, *Hertfordshire*, I, 591.
[6] P. R. O., E. 315/202, pp. 84r-85, E. 315/203, p. 37.
[7] H. M. C., *Salisbury MSS.*, XIII, p. 455.
[8] B. M., *Lansdowne MSS.*, v. 33, f. 70, p. 175.
[9] Joel Hurstfield, *The Queen's Wards* (London, 1958), p. 265.
[10] *Ibid.*, p. 82.

hurst was commonly referred to as Mr. Barnard.[11] It is interesting to note that Dewhurst kept the evidence house when it was uncommon for anyone but the lord to have a key.[12]

The association of Dewhurst with wards, especially with those in Burghley's immediate custody, is substantiated by evidence that in 1577 the Court of Wards paid various sums to Dewhurst for the charges of the Earl of Essex, her majesty's ward, committed to Burghley's care.[13]

A contemporary was aware of Dewhurst's influence with Burghley, grateful for its use on his behalf in the past, and confident of its success in his immediate need. In October, Tristram Conyers wrote Dewhurst at Cecil House in this fashion:

> Old Serjeant Berdlos, of the Common Pleas bar, was wont, at his departure in the end of term, to make a cross upon the bar, and with a solemn kneeling, kiss the bar, praying that once more, if it pleased God, he might come thither again; so I, in every suit wherein I have troubled you, after my despatch, have prayed that once more I might trouble you again. I have sued heretofore for gain, but now it is to get my own without loss.

Dewhurst was to present a petition to Sir Robert Cecil and secure an answer.[14] In this instance we see Dewhurst the patronage dispenser, enjoying one of the most lucrative fringe benefits of service in the household of a great statesman.

While at one of the Cecil manors in December, 1592, Dewhurst sent Burghley a letter by Jennings, the gardner, which contains the sort of information an estate officer might send. Dewhurst described the condition of several of Burghley's estates, reporting the theft of numerous items. He mentioned in passing that he had been at Westminster in connection with the audit of the College possessions.[15] This he did by virtue of his appointment in 1586 as auditor of Westminster College.[16] It is possible that he was doing the same thing for Lord Burghley, even likely considering the character of the letter of December, 1592. This would not, however, have been a full-time responsibility.

Two years after Dewhurst received his Westminster appointment, in October, 1588, he secured a twenty-one year lease "of a tower roofed with lead built on the wall dividing the Palace of Westminster from the Abbey."[17] The same lease was regranted to his widow Anne and to his son Thomas for the term of forty years in April, 1597. This office or residence was very handy to both the Court of Wards and to Burghley's

[11] See Clapham biography.
[12] Banks, "Breviate," p. 328.
[13] P. R. O., Wards 9/381.
[14] Great Britain, *C. S. P. D.*, I (London, 1856), p. 113.
[15] Great Britain, *C. S. P. D.*, III (London, 1867), p. 293.
[16] Westminster Abbey Library, unpublished list of officers.
[17] Westminster Abbey Library, General Catalogue, No. 18076, 18080.

office-residence, St. Albans' House, located just south of the Henry VII Chapel.[18] All of these grants were in the gift of Burghley's faithful friend, Dean Gabriel Goodman.

Dewhurst had other jobs and leases which were also secured by Lord Burghley to provide recompense for an unsalaried servant. In July, 1577, Dewhurst was appointed surveyor over all royal manors and lands in Middlesex and London, an exchequer appointment, for which he received an annual salary of £13.6.8. By March, 1589, Dewhurst had become royal woodward of Hertfordshire, for at that time he was ordered as woodward to repair the paling of Her Majesty's great park of Hatfield by command of Lord Burghley and Sir Walter Mildmay.[19] Thomas Dewhurst received the appointment after his father's death.[20] Together with Robert Taverner, Dewhurst received several manors in Nottinghamshire, Derbyshire and Huntingdonshire for a term of twenty-one years.[21]

Burghley's practice, not neglected in Dewhurst's case, was to dip into the Court of Wards for his gentleman servants. At some time between 1570 and 1581 Dewhurst was granted a lease of the premises of a rather insignificant wardship, the annual value of which was only 8s.11d. He paid a mere 10s. for the lease.[22] The grant of the wardship of Margaret Mitford, for which Dewhurst paid £13.6.8., was conferred on him in 1576.[23] In 1587 Robert Cecil brought Vincent Skynner and Barnard Dewhurst in with him in the obligation of £500, guaranteeing the payment of £250 for the wardship of Giles Allington, worth £66.13s.4 annually. It is doubtful that Dewhurst shared in the annual income from the wardship.[24] In 1591 Dewhurst was given the wardship of a natural idiot, one Frances Hardwyck, orignally granted in 1579 to Frances Southwell for a fine of £23.6.8.[25]

There is also every reason to believe that Dewhurst's admission to Gray's Inn on February 2, 1582 was the work of Lord Burghley who was himself a prominent member of that company.[26]

Two scraps of evidence bear upon Dewhurst's financial capability. One, a controversial recognizance for debt, indicates on the surface that certain parties owed Dewhurst £1000.[27] As we cannot conclude exactly this, the conditions of the contract not having been copied into the

[18] Westminster Abbey Library, Register Book VII, f. 56.
[19] Cecil Papers, Accounts 4/24, p. 168.
[20] P. R. O., E. 315/309; E. 315/319.
[21] P. R. O., Cal. Pal. Rolls, 17-30 Elizabeth, p. 1r.
[22] P. R. O., Wards 9/190.
[23] P. R. O., Wards 9/381.
[24] P. R. O., Wards 9/221.
[25] P. R. O., Cal. Pat. Rolls, 17-30 Elizabeth, p. 11; Wards 9/221.
[26] Joseph Foster, ed., *Register of Admissions to Gray's Inn*, 1521-1889 (London, 1889), p. 60.
[27] P. R. O., L. C. 4/193, ff. 5, 65.

recognizance, it may only be said with some certainty that he was a man of affairs. It is certain, however, that the Earl of Essex had borrowed from Dewhurst. In October, 1600, among Essex's listed debts was one for £120 "due to be paid presently" to the excutors of Barnard Dewhurst.[28]

Dewhurst apparently died toward the last of 1596 or early in 1597, in which year the will was proved. This was the only will, out of more than two hundred examined, which omitted even the suggestion of a religious preamble. His eldest son was left £1,500 to be loaned at interest by Dewhurst's friends, William Pitt and Henry Best, until the son came of age. For their pains, the two friends received £20 and £10 respectively. The second son, Robert, got £300, similarly loaned at interest. From the interest allowances were to be paid the boys "by the consent and good liking of my very good friend Mr. Henry Maynard," who was made the overseer of the will and given Dewhurst's diamond ring.[29]

Henry, Barnard and John, the three younger sons, were given £200 each, allowances to be paid them from the interest until they reached the age of twenty-four. Anne, Dewhurst's wife, got £1,000, all plate, jewels, and household stuff, as well as the leases of his house at Westminster and of the manor of Haddam in Hertford. The profits of certain lands in Essex were also to be hers. Two sons-in-law had their debts cancelled for £220. The vicar of Cheshunt Church, where Dewhurst was buried, was to have £5. In all, Dewhurst left cash bequests of £3,655, excluding the one year's wages to all his servants. The will was witnessed by Thomas Bellot, Burghley's steward; Gilbert Wakering, a clerk in Burghley's service; and John Norton.[30]

John Durninge

One reference only identifies this man as a servant of Lord Burghley and it affords no clue as to what he did, only when he served. The evidence is contained in a copy of testimony offered by Durninge in a Duchy of Lancaster matter in which he was described as servant to the Lord Treasurer. The statement bears the date 1597.[1] As he must have been a young man, he could not have served the Lord Treasurer very long.

Durninge probably came to Burghley's attention as the husband of Burghley's great-niece, Elizabeth, the daughter of Adam Cleypool and Dorothy, daughter of Robert Wingfield and Burghley's sister. An annuity of £50 was granted to Durninge in 1598 for the surrender of certain

[28] H. M. C., *Salisbury MSS.*, X, p. 348.
[29] P. C. C., 7 Cobham.
[30] *Ibid.*

---

[1] H. M. C., *Salisbury MSS.*, XIV, p. 29.

lands.² He sat in the parliament of 1601 for Corfe Castle. He owned lands in Stafford and Essex, buying further property there in 1603 from Michael Hickes, Burghley's secretary.³ When he died in 1623, he resided in Maxey Castle, one of the Cecil manors. His will indicates that Durninge died without living children though not without hope of having one. Several bequests were conditional, to be paid only if he left no issue. The poor of the parishes of Maxey, Northamptonshire and Sifford, Essex received £40, evenly divided between the two parishes. If Durninge had issue, then £1,000 was set aside for the child. Otherwise, various sums were left to relatives and to his wife who was the sole executrix.⁴

Henry Fades

Very little is known about this man who first appeared in Burghley's service on the occasion of the Queen's visit to Theobalds in 1572 when he was assigned "to see about the house."¹ He appeared again as the servant designated to keep the cupboard on the south side of the great chamber on April 30, 1581, when Lord Burghley entertained the French Commissioners at a splendid dinner given in Burghley House, the Strand.² From his assignments on these occasions it may safely be concluded that he was a gentleman.

An undated entry in the Cecil Papers contains a clue as to his regular post in Burghley's service. The entry is an unsigned comment to the effect that Burghley desired to see the rental itself, "by which Henry Fadys (by this time apparently deceased) did gather the rents," in order to know the names of the parcels of ground held by the tenants.³ This position might explain why Fadys or Fades sent details about the swans on the river at Totnam Mill, Enfield, and Spinckford to Sir Robert Cecil in 1595.⁴ It does not necessarily explain why in July, 1593, the Master and Seniors of St. John's College Cambridge should write to Henry Fades about the preaching of the four annual sermons for the late Lady Burghley which, they explained, had been committed to Mr. Neile, the vicar of Cheshunt parish.⁵

It is interesting to note that Henry Fades was another of those servants whose reward came from Westminster Abbey where, in December,

² P. R. O., Cal. and Index, Pat. Rolls, 38-43 Eliz., p. 1r.
³ History of Parliament Trust, unpublished biography.
⁴ P. C. C., 108 Swann.

¹ Cecil Papers, v. 140, p. 20.
² B. M., *Lansdowne MSS.*, v. 33, f. 70, p. 175.
³ Cecil Papers, v. 143, p. 107.
⁴ Cecil Papers, General 67/12, p. 272.
⁵ Cecil Papers, v. 22, p. 103.

1595, he received a patent of appointment to the surveyorship of the College at a fee of £6.13.4. annually.[6] Between 1596 and 1597 Fades was also supervisor of works for the Abbey.[7]

John Floyde

John Floyde, if a Welshman, was one of many fellow countrymen whom Dean Gabriel Goodman attracted to Westminster Abbey. More frequently a person went from Cecil's service to that of the Dean and Chapter of Westminster Abbey. Here is the case of a man who went from the Abbey into Cecil's employ.

On January 16, 1562, Floyde was appointed verger of Westminster Abbey in which capacity he had the custody of the tombs and monuments at a fee of £6.13.4. a year.[1] In August, 1571, a John Floyde received £10 by warrant of the Master of the Court of Wards "for his pains in writing of books for the Queen's Majesty" by the appointment of Mr. Onslowe, late attorney of Wards.[2] We next encounter a John Floyde on the staff at Theobalds, awaiting the Queen's visit there in 1572.[3] Later, in 1572, Floyde received particulars of leases for Lord Burghley, and was described as gentleman servant to the Lord Treasurer.[4] We last meet Floyde doing the same thing in May, 1574.[5]

It is possible that the Sir Thomas Fludd, son of John Fludd of Morton, Salop, was a relative of Burghley's John Floyde. Sir Thomas served as M. P. for Maidstone in 1593, 1597 and 1601, and was receiver of Kent in or before 1585, serving as surveyor as early as 1570.[6]

Barnaby Gooch

Barnaby Gooch was born about 1542, the son and heir of Robert Gooch of Chilwell, Nottinghamshire, and Margaret, the daughter of Sir Walter Mantell of Heyford, Northamptonshire. The Gooch family was earlier settled in the Forest of Dean, in Gloucester.[1] Barnaby's father, Robert, settled in Alvingham, Lincolnshire and became Recorder of

[6] Westminster Abbey Library, Register Book VII, p. 50.
[7] Westminster Abbey Library, unpublished list of officers.

---

[1] Westminster Abbey Library, Register Book V, p. 14.
[2] P. R. O., Wards 9/380.
[3] Cecil Papers, v. 140, p. 20.
[4] P. R. O., E. 315/202, pp. 44r-45.
[5] P. R. O., E. 315/202, p. 79r.
[6] Mort, "Commons," p. 102.

---

[1] Maddison, *Lincolnshire Pedigrees*, p. 408.

Lincoln and receiver of the Court of Augmentations, the latter in 1550-1551. Robert died in 1557 when Barnaby was not quite sixteen years old.[2] Robert was very likely the Mr. Gooch who appeared receiving rents for Cecil in 1556.[3] Barnaby, a kinsman of the Cecils, probably entered the Cecil service shortly after his father's death.

Barnaby presumably remained an unsold ward of the crown for as soon as Cecil became Master of the Court of Wards, Barnaby was allowed to purchase his own wardship for £80, to be paid over an eight year period at the rate of £10 each year. Although the Gooch lands were worth £120.18.4 annually, the Court only allowed Barnaby £26.13.4 annually, the remainder being either the Queen's profit or necessary for the needs of the estate.[4] By September 25, 1570, the last installment had been paid.[5]

On June 26, 1563, the Court of Wards granted Gooch license to enter upon his lands.[6] He had at the same time found someone with whom to share his estate. He sued for the hand of Mary, daughter of Thomas Darell of Scotney Castle, Kent.[7] Unfortunately, her parents were determined to marry her to a certain rich Sampson Lennard whose money was his chief commendation. Mary, to prevent this, privately contracted herself to Gooch. The ensuing tangle was submitted to Archbishop Parker of Canterbury who was requested by Cecil to hear the case according to law and equity. Though the Archbishop's decision is not known, Gooch did take Mary as his wife and they had numerous offspring.[8]

While it is not possible to describe with assurance what position Gooch occupied in the Cecil household, he served on special occasions and was referred to as a retainer.[9] During the Queen's visit to Theobalds in 1572 he was placed high on the list of servants and referred to as the first server for the first meal.[10] In 1581 he was on hand for the feasting of the French Commissioners when he was assigned as a server in the great chamber, along with Walter Cope, another Cecil relation.[11] He again appeared among the servants on the occasion of the Queen's visit to Theobalds in 1591, though in this case the list does not include assignments.[12]

[2] *Ibid.*
[3] P. R. O., S. P. 11/107-108.
[4] P. R. O., Wards 9/156.
[5] P. R. O., Wards 9/380.
[6] Great Britain, *Cal. of Pat. Rolls,* II (London, 1948), p. 596.
[7] George W. Marshall, editor, *The Genealogist* (London, 1882), VI, p. 155.
[8] John Strype, *Life and Acts of Archbishop Parker,* 4 volumes (Oxford, 1821), I, pp. 286-287.
[9] *Ibid.*, pp. 286-287.
[10] Cecil Papers, v. 140, p. 20.
[11] B. M., *Lansdown MSS.,* v. 33, f. 70, p. 175.
[12] Cecil Papers, v. 140, p. 37.

The only clear reward arranged for Gooch outside Cecil's own service was his appointment in 1563 as a Gentleman Pensioner to the Queen.[13] In 1574 Gooch apparently left the employment of Burghley for service in Ireland where, upon arrival, he promptly caught a fever.[14] Gooch provided Burghley with regular reports on the state of affairs in Ireland, not neglecting to complain about the trouble still caused him by his father's debts.[15] Perhaps this caused him to sell one of his paternal estates to a George Darell, possibly his wife's brother.[16]

How long Gooch remained in Ireland at this time is not known. We know, however, that he published a book in 1576, the *Zodiac of Life*, dedicated to his patron and kinsman, Lord Burghley. The book was a translation into English verse of a work by "an excellent Italian, Christian poet, Marcellus Palingenius Stellatus."[17] He also had a reputation as a poet.[18] Wherever he was when he published, we know he was in England in 1581 to wait upon Lord Burghley's French guests.

In 1582 Gooch returned to Ireland, obviously warmly endorsed by Burghley. Several officials, as if in reply to a request, wrote Burghley that they would show favor to Mr. Gooch, Burghley's kinsman.[19] The result was that Gooch was employed in "Her Majesty's service martial, under Sir Nicholas Malbie."[20] By March, 1583, he had apparently been wounded in the leg as he informed Burghley, asking that Burghley be good to his family in England.[21] Gooch complained to Burghley, in October, 1584, that he had been refused license to repair to England for six months to settle his inheritance fallen to him by the death of his mother-in-law.[22] He finally secured leave to come, possibly by Burghley's intervention, for there is a final reference to him as the bearer of a communication from Sir John Perrot to Walsingham, April 23, 1585.[23]

We find Gooch next writing from the Lord Treasurer's Chamber at Court to the Earl of Rutland, relating news of interest to the Earl, June 19, 1587.[24] He is identified with service to the Cecils for the last time in 1591. Gooch died at Alvingham, Lincolnshire, sometime in February, 1594.[25]

---

[13] Strype, *Parker*, pp. 286-287.
[14] Great Britain, *C. S. P., Ireland*, II (London, 1867), p. 8.
[15] *Ibid.*, p. 17.
[16] P. R. O., Cal. Pat. Rolls, 1-16 Eliz., p. 178.
[17] Strype, *Reformation*, II, part 2, p. 81.
[18] *Concise D. N. B.*, p. 510.
[19] Great Britain, *C. S. P., Ireland*, II (London, 1867), p. 392.
[20] Great Britain, *C. S. P., Ireland*, II (London, 1867), p. 397.
[21] *Ibid.*, p. 433.
[22] *Ibid.*, p. 537.
[23] *Ibid.*, p. 561.
[24] H. M. C., *Rutland MSS.*, p. 219.
[25] Maddison, *Lincolnshire Pedigrees*, p. 408.

Gabriel Goodman

Gabriel Goodman, born about 1529 at Ruthin, Denbighshire, in Wales, was the son of Edward Goodman, merchant and burgess of Ruthin, by his wife Cecily, daughter of Edward Thelwell of Plas-y-wad. Gabriel received a B. A. from Christ's College, Cambridge, in 1550 and became a fellow of Jesus College where he served until September 28, 1555, taking his M. A. there in 1553.[1]

Late in 1554 Goodman joined the Cecil household and was to have livery immediately. He entered in the capacity of a schoolmaster, receiving well over twice the salary of any other servant, drawing 33s.4d. each quarter.[2] As one who sympathized with the religious settlement of Edward VI, he could not very well have served as chaplain in a house which ostensibly conformed to the Marian re-settlement and had its priest.[3] This young Welshman, probably not over twenty-five years of age, found a kindred spirit in his master, the still youthful Sir William Cecil. Cecil, we are told, perpetually sent Goodman on confidential missions of importance. The two were so much together that Cecil was later referred to as the Dean of Westminster, for Goodman seemed subject to Cecil's instructions.[4]

On September 30, 1558, just six weeks before the end of Mary's reign, Goodman became rector of the parish of South Luffenham, Rutlandshire. In the following year he became rector of the first portion of the church of Waddesdon, Buckinghamshire, the second portion being added on November 25, 1569.[5] Goodman was further advanced on October 23, 1559, when he received the prebend of Chiswick in St. Paul's Cathedral.[6] When in 1560 Westminster Abbey was refounded as the collegiate church of St. Peter, Westminster, with a priest-dean and twelve priest-prebends Goodman was made one of the twelve prebends.[7] On August 13, 1561, after the first dean's death, Goodman was made the dean of Westminster for life, and held it for almost forty years.[8]

Many reasons are given or Goodman's failure to reach the episcopal bench. The anonymous author of the article about him in the *Dictonary of Welsh Biography* gives three reasons: Goodman's opposition to Leicester, his prominence on the Court of High Commission, and his reputa-

---

[1] Sidney Lee, "Gabriel Goodman," *DNB*, VIII, p. 130.
[2] B. M., *Lansdowne MSS.*, v. 118, f. 42r.
[3] Sir John Edward Lloyd, editor, *Dictionary of Welsh Biography* (London, 1959), p. 283.
[4] Richard Newcome, *A Memoir of Gabriel Goodman* (Ruthin, 1825), p. 13.
[5] Lee, "Goodman," p. 130.
[6] Great Britain, *Cal. of Pat. Rolls,* Elizabeth, I (London, 1939), p. 125.
[7] *Ibid.*, p. 397.
[8] *Ibid.*, v. II (London, 1948), p. 95.

tion as a grave, solid, severe man.⁹ The latter reason was said to have been the verdict on him by Archbishop Parker when it was proposed that Goodman succeed Grindal as Bishop of London. None of several suggested bishoprics was conferred upon him.¹⁰ When one observes the close association and interplay between Burghley and Goodman, it is not too difficult to imagine that Goodman was most conveniently located where he was. His proximity to the court, his authority in Westminster, and the patronage at his disposal must have made him indispensable to Burghley where he was.

Goodman's responsibilities at Westminster included a boys' school, the statutes for which Goodman himself completed in such a way that they remained in force for three centuries. Goodman had also to give final approval to the appointment of headmaster whom the Dean of Christ Church and the Master of Trinity alternately selected.¹¹ Lord Burghley himself became interested in the school and provided an annual gift of 20 marks toward the purchase of books for such scholars as were elected to the universities.¹²

It was his responsibility for the school that Goodman had in mind when in April, 1570, he leased his prebendary of Chiswick in St. Paul's Cathedral to William Walter of Wimbledon, an attorney for the college, and to George Burden, a Cecil servant and Abbey employee, for ninety-nine years at £17.19. a year. The condition was that the leasees, within twenty-one years and at their expense, add to the mansion house sufficient facilities for the lodging of one of the prebends of Westminster, the schoolmaster, usher and forty children of the grammar school when in times of sickness they would repair there for safety. For some reason, on June 12, 1570, the lease was re-assigned by the leasees to the Dean and Chapter of Westminster but the house was eventually built.¹³

Goodman, as well, enjoyed all the manorial rights belonging to the old abbots of Westminster and, acting as lord of the manor, carried on the government of Westminster.¹⁴ Only in 1585 was there drafted an act of municipality. Even then, though there were twelve burgesses and twelve assistants to preside over the twelve wards, the power still lay mainly with the Dean as president of the Court. In fact, the Dean and High Steward, usually a high nobleman and in this case Lord Burghley, chose the burgesses while the High Stewardship was the gift of the Dean.¹⁵ Thus the Dean continued to rule Westminster for practical purposes even after the municipality act of 1585.

⁹ *DWB*, p. 95.
¹⁰ Lee, "Goodman," p. 130.
¹¹ John Sargeaunt, *Annals of Westminster School* (London, 1898), pp. 10-12.
¹² Lawrence E. Tanner, *Westminster School* (London, 1951), p. 25.
¹³ Westminster Abbey Library, Register Book VI, p. 8.
¹⁴ W. H. Manchee, *The Westminster City Fathers, 1585-1901* (London, 1924), p. 4.
¹⁵ *Ibid.*, pp. 5-6, 211.

While the Dean had these responsibilities at home, he was repeatedly used as commissioner for ecclesiastical causes in the Court of High Commission in which capacity he assisted in the condemnation of the Dutch Anabaptists in 1575; he aided Burghley in settling a Cambridge dispute; he translated the first epistle to the Corinthians for the Bishop's Bible; and he helped Dr. William Morgan in his Welsh translation of the Bible with literary aid and with money.[16] Goodman also had time to act on more than one occasion as a commissioner for the Queen in the collection of the Westminster subsidy.[17] Lady Burghley used him as her advisor in the bestowal of her charities. In fact, when she chose anonymously to endow two places at St. John's College, Cambridge, she caused some lands to be purchased in the name of Goodman, who himself assured them to the College as a perpetual maintenance for the two scholars. She also gave to the Haberdashers Company of London a good sum of money through the assistance of the deans of St. Paul's and Westminster. It must be said for Lady Burghley that she gave these gentlemen five pieces of plate to express her thanks for their pains.[18]

The continued exchanges between Burghley and Goodman, commented upon by contemporaries, are from time to time documented. Goodman gave a number of Burghley's servants lucrative sinecures on the Westminster staff. In 1576, Goodman served as a witness to the will of Sir Anthony Cooke, Burghley's father-in-law.[19] In 1570, Burghley committed a crown ward to Goodman's care for an indefinite period of time, paying Goodman the first year £10 for William Vaughan's charges.[20] The next year the fee for Vaughan's care was £20 and Vaughan was committed to Goodman's care for his education.[21] In 1572 the fee climbed to £26.[22] When there is another record of payment for Vaughan's charges, in 1577, the fee was £13.6.8.[23] Whether or not this was intended as a reward for Goodman, it is certainly an instance of the closeness with which the two men worked.

A further illustration of their friendship is the founding by Goodman in 1590 of Christ's Hospital in Ruthin, his native town, for a president, a warden and twelve poor inmates. He added a grammar school to the foundation in 1595.[24] In 1601, the last year of his life, the aged Goodman wrote to Robert Cecil, acknowledging his obligations to the late Lord Burghley, declaring that the means by which he had aided his native soil

[16] Lee, "Goodman," p. 130.
[17] P. R. O., E. 179/142/202; E. 179/253/1a. Subsidy rolls.
[18] Strype, *Reformation,* III, Part II, pp. 126-128.
[19] B. M., *Lansdone MSS.,* v. 23, f. 64, p. 142.
[20] P. R. O., Wards 9/373.
[21] P. R. O., Wards 9/380.
[22] *Ibid.*
[23] P. R. O., Wards 9/381.
[24] Lee, "Goodman," p. 130.

by founding a school and hospital were Burghley's. Goodman wrote especially to obtain Cecil's help in obtaining a corporation for the town, the chief market town of Denbigh.[25]

A final and conclusive mark of the relationship between Burghley and Goodman was the latter's appointment in 1598 as one of Burghley's executors. He shared the responsibility with another Welshman, Thomas Bellot. Goodman's recompense for this service was the annual income from all Burghley's lands belonging to the Neate near Westminster.[26] Actually the task was a heavy one for the estate was large and the provisions of the will complicated and numerous. A year later, the two executors stood as bondsmen guaranteeing that Sir Robert Cecil would perform a certain contract.[27] There were doubtless many other occasions when this posthumous service to Lord Burghley demanded their energy.

Nor was Lord Burghley's the only estate requiring Goodman's attention. In 1596 a friend and employee, Thomas Fowler, the supervisor of works for Westminster Abbey since 1583, and Comptroller of Her Majesty's Works, died leaving his dwelling-place in St. Martin's-in-the-Fields to the Dean and Chapter.[28] The gift was conditioned by the request that several annuities be paid from the income, one of 40s. to Goodman himself and to his heirs forever.[29] Goodman, an overseer of the will, thereupon called upon his good friend Thomas Bellot to make an inventory of the fixtures remaining in the house and intended by Fowler as furnishings for it.[30]

Goodman died in 1601, having served in one place as dean for forty years. His will bespeaks his devotion to God without much of the fervor which is associated with puritanism. To his friend William Camden, an associate in the service of Westminster Abbey, Goodman intrusted the plans for his funeral and burial which took place in the Abbey. Camden's reward was a "ring of gold with turkey stone." To the second Lord Burghley Goodman gave two pictures, one of the first Lord Burghley, the other of Lady Burghley, "my lady and mistress." His executors were his servant Richard Williams, and Mr. George Bellot, receiver-general of the college lands and brother of Thomas Bellot, Burghley's steward.[31]

Goodman admitted to Sir Robert Cecil that while he endeavored to do all the good he could to all, he principally had in mind his native soil.[32]

[25] H. M. C., *Salisbury MSS.*, XI, p. 5.
[26] Collins, *Burghley*, p. 97.
[27] P. R. O., L. C. 4/194, Recognizances for Debt, f. 73.
[28] Westminster Abbey Library, unpublished list of officers.
[29] P. C. C., 8 and 9 Drake.
[30] Westminster Abbey Library, Gen. Cat., No. 17215.
[31] Newcome, *Goodman,* appendix A, p. 1.
[32] H. M. C., *Salisbury MSS.*, XI, p. 5.

Certainly his influence with the Cecils must have made him important as a link between Wales and the Court. The Abbey records for his tenure as dean are filled with the names of Welshmen to whom he gave positions. Among the eager Welsh was probably Thomas Bellot, whom Goodman was able to locate in 1566 in Cecil's household as steward. Goodman subsequently gave employment to Cuthbert, George and Owen Bellot and was a great friend of another of Thomas's brothers, Hugh, Bishop of Bangor and later of Chester. Nor did Goodman neglect his own family. His only brother Godfrey was employed as Chapter Clerk from 1571 until his death in 1585, only to be succeeded by his son Gabriel, the dean's namesake, and already employed as a prelector. At least two other Goodmans served, each as sacrist for a time.[33] One nephew eventually rose to the episcopal bench.

Thomas Gresham

This servant, who bears the name distinguished by the Queen's financial agent, Sir Thomas Gresham, cannot be linked with Sir Thomas, who had no sons, nor with any other Gresham family. Nothing is known about him outside the few references to him in connection with Lord Burghley. In December, 1576, and again in May 1578, Gresham had delivered to him, as gentleman servant to the Lord Treasurer, three different items or particulars about estates. This suggests some form of service to Burghley, perhaps merely as a retainer, taking his turn in the chamber and running the errands that developed during his vigil in the Lord Treasurer's outer chamber.[1]

On October 27, 1579, a marriage license was granted to Thomas Gresham, "*unum ex familia* of Lord Burghley" and Jane Parratt, spinster, of St. Alban's, Wood Street, to marry there.[2]

In 1581 a Gresham was appointed to serve with Hickes, Maynard, Skynner, Windebank and others as translators for the middle table during the banquet for the French Commissioners given at Burghley House, in the Strand.[3] Finally, a not very promising wardship was granted to a Thomas Gresham of Brasebourghe, Lincolnshire, gentleman, in 1595. For a fee of £30 Gresham could expect an annual return of £6.13. Unhappily the ward was already twenty years old.[4]

[33] Westminster Abbey Library, unpublished list of officers.

[1] P. R. O., E. 315/202.
[2] *London Marriage Licenses,* p. 91.
[3] B. M., *Lansdowne MSS.,* v. 33, f. 70, p. 175.
[4] P. R. O., Wards 9/157; Wards 9/158.

Ralph Grey

Ralph Grey was born about 1552, the son of Sir Ralph Grey of Chillingham, Northumberland, and Isabel, daughter of Sir Thomas Grey of Horton. The Greys were a prominent English border family whose influence was increased by the decline and disrepute into which the Percys and Nevils, Earls of Northumberland and Westmoreland respectively, fell. Ralph's father died at Chillingham in December, 1564, leaving his sons under age and royal wards. Only the eldest son, Thomas, can be traced through the Court of Wards records. Born in April, 1549, he was fifteen years old when he became a ward of the crown.[1]

Thomas apparently was never granted or sold to anyone. Rather he was retained by the crown and entrusted to the care of Sir William Cecil, Master of the Court of Wards. It must be assumed, since he appears in the same accounts as the Earls of Oxford and Rutland, Henry Grey and William Carr, that Thomas took up residence with them in Cecil's home. John Hart, Chester Herald, for five years received the exhibitions for Thomas Grey, usually over £70 a year. In April, 1570, Thomas was twenty-one and the exhibition was paid only for the first quarter of the year. At £26.16, it was larger than ordinary, aggravated by the hurt in his head which required surgery and a special diet and by the necessity for supplying the youth with appropriate clothes in which to assume his place among the border gentry.[2] Within four years, Thomas had served as sheriff of Northumberland. In 1585 he married Lady Katherine Nevil, daughter of the late Earl of Westmoreland, and by 1590 he was dead.[3]

Where Ralph was during the minority of his brother is not known. Perhaps he, too, was lodged in Cecil's house and occupied in Cecil's service. When in 1570, Sir Thomas Grey, Ralph's maternal grandfather, died, leaving Ralph an inheritance, Sir John Forster wrote to Cecil in October, 1570, that he had acted according to Cecil's letter and had delivered to Cecil's servant, Ralph Grey, Sir Thomas Grey's land. One wonders if Cecil's directions were contrary to the normal expectations of the other heirs for Foster noted that the gentlemen who married the daughters and heirs of Sir Thomas Grey were unhappy with the arrangement.[4]

It is interesting to note that Cecil followed Sir Thomas Grey as Steward of Dunstanburgh, becoming also Constable and Receiver, all

---

[1] Madeleine H. Dodds, ed., *A History of Northumberland*, 15 volumes (Newcastle upon Tyne, 1935), XIV, p. 328.
[2] P. R. O., S. P. 15/19, ff. 78-79; Wards 9/373.
[3] Dodds, *Northumberland*, p. 328.
[4] Great Britain, *C. S. P. D.*, VI (London, 1870), p. 321.

offices within the Duchy of Lancaster. In 1578, however, Ralph Grey and Edward, his brother, became Constable and Steward for life, Ralph having been named Bailiff of Dunstanburgh Castle and lordship on June 22, 1571. Ralph later served Northumberland as sheriff in 1582-1583, 1591-1592 and in 1593-1594.[5]

Ralph's career well illustrates the contentiousness to be found in sixteenth century England, and particularly on the borders where the unruly were less likely to be restrained by a distant and nearly impotent government. On October 7, 1592, Ralph outlined in a letter to Lord Burghley the quarrel he had already mentioned between himself and Sir Henry Woodrington over lands inherited by Ralph in 1591 from his brother Henry who had brought them from Hector Woodrington, who ten years earlier had bought them from Sir Henry. The quarrel concerned Sir Henry's illegal attempts to regain possession. When the justices of the peace, at their own request guarded by two-hundred of Ralph's men, went to the lands in question, they were withstood by men sent from Sir Henry. Ralph concluded his letter to Burghley with the explanation that for these and similar abuses offered by young Henry Woodrington and his assistants, he had exhibited a bill against them in Star Chamber.[6]

The facts in the Star Chamber petition extend the story. About forty Woodrington men actually entered the property in dispute, drove off Ralph's cattle and took possession while Ralph was away. The petition, citing other grievances, requested that subpoenas be delivered to these riotous people to cause them to appear before the Court of Star Chamber.[7] Unfortunately, only the petition exists. Perhaps the Court did not hear the case. On May 30, 1593, John Carey, a younger son of Lord Hunsdon, wrote Lord Burghley that "thanks to God, there is settled within these few days, one of the greatest causes on Northumberland for these forty years. . . ." The quarrel, he said, endangered most of the principal houses in the area. While the gentlemen of the shire were unable to do anything to stop it, "it hath pleased God to raise up a meaner instrument to bring this great matter to quietness and friendship. . . ."[8]

In 1594 there was hard feeling between Grey and Sir John Forster, Warden of the Middle Marches and member of the Council of the North. Forster, in carrying out a royal commission, had searched the homes of Ralph and his relatives for "papisting." Ralph thereafter bore a grudge against Forster which did not diminish when Forster bought a farm of which Ralph had the lease.[9]

[5] Somerville, *Lancaster*, p. 537.
[6] Great Britain, *C. S. P. D.*, XII (London, 1872), p. 340.
[7] P. R. O., Star Chamber 5/G9/5.
[8] Great Britain, *C. S. P., Borders*, I (Edinburgh, 1894), p. 463.
[9] Great Britain, *C. S. P. D.*, XII (London, 1872), p. 367.

On another instance, Ralph, seeking to be made treasurer of Berwick, a post several ancestors had held, used a member of the Selby family to present a full explanation of his case before Sir Robert Cecil in 1596.[10] But by February of the following year the Selbys and Ralph Grey were at odds, even resorting to the use of force against one another. The Selbys eventually capitulated and made their peace. They acknowledged, in an ingratiating manner, that it was hopeless to oppose a friend of the Cecils.[11] Clearly it paid to stand well with so influential a family.

In spite of frequent quarreling, when Lord Eure had to return to London from his post as Lord Warden of the East March and was asked to suggest suitable deputy wardens to Lord Burghley in 1597, he mentioned first Mr. Ralph Grey of Chillingham whose house was in the March and whose strength was the greatest of any of the East March.[12]

This influential borderman, in September, 1597, had to answer certain questions put to him by the Lord Bishop of Durham and Sir William Bowes as a result of the presentments of the East and Middle March juries given the previous year. In response to a question about the levy of excessive fines, Ralph replied that he usually took none. And for certain lands held since the deaths of his grandfather and his brother, the rental assize of which was £380, he had never taken more than £380. He also denied ever renting lands to Scots. Some land, he admitted, had been let to Scots before his time, but they were Scots who regularly helped Englishmen.[13]

Only one valuable award can be traced to Lord Burghley. Shortly before Burghley's death, Ralph was granted the wardship of his sister's son, Robert Collingwood, whose lands were worth £105.7.6 annually. Ralph paid £120 for the grant.[14]

Ralph, sometime prior to October 6, 1581, married Jane, daughter of William Arthington.[15] When their son William was born in 1593, Lord Burghley and the Lord Chamberlain, Lord Hunsdon, were the godfathers, represented by Sir William Reed and John Carey, Hunsdon's son. When Reed wrote Burghley that he had done as Burghley directed "touching Ralph Gray's son," he added that he had dealt liberally with the nurse and the midwife.[16] This son was to honor both his sponsors and his family by being in turn knighted, made a baronet, and finally first Lord Grey of Wark. Lord Grey's grandson became the first Earl of Tankerville and a First Lord of the Treasury. Ralph Grey himself was among those knighted in 1603. He died in 1623.[17]

[10] Great Britain, *C. S. P., Borders,* II (Edinburgh, 1896), p. 98.
[11] *Ibid.,* pp. 250-251, 278.
[12] Great Britain, *C. S. P., Borders,* II (London, 1896), p. 364.
[13] *Ibid.,* p. 401.
[14] P. R. O., Wards 9/158.
[15] Dodds, *Northumberland,* p. 328.
[16] Great Britain, *C. S. P., Borders,* I (Edinburgh, 1894), p. 485.
[17] Dobbs, *Northumberland,* p. 328.

In Ralph Grey Lord Burghley had an able and energetic partisan on the border. It is possible that Burghley deliberately received the Greys into his own household in order to plant on the borders a faction loyal to himself. Certainly from Burghley's standpoint, friendship and support on the borders were needed. One of the causes of the disturbance in the North in 1569 had been intense dissatisfaction with the influence of Sir William Cecil on the government. In any case, he well knew what family he sheltered and how they were related to other prominent border families. Burghley noted in the margins of the 1595 musters of the Middle Marches just how the principal families were interrelated.[18]

Arthur Hall

Authur Hall was born about 1540, son of Francis Hall of Grantham, Lincolnshire, and Calais.[1] The Hall family had long distinguished itself in the two areas, and Arthur would likely have succeeded to the role of officer of Calais had he been born earlier. England had, however, lost Calais before Arthur had come of age. Arthur's great grandfather, Thomas Hall, was a Merchant of the Staple of Calais, and one of the magnates of Grantham.[2] Francis Hall, father or grandfather (both named Francis), was in the service of the Duke of Suffolk in 1518. The Francis Hall at Calais in 1528 was the father of Arthur. He remained in Calais until his death nearly twenty-five years later, moving from the rank of spear to that of Comptroller of the town and marches.[3] Francis Hall's uncle was Sir Robert Wingfield, appointed deputy of Calais in 1526.[4] Wingfield was also the father of Robert Wingfield who married Cecil's sister, Elizabeth. Francis Hall was something of a man of the world who adjusted easily to the changes in religion and purchased from the Crown extensive Lincolnshire estates, formerly the property of the church.[5]

When Francis Hall died, June 10, 1552, he left behind his wife, Ursula, thirteen-year-old Arthur, three daughters, land in France worth £52 annually, and Lincolnshire lands worth £148.9.3 annually.[6] Cecil showed great interest in the wardship and sent an agent to the inquisi-

---

[18] Great Britain, *C. S. P., Borders*, II (London, 1896), p. 72.

[1] Sidney Lee, "Arthur Hall," *DNB*, VIII, p. 940.
[2] H. G. Wright, *The Life and Works of Arthur Hall of Grantham* (Manchester, 1919), p. 4.
[3] *Ibid.*, pp. 5, 16.
[4] *Ibid.*, p. 5.
[5] *Ibid.*, p. 6.
[6] *Ibid.*, pp. 18, 24.

tion. Ursula was reluctant to give up her son, though the advantages of his upbringing in Cecil's household were suggested to her.

She consented and in the fall of 1552, Hall became a member of the Cecil family circle. "He was," said Wright, "one of those numerous gentlemen who helped make up the household of an Elizabethan nobleman, a survival of the armed retainers of the Middle Ages. Their duties were to appear with their lord in public and thus add to the splendour of his train. They carried messages for him, and, if necessary, defended his name against the malice of enemies."[7] It seems questionable, however, whether this definition suits a thirteen-year-old ward. The legal tangle was not worked out until the following year when on May 9, 1553 the patent granting Cecil an annuity of £50, assigned on specified Hall manors, was issued, coupling with the annuity the custody of the body and the marriage.[8]

How long Hall remained in Cecil's household is not known. While there he received a quarterly allowance of 4s. which was 8d. more than Cecil gave his own son Thomas, Hall's contemporary, fellow student and good friend. In addition to Thomas Cecil, future Earl of Exeter, the household at Wimbledon in 1555 contained John Stanhope, nephew of Protector Somerset, third cousin once removed of Lady Cecil, and future Baron Stanhope of Harrington; Elizabeth Cooke, Lady Cecil's sister, who later married Sir Thomas Hoby and, second, Lord John Russell; Elizabeth Cecil, who later married Hall's cousin, Robert Wingfield, and second, Hugh Allington; Gabriel Goodman, future Dean of Westminster; Roger Alford, teller of the Exchequer; Quinten Sneynton, usher of the Court of Wards, who may have married Hall's sister; and others of less interest, not omitting mention of a priest.[9]

Cecil not only favored Hall with such associates but sent him off to his own college, St. John's, Cambridge, where Hall apparently remained for some time but did not take a degree. Hall commented upon the encouragement he received from Roger Ascham, associated with St. John's. With such aid he eventually became proficient in classics.[10]

Hall came into his estates in 1560. By 1564 or 1565 he had exchanged Cecil's service for that of the Queen. Perhaps he had already met and married Mary Denys, the daughter of a London goldsmith. Their son, Cecil, born in 1567, was the godson and subsequently the servant of Sir William Cecil.[11] During these years Hall travelled in Italy and southeastern Europe, returning in January, 1569 from Constantinople. Though he inherited more property in 1582 on the death of a relative,

[7] Wright, *Hall,* pp. 25-26.
[8] Great Britain, *Cal. of Pat. Rolls,* Edward and Mary, V (London, 1927), pp. 136-137.
[9] B. M., *Lansdowne MSS.,* v. 118, p. 36.
[10] Lee, "Hall," p. 940.
[11] Wright, *Hall,* p. 37.

he continued spending recklessly and so lived precariously, usually residing in London when not travelling.[12]

First elected to parliament in 1571, his second election as M. P. for Grantham in 1572 discloses another aspect of Hall's character. Nine days after the election he was called to the bar of the House to answer a charge of having made lewd speeches. Hall apologized and was pardoned. During a card game in 1573, Hall accused another of cheating. The issue was a public brawl, a libel suit, and finally a book of explanation by Hall for which the Privy Council demanded an apology. In this case, the result was imprisonment in the Tower and expulsion from the House of Commons.[13] In 1588 Hall was in the Fleet, sorry that he ever had left Burghley's service.[14]

He went to prison almost as a matter of routine for the rest of his life. In 1604, the year before his death, Hall said he had spent the past three years in the Fleet for debt.[15] Likely there were many people who shared the view of Hall expressed by Sir Julius Caesar, Master of Requests, in a letter to Sir Robert Cecil: ". . . I hear that Mr. Arthur Hall, whose tongue has been accustomed to slander, has written or intends to write some bitter and slanderous letter against me. I pray you, if you shall receive this, to esteem it as an ordinary work of his distempered brain."[16]

Lord Burghley must have been sadly disappointed in the outcome of this offshoot of his household. From the evidence it is clear that Burghley did his best for Hall. And he continued, from the early grant of a wardship worth £15 annually until his own death in 1598, to help Hall in his distress.[17] Hall's gratitude was the complaint that he had not received enough.[18] The Cecils and the Halls remained friends. Hall's uncle, Edmund, was one of Burghley's mother's friends and a trustee of her foundation for the poor artificers of Stamford.[19] And young Cecil Hall, Authur's son, was in Burghley's service, though there is no evidence as to how he served.

Perhaps Hall's literary efforts ultimately redeemed him. In 1563 he began the translation of the ten books of Homer's *Iliad* into English, a task he completed in 1581 and dedicated to his old friend, Sir Thomas Cecil.[20] Hall died December 29, 1605 and was buried at Grantham, January 7, 1606. His wife had died in 1582. Hall left a son, Cecil, and two daughters.[21]

[12] Lee, "Hall," p. 940.
[13] Lee, "Hall," p. 940.
[14] Great Britain, *C. S. P. D.*, II (London, 1865), p. 554.
[15] H. M. C., *Salisbury MSS.*, XVI, p. 147.
[16] *Ibid.*, pp. 154-155.
[17] P. R. O., Wards 9/373.
[18] Great Britain, *C. S. P. D.*, V (London, 1869), p. 11.
[19] P. C. C., 23 Rutland.
[20] Lee, "Hall," pp. 940-941.
[21] Maddison, *Lincolnshire Pedigrees*, pp. 441-442.

John Hart

The biographical data on John Hart is questionable. Bror Danielsson, who was interested in Hart's literary efforts, did a painstaking job of searching for the right Hart family with which to link John. His success is doubtful. Danielsson concludes that John's father was a John Hart of Northolt, Middlesex where he was headborough from 1461 until 1477. This John was dead by 1500.[1] Our John Hart, appointed Chester Herald in 1567, was still going strong in 1574, without any sign of advanced age.[2] If indeed John Hart was the son of the Northolt Hart, he must have been at least sixty-seven when appointed Chester Herald, an unlikely age for a royal agent expected to travel regularly.

Judging from his *Orthographie,* published in 1569, Hart had a good grounding in Greek, Hebrew and Latin. He seems also to have been influenced by the theories of two distinguished Cambridge scholars, Sir John Cheke and Sir Thomas Smith. Since he served under Sir William Cecil, a third member of that able Cambridge group, it is tempting to conclude that Hart studied at the University.[3] Hart was also acquainted with the Spanish, French, Italian, Dutch, and German languages, perhaps equipping himself with them while on his travels.[4]

There is no record of Hart having been a Marian exile. A John Hart, yeoman of London, was pardoned by the Queen on October 6, 1561, for having lawfully defended himself and killed an assassin with a rapier, an incident he mentioned to Cecil in a letter.[5] Hart is first mentioned as an official of the Court of Wards on October 6, 1563, when he received payment from the Court for the diet and entertainment of Edward de Vere's schoolmasters and servants. There is evidence of similar receipts until 1570. Hart received, as well, money for other wards of the Crown, as the third Earl of Rutland, Henry Grey, Thomas Grey, William Carr, and Lord Zouch, the latter purchased in the name of Thomas Cecil.[6] All of these wards at one time or another lived in the Cecil household. It has been suggested that John Hart was the tutor in an elaborate school for wards conducted by Cecil. While Hart obviously possessed the talents for such a job, there is not any evidence, beyond the accounts, which suggests such a possibility.

Hart certainly worked closely with Cecil. It was Cecil who had Hart created Chester Herald, a position which entitled the possessor to

---

[1] Bror Danielsson, *John Hart's Works on English Orthography and Pronunciation* (Stockholm, 1955), pp. 13-14.
[2] P. R. O., S. P. 15/23/f.132.
[3] Danielsson, *Hart,* p. 21.
[4] *Ibid.,* p. 24.
[5] Danielsson, *Hart,* p. 25.
[6] Hurstfield, *Wards,* p. 249.

occupy apartments in Derby House.[7] There Hart and his wife were living in 1573 when Mary Hart complained of the misbehaviour of Garter-king-at-arms' son, William Dethick, York Herald. She insisted that he mistreated her and that his parents had tried to destroy her marriage to John Hart. Mary corresponded with Lord Burghley after her husband's death, referring to him as Burghley's servant.[8]

Occasionally John Hart was linked in the performance of duties with Quyntyn Sneynton, usher of the Court of Wards and a former domestic employee of Lord Burghley. For instance, in 1563, the warrents or bills for the needs of the Earl of Oxford were paid in four instalments, as though quarterly payments, to Quyntyn Sneynton first, then to Morris Tompson, and the two last ones to John Hart. The warrants for the Earl of Rutland were handled similarly.[9] Morris Tompson had no known place in the Court of Wards. He does appear as keeper of the plate in a household list prepared for the Queen's visit to Theobalds in 1572.[10] By 1570, the accounts for several consecutive quarters are all in Hart's hand.[11]

Hart and Sneynton also appeared together as recipients of fees for carrying money in 1569-1570 during the northern rebellion. On November 30, 1569, the Council approved the payment of £26.14.4 to them as expense money for carrying £4,000 "during the late rebellion." The Council approved another £23.10 on December 20, 1569, for carrying £4,000. To John Hart alone the Council, on January 14, 1570, awarded £10 for carrying £5,000 to Ralph Sadler.[12] Here they appear as Crown officials, loaned by the Court of Wards for an extraordinary task, perhaps carrying money provided by the Court of Wards.

Hart concerned himself with language and produced three works on the subject. The first, "The Opening of the Unreasonable Writing of Our English Toung: Wherein is shewid what necessarily is to be left, and what followed for perfect writing thereof," was completed in 1551. The second, "An Orthographie," appeared in 1569; the third, "A Method," in 1570.[13]

Michael Hickes

Michael Hickes came from a Gloucestershire family which eventually sent a member to the metropolis. Michael's father, Robert, was a citizen

[7] Danielsson, *Hart*, p. 14.
[8] *Ibid.*, pp. 26, 28.
[9] Danielsson, *Hart*, p. 72.
[10] Cecil Papers, v. 140, p. 20.
[11] P. R. O., S. P. 15/19/ff. 85, 83.
[12] P. R. O., E. 403/2259.
[13] Danielsson, *Hart*.

of London and a mercer, living over his shop in Cheapside. Michael's mother, Julian, was the daughter and heir of William Arthur of Clapham, Somerset. Michael was the eldest of their three sons, arriving on October 21, 1543. His brothers were Baptist Hickes, who succeeded his father in the mercer's trade and profited greatly, becoming in time Viscount Campden; and Clement Hickes, who settled in Chester and married a girl from Wales.[1]

Nothing is known of Hickes before his matriculation as a pensioner of Trinity College, Cambridge at Michaelmas, 1559.[2] There is no record of his having taken a degree. No information survives for the ensuing period until Hickes was admitted to the fellowship of Lincoln's Inn, one of the schools of law, on March 20, 1565, following only a few months after Vincent Skynner's admission. Skynner was also a secretary to Lord Burghley and a Trinity College man. Another member of the Inn was George Blyth, Burghley's nephew and secretary, also a friend of the Penns into whose family Michael's widowed mother had married. He was likely an instructor of Hickes at Trinity College.[3] It is quite possible that Michael occupied chambers in the Inn as, some years later, letters were addressed to him there.[4]

It is impossible to say which, of a number of circumstances, brought Hickes to Burghley's notice and into his service. It would be pleasant to argue that George Blyth, when advanced to the secretaryship of the Council of the North, suggested Hickes, remembering the bright student he had taught at Cambridge. Yet we know that Burghley himself knew the Hickes family, probably made purchases in their Cheapside shop. Burghley considered Hickes' mother his friend. To her he turned while still in his youth with the request of a loan for £50.[5] Still another possibility is the connection between Hickes and Skynner, at College and Inn.

Although there is also difficulty in establishing precisely when Hickes entered Burghley's service, Hickes' biographer, A. G. R. Smith, asserts that Hickes' employment began in 1573. There is apparently no record of the character of Hickes' work until his appointment as personal secretary in 1580.[6] When mentioned in the list drawn up to describe the overall operation of the household during the dinner for the French Commissioners, April 30, 1581, Hickes appeared toward the bottom of a list of thirty-five named to attend upon the servers. Skynner headed this

[1] John Maclean and W. C. Heane, editors, *The Visitation of the County of Gloucester*, 1623, Harleian Society Publications, XXI (1885), pp. 80-81.
[2] *Alumni Cantabrigiensis*, II, p. 365.
[3] See Blyth biography.
[4] *The Records of the Honorable Society of Lincoln's Inn*, 2 volumes (London, 1896), I, p. 73.
[5] Read, *Cecil*, p. 32.
[6] A. G. R. Smith, "Portrait of an Elizabethan," *History Today*, XIV (Oct., 1964), p. 717.

list while Maynard was third. While it may not be sound practice to deduce status from such a list, yet most of the charts preserved obviously begin with the most important persons. Hickes was also stationed at the middle table as a translator. At the same table were Skynner, Maynard, Arundell, Gresham and Windebank.[7] Hickes was not included in the list drawn up in October of the same year for the Queen's entertainment at Theobalds, while Maynard was specifically mentioned as secretary.[8]

Because Maynard was mentioned as secretary in October, 1581, we need not preclude Michael Hickes from consideration. It may only indicate the manner in which secretaries were called upon to serve. Since Lord Burghley required almost continuous service, there was little time for the personal affairs of servants while on duty with the Lord Treasurer. The extant correspondence involving Hickes and Maynard lends credibility to the theory that the secretaries served periodically, perhaps a quarter at a time. Certainly this was the accustomed division of a chaplain's service period. Richard Neale, wishing to accompany Robert Cecil on a journey to France, explained that "my attendance upon my Lord your father will afford me this liberty, my waiting-quarter being now expired, and Mr. Thompson come up to wait."[9] Both men were chaplains.

By 1582 Hickes was active in Burghley's service. Strype preserves the record of John Stubbs, the noted puritan pamphleteer and fellow member of Lincoln's Inn, who was freed from prison in 1582, partly because his friend Michael Hickes interceded with Burghley for Stubbs. In an interesting letter, written from the home of Lord Rich, another friend of Hickes, Stubbs thanked Hickes especially for the speed with which he procured the release. Then he wished for Hickes:

> That when it shall please God to single you out to another estate and condition of life, you may depart thence with the spoil of those riches and virtues, which the place and people where you are may yield you; and wholly shake off from your feet that corruption and dross, which without grace, and great heed and watchfulness might easily creep upon you....[10]

Likely Stubbs was the man about whom Skynner addressed Hickes in July, 1581. Writing rather mystically and piously from Theobalds to Hickes at Lincoln's Inn, Skynner spoke about the ill fortune and suffering of a mutual friend, able, "with parts admirable for church and state." Hickes was urged to come to the country so that they could talk together.[11] Possibly both men worked on Lord Burghley who in turn charmed the Queen.

[7] B. M., *Lansdowne MSS.*, v. 33, f. 70, p. 175.
[8] Cecil Papers, v. 140, p. 25.
[9] H. M. C., *Salisbury MSS.*, VIII, p. 35.
[10] Strype, *Reformation*, III, part I, 214.
[11] B. M., *Lansdowne MSS.*, v. 33, f. 79, p. 193.

In 1586, Skynner and Hickes were still serving together. Skynner wrote from Enfield House to Hickes in March, 1586, sorry that he had missed Hickes before his departure into Lincolnshire. Skynner was principally anxious to introduce Hickes to Dr. Bright whom they both knew at Cambridge. Skynner, not then on duty, was eager to have Hickes present the impatient Dr. Bright to Robert Cecil so that he could demonstrate his invention, a kind of shorthand. Bright hoped he could teach Robert this method while Lord Burghley secured some privilege for him from the Queen.[12]

Very early in the next decade Skynner received a promotion, apparently the last secretary to leave Burghley's service in this way during Burghley's life. This left two powerful and able assistants, Michael Hickes and Henry Maynard, linked together in service for the remainder of Burghley's lifetime. It is clear that their position with Burghley gave them a recognized place in society. If there were others who shared the eminence of Hickes and Maynard, and Barnard Dewhurst possibly did, they were not publicly associated with Burghley's secretariat in the evidence that survives.

Since much of Hickes' carefully preserved correspondence survives, it is tempting to overestimate his importance. The cumulative effect of the evidence is to suggest the primary importance of Henry Maynard, certainly the more influential of the two. Whereas Hickes became the confidant of Robert Cecil during the years of Burghley's decline, Maynard ingratiated himself with the Queen to such an extent that it was thought he would presently be made secretary of state. Nonetheless Hickes had his place and has now his biographer.[13]

Professor Hurstfield states that Hickes was often the principal channel through whom suitors for wards made their pleas. Even the great in the land bestowed a friendly greeting, and frequently a gift, upon this "astute and cynical trader in wards."[14] One suitor, unrequited, requested the return of his gift to Hickes.[15] The task of appointing escheators, the responsibility of Lord Burghley as Lord Treasurer, passed from Vincent Skynner to Hickes in the last decade of the sixteenth century.[16] These responsibilities, if only partially his, gave Hickes great influence and access to considerable wealth. The vital character of Hickes' association with Burghley can be understood by reference to the contemporary presidential assistants through whom virtually every piece of information passes on its way to the President. And in Burghley's time, one expected to "gratify" the servants, especially the secretary, to

[12] *Ibid.*, v. 51, item 27, f. 55.
[13] A. G. R. Smith, "Sir Michael Hickes and the Secretariat of the Cecils, c. 1580-1612" (London Ph.D. thesis, 1962).
[14] Hurstfield, *Wards*, p. 68.
[15] *Ibid.*, p. 69.
[16] Hurstfield, *Wards*, p. 232.

insure the success of a petition or project. To such a degree was this the custom that Burghley did not even pay many of the gentlemen who served him, doubtless aware that others would do it for him. Even relatives, as Lady Burghley's first cousin, Sir William Fitzwilliams III, approached Burghley through his secretary, in this instance Hickes, to whom Fitzwilliams gave gifts.[17]

Hickes and Henry Maynard worked closely and well together. Hickes was not present during an undated visit of the Queen to Theobalds, probably enjoying his respite from continuous service. Maynard wrote that since the Queen came, he had been "unreasonably troubled, more than you would easily believe." He wished that some honorable person could be brought in to assist him. Presumably someone they both knew wished the job but Maynard thought he would find the burden greater than he had imagined. Maynard concluded his letter to Hickes, whom he always calls Mr. Michael, with thanks for a gift of wax.[18] Letters from Maynard to Hickes in September and early November of 1594 indicate that Hickes was again absent. In that of November 1, 1594, Maynard anticipated Hickes' return within a few days, when they would have leisure to dispose of "all matters."[19]

By August 11, 1597, Hickes was again on leave in the country. Maynard wrote appreciatively of recent kindness, perhaps on a visit to the Hickes, and expressed the hope that Mrs. Maynard might greet Mr. and Mrs. Hickes in the Maynard home.[20] Five days later Hickes received warning that the Queen might visit the Hickes' home while on progress.[21] Presumably Elizabeth did visit the Hickes' estate, Ruckholt, in Essex, August 17 to 19, 1597.[22] Hickes, surviving the visit, was back on the job at court by August 25, and Maynard released to enjoy the country air at his estate, Easton Lodge, Essex. Maynard took time out to write Hickes a letter requesting that a petition be passed to Burghley for the excuse of a poor sick person from a required loan to the Queen.[23]

The last tour of duty fell to Maynard whose letter of June 16, 1598 allowed Hickes to share the melancholy of it. Burghley was pretty much in seclusion and in ill health. Only the importunities of a suitor anxious to wring a last favor from the dying statesman, disturbed the calm.[24] Maynard was still serving when Burghley died.

[17] Mary E. Finch, *The Wealth of Five Northamptonshire Families*, 1540-1640, Northamptonshire Record Society Publications, XIX (Oxford, 1956), p. 105.
[18] B. M., *Lansdowne MSS.*, v. 68, item 98, f. 220.
[19] *Ibid.*, v. 77, item 67, f. 170.
[20] *Ibid.*, v. 85, item 23, f. 45.
[21] *Ibid.*, f. 49.
[22] Edmund K. Chambers, *The Elizabethan Stage*, 4 volumes (Oxford, 1923), IV, p. 111.
[23] B. M., *Lansdown MSS.*, v. 85, item 29, f. 57.
[24] B. M., *Lansdowne MSS.*, v. 87, item 22, f. 71.

Not only did the two secretaries collaborate in the course of their work. Both served as Members of Parliament. Hickes sat for Truro in 1584, for Shaftesbury, 1588, 1593; for Gatton, 1597; for Horsham, 1601, and 1604.[25] Only in 1593 and in 1604 was Maynard not a fellow M. P. It may be assumed that the two worked closely with Lord Burghley on the government's strategy for the lower house. It is not clear why a speech, made on behalf of old soldiers, and endorsed as Maynard's speech should nonetheless be preserved in Hickes' handwriting. Hickes may either have written the speech or simply have made a copy.[26]

The two men maintained cordial relationships after Burghley's death dissolved their working partnership. In August, 1599, after Maynard had taken an administrative post with the forces mobilized to meet an expected Spanish invasion, he wrote humorously to Hickes urging him to comfort the gentlewomen who were made fearful by the danger, assuring them that so long as such as Maynard were soldiers, all would be well. Then, in a more serious vein, he discounted the report of Spaniards in England.[27]

It is very difficult to estimate or evaluate the extent of Hickes' rewards for his services. There is no evidence that he ever received a salary. The position he occupied, while strategic, was purely private and unofficial. In fact, had there been an official salary, we would still be left with the problem of accounting for the major part of his income, for official salaries were notoriously inadequate. The opportunity to enrich himself was inherent in his position. And undoubtedly Lord Burghley expected him to use it, but with discretion. The only reward from Burghley of which there is evidence was a piece of plate, worth £3 or £4, left in his will.[28] And Hickes was not specifically mentioned by name in the will, a factor suggesting the amplitude of his reward during Burghley's life through the normal perquisites of office.

Burghley provided Hickes with two wardships which can be traced in the Wards' records. The first, the wardship of Thomas Gardiner, worth only £5 annually, was granted in 1591.[29] In 1596 Hickes received the wardship of Gabriel Parvis, unquestionably Hickes' wife's son who later served as one of the witnesses of Hickes' will.[30] This was a nice gesture on Burghley's part for it assured his faithful secretary the full benefits of his marriage to a wealthy widow. No other reward can be traced from Burghley to Hickes.

The evidence of Hickes' loans, assuming them to be such, is too sparse to shed much light on his capabilities as a money lender or as a

---

[25] Mort, "Commons," p. 145.
[26] B. M., *Lansdowne MSS.*, v. 73, item 38, f. 130 and reverse.
[27] *Ibid.*, v. 87, item 58, f. 164.
[28] Collins, *Burghley*, p. 96.
[29] P. R. O., Wards 9/221.
[30] P. R. O., Cal. and Index, Pat. Rolls, 38-43 Eliz., p. 17r.

man of wealth. Nonetheless, there are the ambiguous recognizances for debt from the later years of Elizabeth's reign, four of them, which suggest Hickes' relationship to large sums of money.[31] There is also the request of Francis Bacon for a loan, and finally the suit of the Earl of Pembroke requesting that his loan from Hickes be extended.[32] The survival of this evidence suggests an even wider scope of operation. In so far as it indicates large sums of money available for investment, it may also suggest the effectiveness of the Tudor system of reward.

In the process of evaluating the profits accruing to Hickes by virtue of his connection with the Cecils, something must be said about the favors awarded Hickes by his master's son and his bosom friend, Sir Robert Cecil. In spite of the twenty years' difference between their ages, the two men became fast friends, even accomplices, during the last years of Lord Burghley. Hickes became feodary for the Court of Wards in Essex in or before 1600 and Receiver General in Essex and Middlesex, for the Exchequer, in 1604.[33] Hickes received a knighthood on July 31, 1604, in the King's bedchamber at Ware.[34] In the same year he received the grant of the site and demesnes of the priory of Lenton, in Nottinghamshire.[35] When Cecil, now Earl of Salisbury, went down to Bath to recover his health, Hickes accompanied him and was the only friend with him when he died in the summer of 1612, at Bath.[36]

Hickes remained cordial with Burghley's old steward, Thomas Bellot, who remembered Hickes with a 70s. bequest when he died in 1611, including a "hope ring" of sixteen ounces with the money bequest.[37]

Hickes himself died on August 15, 1612, aged sixty-nine, and was placed in a splendid marble and alabaster tomb in the parish church of Ruckholts, Essex. The inscription suggests that he achieved and enjoyed all that he desired in life.[38] Chamberlain's account of the manner of Hickes' passing will draw smiles today. He reported to Dudley Carleton, in a letter of September 11, 1612, that "Sir Michael Hickes died not long since at his house in Essex of a burning ague, which came as is thought of his often going into the water this hot summer, which though it might seem to refresh him for the time, yet was thought unseasonable for a man of his years."[39]

A widow, twin sons and a daughter were Hickes' beneficiaries. He did not marry until past fifty. Then his bride was a wealthy widow with

[31] P. R. O., L. C. 4/193, ff. 35, 172; L. C. 4/194, ff. 165, 401.
[32] Mort, "Commons," p. 145.
[33] *Ibid.*
[34] Maclean, *Gloucester*, pp. 80-81.
[35] Great Britain, *C. S. P. D.*, VIII (London, 1857), p. 125.
[36] McClure, *Chamberlain*, I, p. 379.
[37] P. C. C., 81 Wood.
[38] Frederic Chancellor, *The Ancient Sepulchral Monuments of Essex* (London, 1890), p. 305.
[39] McClure, *Chamberlain*, I, p. 379.

young children. Henry Parvis, merchant, died in 1593. Sometime after his death, Elizabeth Colston Parvis, his widow, married Hickes and Parvis' son Gabriel became Hickes' ward. Hickes purchased the Parvis estate, Ruckholt, the Essex property which Henry Parvis had only bought the year before his death. This became the family home, remaining in the Hickes family until 1720.[40] Hickes also resided at Beverstone Castle, Gloucestershire, and in a house in Austin Friars, London.[41] He owned, in addition, several other houses in London and Lenton Priory, Nottinghamshire.[42]

The will left by Hickes is a disappointing document. It is brief, apparently making only legal arrangements following upon an earlier disposition of property. The religious statement is correspondingly brief yet unmistakably protestant in tone. Only two specific money bequests are mentioned. His daughter Elizabeth was to get a marriage portion of £1,500 plus a wardship then in Hickes' possession. The wardship was calculated to bring the value of her portion to £2,000. Mary Parvis, Hickes' step-daughter, was to have £200. Hickes' wife; his brother, Sir Baptist Hickes; his brother-in-law, Sir Thomas Lowe; and later his son, William, were made executors.[43] William eventually became a baronet, probably by purchase, for Chamberlain said "that [he] comes to it I know not by what title."[44]

Thomas Holcroft

We know from contemporary evidence that there were Holcrofts in the Cecil household continuously, beginning in 1550 when the first Holcroft began his service.[1] When fully named, the Holcroft was consistently a Thomas Holcroft. As there is no evidence linking these men with a family of that name, one has simply to deduce the most likely family tree on which to hang these men. As Thomas Holcroft usually appeared at or near the top of household lists, it may safely be assumed he was a gentleman. When the Queen visited Theobalds in 1572, Thomas Holcroft appeared fifth in a list of fifty-eight, and was designated an usher for the parlor, a position undoubtedly taken by a gentleman.[2] The most gentle Holcrofts available are those of the Cheshire family, in many respects the most likely supplier of Cecil household servants.

[40] Thomas Wright, *History of Essex*, 2 volumes (London, 1831-1835), II, p. 498.
[41] Mort, "Commons," p. 145.
[42] P. R. O., I. P. M., C 142/327/132.
[43] P. C. C., 110 Fenner.
[44] McClure, *Chamberlain*, II, 260.

[1] B. M., *Lansdowne MSS.*, v. 118, p. 35.
[2] Cecil Papers, v. 140, p. 20.

The first Sir Thomas Holcroft was the second son of John Holcroft of Lancashire. Sir Thomas became an esquire of the body to Henry VIII, was knighted in Perth, Scotland in 1544, and received from his royal master the dissolved monastery of Vale Royal in Cheshire. He married Juliana, daughter and heiress of Nicholas Jennings, Alderman of London. Thomas also served as Marshall to Queen Mary. Their children were: Isabella, who married Edward Manners, third Earl of Rutland and Lord Burghley's ward, the daughter of which union married the eldest son of Thomas Cecil, Earl of Exeter; and Sir Thomas Holcroft, son and heir, one of the privy chamber, living in 1613. This Sir Thomas married Elizabeth, daughter of Sir Edward Fitton. After her **death in 1595, he** married Elizabeth, daughter of Sir William Reyner. They had a son also named Thomas.[3] The issue is therefore clouded by three Thomases, at least two of whom may have served Lord Burghley.

The first Thomas was M. P. for Cheshire in 1553. He was first cousin to Sir Gilbert Gerrard, Master of the Rolls and member of an important administrative family. Thomas died in 1564.[4] The wardship of Thomas Boydell was presumably sold to him for £13.5.4 sometime within the first four years of the reign of Elizabeth. The ward was a little over fourteen years of age when his father, John, a Cheshire landowner, died.[5]

The second Thomas, our most likely candidate, became an M. P. for Cheshire in 1593, representing Cheshire again in the parliaments of 1597, 1601, and 1604. He was admitted to Gray's Inn in 1598 by the means of Lord Burghley, serving in the same year as sheriff of Chester. Knighted in 1603, he became a gentleman of the privy chamber soon after, then baron of the Exchequer for the County Palatine of Chester in 1605. In 1604 he was mentioned as one employed by Robert Cecil on private and public business.[6] It was likely this Thomas Holcroft to whom Burghley granted the wardship of Thomas Brokholes in 1569.[7] No sooner had Holcroft completed payment on Brokholes' wardship in 1572, when in the same year he received another, the wardship of Elizabeth Cathornes.[8]

By 1601 Thomas had become a J. P. in Cheshire, where he had inherited Vale Royal, his father's estate. Death came in 1620 through falling downstairs and breaking his neck.[9] This may or may not be the

[3] Ormerod, *Chester*, I, p. 154.
[4] John P. Rylands, ed., *The Visitation of Chester in 1580*, Harleian Society Publications, XVIII (1882), p. 124.
[5] P. R. O., Wards 9/156.
[6] Mort, "Commons," p. 150.
[7] P. R. O., Wards 9/373.
[8] P. R. O., Wards 9/380.
[9] Mort, "Commons," p. 150.

same Thomas Holcroft who in 1582, while serving as bailiff of Westminster, wrote Lord Burghley about the water situation there.[10]

Roger Houghton

From Roger Houghton's monument in St. Clements Danes church, in the Strand, we learn that he died in 1617, aged sixty-four, after serving Robert Cecil forty-two years, faithfully and well.[1] Using these figures as a guide, he must have been born around 1553. As the monument also attributes his origin to an ancient Lancaster family, perhaps he was a younger brother or nephew of Thomas Houghton, M. P. for Lancashire in 1553. The heir of Thomas Houghton of Houghton Towers, Lancashire, was his son Richard, under age at his father's death in 1589, and given as ward to Sir Gilbert Gerrard whose daughter he married. This family, in any case, had a long tradition as knights of the shire.[2] If not an immediate member of this family, Houghton likely sprang from a junior branch.

If we take the facts inscribed on the monument at face value, perhaps Roger Houghton did enter Burghley's servic in 1570. Only seventeen at the time, his service may have been directly upon Robert Cecil, seven years old and in need of a squire or associate. The inscription suggests continuous service to Cecil and there is no good reason to doubt it. Most of our information about Houghton relates him to Robert Cecil whom he later served as steward. Even so, until Cecil established a separate household, Houghton would have been employed by Burghley and in his establishment. Very likely Thomas Bellot, who had entered Burghley's service as steward four years earlier, detected ability in the young man and took him under his wing. Certainly the evidence suggests that Bellot and Houghton became and remained very good friends.

Houghton was first mentioned in a household list in 1581 when the list drawn up for the Queen's visit in October included his name.[3] When mentioned next, in 1593, Houghton seems to have become head of the Robert Cecil household at Theobalds. Writing to Cecil, Houghton asked for money to pay the servants, reported on the welfare of Cecil's two children, William and Frances, and relayed Bellot's thanks for the gift of a spaniel.[4] On July 28, 1598, just days before Burghley's death, Houghton informed Cecil of his father's decline, repeating what George

---

[10] H. M. C., *Salisbury MSS.*, XIII, pp. 205-206.

[1] John Le Neve, ed., *Monumenta Anglicana, 1600-1649* (London, 1719), p. 65.
[2] Mort, "Commons," p. 155.
[3] Cecil Papers, v. 140, p. 25.
[4] *Ibid.*, General 19/1/106.

Coppin had said about Burghley's lack of appetite but that they hoped Burghley would "fall to his meat today. . . ."[5]

Houghton appeared regularly in the financial dealings of Robert Cecil. There is a receipt from October, 1598 for £100 paid out by Houghton at the direction of Cecil.[6] There are also notes of sums paid by Houghton and Cecil's secretary, Richard Percival, to "intelligencers," between July 9, 1597 and July, 1599, the total of which was £1195.13. Besides these, there were payments at Court from March 1597 to June, 1598, exceeding £1,302.[7] Writing from Court in June, 1600, Cecil instructed Houghton, at Cecil House in the Strand, to pay the bearer of the note certain funds to be used for victualling the Lord Admiral's pinnace.[8]

On August 12, 1600, the forty-seven year old Roger Houghton was admitted to Gray's Inn, obviously not simply to continue his education. As the normal admission to an inn followed university training, this unusually late admission must have been an honor or perhaps recognition of legal training secured outside the inns of court. On the same day, Francis Roberts, another Cecil employee, gained admittance, presumably under the sponsorship of Cecil as this was the inn favored by the Cecils.[9]

The most signal reward conferred upon Houghton, if appearances are correct, joined him with Thomas Bellot. Probably the two were acting as agents for the Cecils when on January 9, 1601, they received from the Queen a lease of the customs and subsidies on imported goods, for the yearly rent of £8,882.[10] Indeed, the sums involved are so large it is tempting to deny outright that this was intended for them alone. A letter from Walter Cope to Robert Cecil, in September, 1601, touched on the custom of all "tufflaffetayes" and satins wrought with cloth of gold and silver which Cecil himself possessed.[11] On the other hand, the patent granted to Bellot and Houghton specifically excepted cloth of gold and silver, thus suggesting the existence of two separate patents.[12] Possibly the machinery of collection, the general administration, was a collective enterprise. The two men received an enlargement of their patent in March, 1602, to include all kinds of silks, adding at the same time £500 yearly to their rent.[13]

At this time, or a little before, Houghton appeared in the enigmatic recognizances for debt, mentioned in two transactions. He seemed to be lending sums of money or acting as guarantor for the performance of a contract. Perhaps this can be said to be evidence, though quite incon-

[5] H. M. C., *Salisbury MSS.*, VIII, p. 280.
[6] Great Britain, *C. S. P., Ireland,* VII (London, 1895), p. 303.
[7] Great Britain, *C. S. P. D.,* V (London, 1869), p. 275.
[8] H. M. C., *Salisbury MSS.*, X, p. 194.
[9] Foster, *Gray's Inn Admissions,* p. 100.
[10] H. M. C., *Salisbury MSS.*, XI, p. 7.
[11] *Ibid.,* p. 396.
[12] H. M. C., *Salisbury MSS.*, XII, p. 77.
[13] *Ibid.*

clusive, of a financial strength which does not make purchase of the customs lease seem quite so unlikely.[14]

In 1610 Roger Houghton was joined with Lord Salisbury and one other in a grant of the rectory and certain tithes of Ormskirk, Lancaster, valued at £47.7.6.[15] No other rewards or grants can be found for Houghton. Two years later Salisbury himself was dead. Houghton served as one of the executors, filling to the last the role of trusted servant.[16]

Houghton must have been an unusually trustworthy man. We have Thomas Bellot's word that he was. So highly did Bellot regard "my special friend Mr. Roger Houghton" that he did not appoint an overseer after making Houghton an executor, saying: "And as for the appointing of an overseer as is usual, I have and ever had such confidence and trust in Mr. Houghton and also well acquainted with his integrity and wisedealing that I leave all to God and his own conscience without naming an overseer." Bellot left Houghton £5 in consideration of this assignment. In the body of the will both Houghton and his wife were recipients of unusual legacies. Houghton was to have the cabinet or Flanders desk in Bellot's chamber, complete with its contents, also a Flanders bowl plated and in a case of red leather. Mrs. Houghton got seven gold 30s. pieces (£10.10s.) and a cypress chest to be delivered from his bedchamber unopened and accompanied by a certain key.[17] Such a bequest, even without the flattering remarks about integrity, bespeaks a close friendship between Bellot and Houghton.

Houghton died in 1617, a fervent protestant, and asked to be buried near his daughter Susan, apparently his only child, in St. Clement Danes. He left £1562 to various relatives and friends, the largest sum, £500, going to a nephew, Sheth Houghton. The poor of several parishes were very well remembered, and £200 was designated for them after his wife's death. The sum of £100 was to go to poor relatives in the parish of Winwicke, Lancashire, besides £40 to the ordinary poor of the parish. Anne, his wife, left the lease of their house in St. Martin's and the residue of estate, was made executor.[18]

Peter Kemp

The author of a history of the Kemp family confessed his inability to connect Lord Burghley's Peter Kemp with any known family of Kemps. He lamely presumed Peter was one of the Kentish Kemps

[14] P. R. O., L. C. 4/194, ff. 99, p. 312.
[15] Great Britain, *C. S. P. D.*, VIII (London, 1857), p. 613.
[16] McClure, *Chamberlain*, I, p. 351.
[17] P. C. C. 81 Wood.
[18] *Ibid.*, 22 Weldon.

because the name Peter was in use there after 1564.¹ Peter lived in Stamford and apparently served Burghley as steward of his possessions there, including the establishment in which Burghley's mother lived. It is quite likely that he succeeded Sir John Abraham in this capacity.

Kemp's first appearance in history is as Cecil's attorney in the transfer to Cecil by the Dean and Chapter of Peterborough of the manor of Stamford Baron, in October 1560.² Throughout the following year Kemp kept Cecil abreast of progress in the building program at Burghley. He sent Cecil a plan of a proposed brewhouse and discussed the felling of timber. The letter of December 13, 1561, contained Kemp's proposal to Cecil for the reduction of the household and renting of the land, made necessary because of Cecil's financial difficulties of that year. The same letter related family news in such a way as to suggest Kemp's place entitled him to comment on private affairs.³ Seizing the opportunity of a letter of January 27, 1562, devoted to reports of cattle sales and payments to be made, Kemp included a request that he be appointed bailiff of Stamford.⁴ The letters that follow deal with opportunities to buy land and with estate business. In one of them, Kemp added that he would not get the farm of a certain piece of land unless Cecil assisted him.⁵

As Kemp did not hesitate to ask for himself, neither did he refrain from pressing the case of another. On May 16, 1562, he recommended Mr. Anthony Burton, chancellor to the bishop of Peterborough, and a very fine, learned man, for the parsonage of Luffenham.⁶ Kemp appealed again for himself in November when he requested a wardship, saying "If it pleasure your honor to stand my good master touching Mr. Wilton's ward. . . ." He wanted the wardship and the lands by lease, worth about 20 marks a year, not to make money but "to do me good in mine age."⁷

Two letters, from December, 1562, are interesting. In the first, Kemp said that Mrs. Harrington recommended her son John as M. P. for Stamford in spite of the fact that Cecil had preferred Mr. Robert Wingfield. The former was a cousin, the latter a brother-in-law of Cecil's. The letter concluded with the lamentable news that Cecil's priest was daily intoxicated.⁸ The second letter, written December 20, indicates

---
¹ Frederick Hitchin-Kemp, *A General History of the Kemp Families* (London, 1902), p. 30.
² W. T. Mellows and Daphne H. Gifford, editors, *Elizabethan Peterborough*, Northamptonshire Record Society Publications, XVIII (Ashford, Kent, 1956), pp. 17-18.
³ Great Britain, *C. S. P. D.*, I (London, 1856), p. 189.
⁴ *Ibid.*, v. XXI, p. 193.
⁵ Great Britain, *C. S. P. D.*, I (London, 1856), p. 194.
⁶ *Ibid.*, v. XXIII, p. 20.
⁷ P. R. O., S. P. 12/25/f. 100.
⁸ Great Britain, *C. S. P. D.*, I (London, 1856), p. 212.

the breadth of Kemp's authority. He wrote that he had delayed the election of the burgesses of Stamford until Cecil's pleasure could be known.[9]

There are two more letters in this span of correspondence, extending from 1561 to February, 1563. At this point the letters between Cecil and his factor in Stamford cease. How this series found its way into the *State Papers* is not known. No other letters, so far as is known, survive from Peter Kemp to Burghley save one in the *Salisbury Manuscripts*. Dated September 15, 1575, it was written to Burghley from Stamford where the plague was raging fiercely. Kemp felt that the leading citizens should return to Stamford, from which they had fled, to handle the situation. Citizens persisted in coming and going from the town in violation of the law and to the danger of neighboring towns. Kemp mentioned the care he took to provide for St. Martin's parish, to isolate it, but some people continued to go into town. He hoped that Lord Burghley would take action to insure the safety of all.[10]

Nothing further is heard from Kemp. We know that he joined the staff at Theobalds when it was augmented for the Queen's visit in 1572. On that occasion he served as clerk of the kitchen for the Lord's first table.[11] How Kemp's situation was altered by Jane Cecil's move into the Sir Thomas Cecil household in June, 1573, is not known. Jane, who suffered from advancing age and greatly impaired vision, was persuaded to join her grandson's household with her two maids and a man. This was the mansion that Lord Burghley was building and in which Kemp presumably lived and served.[12]

In 1578 the will of a Peter Kemp of Stamford was filed for probate. Very, very brief, with little apparent wealth to dispose of, Kemp bequeathed first his soul to God, then the lease of his house to a Peter Oxley, £20 to another, and a white silver cup to someone else. Nicholas Wolriche and Richard Shutt were appointed executors. Witnesses were William Atkinson, William Hoghand and Thomas Clerk.[13] Richard Shutt is almost certainly the same Shute Burghley employed while William Atkinson and Thomas Clerk are probable servants of Burghley.

Burghley let fall to Kemp some of the lesser plums from the Court of Wards. In 1567, upon payment of £5.6.8, Peter Kemp was given the wardship of Christopher Bedingfield.[14] Two years later he paid a mere £1.3s.4 as his whole fine for the wardship of Mary Conye. One year later still, Kemp was given the wardship of Peter Peres, the total cost of which was £5.[15] With only the price to judge by, each grant

[9] *Ibid.*, v. XXVI, p. 213.
[10] H. M. C., *Salisbury MSS.*, II, p. 111.
[11] Cecil Papers, v. 140, p. 20.
[12] Great Britain, *C. S. P., Scotland*, IV (London, 1905), p. 581.
[13] P. C. C., 1 Daughtry.
[14] P. R. O., Wards 9/373.
[15] P. R. O., Wards 9/373.

might aptly be described as modest unless, of course, the purchase price does not represent the normal charge.

Henry Lacy

A Mr. Lacy was identified as steward of Cecil's estates on an undated list clearly belonging to the 1550's. For his pains he received an annual salary of £2, considerably under the £5 paid George Williams, probably a receiver-general.[1] A Mr. Henry Lacy, possibly the steward, wrote Cecil from Stamford on January 27, 1554, that he and his fellow burgesses had received Cecil's "gentle" letter to them directing the election of Sir. Anthony Cooke, Cecil's father-in-law, as an M. P. for Stamford. They had with a whole consent agreed to the proposal. As Cecil had written that the Lord Admiral was writing in favor of another for the other place, he should know that the burgesses favored Henry's son, Robert Lacy of Lincoln's Inn. As Robert was in the Lord Admiral's service, Cecil's aid was solicited to assure the Lord Admiral that both Lacys would perform what service they could for the Lord Admiral.[2]

In February, 1554, a Henry Lacy was appointed a justice of the peace for Lincolnshire.[3] On November 28, 1554, Henry Lacy and George Williams wrote Cecil about estate business.[4] Finally, Henry Lacy's signature appears on a letter from the officials of Stamford to Cecil in May, 1557.[5]

The deaths of two Henry Lacys of Stamford are recorded. A Henry of St. Martin's died January 1, 1559, leaving as heir a son named Thomas.[6] The second Henry died in 1564, leaving to a servant, William Atkinson, ten marks; to another servant, Robert Wilson, five marks. He appointed his son, William Lacy, as his sole executor.[7] Neither of these Lacys has any clear connection with the Cecil family.

Henry Maynard

Henry was the son of John Maynard of St. Albans, Hertfordshire, and Mary, John's second wife, daughter of Robert Perrot of Oxfordshire and widow of John Bridges. If the 1547 date of the death of John's

[1] B. M., *Lansdowne MSS.*, v. 118, p. 36.
[2] Samuel Haynes, ed., *Collection of State Papers Relating to Affairs in the Reigns of Henry, Edward, Mary and Elizabeth,* 2 volumes. (London, 1740-1759), I, p. 201.
[3] Great Britain, *Cal. of Pat. Rolls,* Philip and Mary, I (London, 1937), p. 21.
[4] Great Britain, *C. S. P. D.,* I (London, 1856), p. 63.
[5] B. M., *Lansdowne MSS.,* v. 3, f. 68.
[6] Maddison, *Lincolnshire Pedigrees,* p. 576.
[7] P. C. C., 2 Morrison.

first wife, Margery Rowlett, is correct, then Henry must have been born about 1550.[1] The family had been inhabitants of Stoke Dameral, Devon, for several generations. A seaport, now a part of Plymouth, Stoke Dameral was the home of seamen-merchants like the Maynards, who engaged in the wool and cloth trade. The expansion of trade in the late fifteenth century drew the younger men to London. A branch of the family became London mercers, one serving in 1552 as sheriff.[2] John Maynard settled in St. Albans and became a respected, successful member of the community. He married into one of the prominent local families, ancestors of the Dukes of Marlborough, when he married, first, Mary or Margery Rowlett, daughter of Robert, a merchant of the Staple of Calais, and sister of Sir Ralph Rowlett, longtime M. P. from St. Albans.[3]

John Maynard had early cast his lot with the new religion as a despoiler of the church, one who profited from the confiscation of church property. During the last years of Henry VIII and after, John either purchased or entered into negotiations for a vast quantity of ecclesiastical property, sometimes acting with a Henry Audeley, whose name appears in the Cecil household lists more than once. In 1546 John was made understeward and keeper of eighteen lordships and manors in several of the central counties. It was therefore not surprising to find John among the thirty-nine members of parliament who walked out of the Commons rather than re-admit the pope's authority in 1553.[4]

When St. Albans received a charter, Sir William Cecil became the Chief Steward and John Maynard the first Steward of the town, an appointment for life. Described in his epitaph as a man learned in the law, Maynard became Steward in 1553 and served until his death in 1556.[5] Upon his death he left an annuity of £10 to his eldest son with which to study law. Other bequests amounted to £163. Strangely, the least inheritance was that set aside for Henry. It consisted simply of one bed.[6] One wonders if his father had made arrangements for him earlier.

Who got the wardship of young Henry Maynard, where and how he spent the intervening, unillumined years, in what manner and place he received his education, are questions that remain unanswered. Although the probability is great that Cecil knew young Henry and was his own agent in securing his services, we cannot be sure this was the way of introduction to Cecil's service nor do we know when he first appeared.

A Mr. Maynard, whom we would like to identify as Henry, turned

[1] C. Demain-Saunders, "The Early Maynards of Devon and St. Albans," *The Genealogists' Magazine*, VI (December, 1934), p. 636.
[2] *Ibid.*, pp. 603, 605.
[3] *Ibid.*, p. 635.
[4] Demain-Saunders, *Maynards*, pp. 636-637.
[5] Clutterbuck, *Hertford*, I, pp. 50, 103.
[6] Demain-Saunders, *Maynards*, p. 639.

up in company with Mr. Blythe (perhaps George), and the Dean of Westminster as gentleman mourners at the funeral of Matthew Parker, Archbishop of Canterbury, in 1575. Perhaps Maynard came then as a member of Burghley's household.[7] On July 14, 1580, Henry Maynard received 100s.5d. as a fee by mandate of the Lord Treasurer.[8] After October 12, 1581, there can be no question of his position in Burghley's household. Noted as secretary in the household list prepared for the Queen's visit to Theobalds in that year, he is second on the list, following after the chaplain.[9]

As secretary, Maynard had to know the Lord Treasurer's business almost as well as the Treasurer knew it himself. The secretary was the man who kept the papers, who maintained order in the conduct of affairs. He determined what applicants, what petitions reached Lord Burghley. Often the decision was facilitated by the offer of a very good fee, indeed usually it was so aided. Even the great who curried Burghley's favor in a project condescended to the secretary, spoke and wrote ingratiatingly to him. In 1586, Sandys, Archbishop of York, wrote to his "loving friend" Maynard, asking him to secure access to Lord Burghley for the bearer of the letter, a learned and goodly preacher. Sandys feared he himself had troubled Burghley too much with his letters.[10] Sir John Hawkins wrote gently in 1589, after Lady Burghley's death, asking Maynard to take a convenient opportunity to remind Burghley of his letters for payment of the ships in the Narrow Seas, and for the ships in dock because the creditors importuned him daily.[11] All those things approved by the Treasurer were noted in books kept for the Treasurer's convenience by the secretary.[12]

Even though the place was a profitable one, the load was heavy. When Maynard was on duty and Hickes away, during the Queen's August, 1591 visit, Maynard wrote to Hickes that he really could use assistance and thought the choice would fall upon "our honorable friend," who may have been John Clapham whose work as a clerk commenced in 1591.[13] Nor did the fact that Burghley was an aging, often ill man, make working with him easy.

There is only one recorded instance of ill feeling between secretary and master, accompanied in the record by Maynard's rebuttal. Maynard had been openly rebuked by Burghley. Furthermore, Maynard felt that for the past two or three years former favors had been withdrawn, all because someone whom Maynard would not cater to sought to bring

[7] Strype, *Parker*, II, p. 432.
[8] P. R. O., E. 403/2268.
[9] Cecil Papers, v. 140, p. 25.
[10] Strype, *Reformation*, III, Pt. I, p. 588.
[11] Great Britain, *C. S. P. D.*, V (London, 1869), p. 588.
[12] Great Britain, *C. S. P., Scotland*, XI (London, 1936), p. 37.
[13] B. M., *Lansdowne MSS.*, v. 68, item 98, f. 220.

about Maynard's disgrace by insinuating to Burghley that Maynard sought to govern him. Maynard stoutly maintained that, far from seeking to govern Burghley, he had declined to move him for friends or kinsman, to show that he served from true love for former favors. Finally, Maynard confessed he was sorry to use such means to justify himself and recover Burghley's good opinion, without which he would take no comfort in serving.[14]

Maynard may well have been at the end of his tether, for he said to Burghley in the letter above that he felt his diligent service was performed at the cost of good health. Soon afterward Maynard must have fallen seriously ill. On August 16, 1593, however, he assured Sir Robert Cecil that he had fully recovered both health and strength. Nonetheless he accepted Cecil's offer of the use of his coach in order to meet Cecil for the transaction of business.[15] Perhaps we should not blame Burghley too much, for the old gentleman was at the time suffering terribly from gout in his hands and feet.[16] One would like very much to know what member of the household agitated against Maynard, what member Maynard spoke of as the monarch who left this throne "and now humbleth himself to dine in the coldhouse every day with his fellows."[17]

It is tempting to see something in the charge that Maynard was governing Lord Burghley, or at least making the attempt. The language of a statement to Hickes in a letter of November, 1594, might be construed to support such a charge. He said "my Lord will not fail, if you let him not, to be at London on Monday, when we shall have leisure to dispose of all matters." The letter was concluded with a mystifying postscript in which Maynard said that he did not yet know whether he was to be of the council (what council?).[18] Actually there was probably more reason to pin such a charge on Hickes and Robert Cecil who certainly connived to fool Burghley.

During the last years of Burghley's life, Robert Cecil assumed as much of the burden of office as he could reasonably do for his father. Consequently Maynard was, in those days, more closely associated with Robert Cecil. We see him communicating with Cecil and performing tasks for him. It was to Cecil that Maynard turned in November, 1594, when he heard that the Queen might dine with him in the course of her progress. Maynard, appalled, asked Cecil to do what he could to alter her purpose for he had not even decided to take the house in question.[19] Maynard was, at the same time, assiduous in his preparation for the Queen's visit to Theobalds. He urged Robert Cecil to speak to Duck the

[14] Great Britain, *C. S. P. D.*, III (London, 1867), p. 361.
[15] H. M. C., *Salisbury MSS.*, IV, p. 357.
[16] Great Britain, *C. S. P., Ireland,* V (London, 1890), p. 186.
[17] B. M., *Lansdowne MSS.*, v. 77, item 55, f. 149.
[18] *Ibid.*, item 67, f. 170.
[19] H. M. C., *Salisbury MSS.*, V, p. 19.

waymaker or else the Queen would find the drive deep in water. And Cecil might befriend the ladies by urging them to ride rather than to drive.[20]

In 1596 Maynard was asked by Cecil to survey the book of Privy Seals and send some "short abbreviates" as the Queen requested Cecil to deliver to her monthly a docquet of all warrants signed for money.[21] The last note from this period of service was sent from a sorrowful Maynard, at Burghley House in the Strand, to Robert Cecil, on August 5, 1598, just after Lord Burghley's death. Maynard asked to be excused for a few days to go to his home in Essex, just twenty-four miles away. In case he was needed Clapham, well acquainted with the books, was on hand.[22]

Maynard's career did not end with the passing of his querulous old master. Dudley Carleton was made aware of this fact by all his correspondents. Robert Lytton, writing to him on August 29, 1598, reported that Maynard's deserts were not unrewarded even from Her Majesty's own hands. Already he was sworn her servant.[23] And on the following day, August 30, John Chamberlain wrote Carleton describing the funeral of Lord Burghley, the sad state of the Treasury, the attempts to make Robert Cecil Lord Treasurer or Master of Wards, and finally that "Mr. Maynard is become the Queen's man, is in high favour, and nearest in election, it is thought, to be secretary."[24] Even with the support of Robert Cecil, Maynard was not destined to hold so high an office. Probably it was contingent upon Cecil's promotion which did not occur.

A place was, however, quickly found for Maynard, one utilizing the bookkeeping skills he had developed as secretary. By November 8, 1597, he was spoken of as General Overseer of the Checks and Musters in Ireland. He thus became a civilian administrator attached to the military.[25] After two and one half years of service, Ralph Birkinshaw, comptroller and Maynard's associate in the work, submitted a brief declaring that £60,030 had been saved for Her Majesty by their employment. The declaration was intended, however, to counter charges of corruption levelled against Birkinshaw.[26] Maynard was not included in the charges.

Our priceless gossip, Chamberlain, on August 9, 1599, reported further news of Maynard in connection with the fear of a Spanish invasion. In the sixteenth century manner of meeting such an emergency, an

[20] *Ibid.*, p. 378.
[21] Great Britain, *C. S. P. D.*, IV (London, 1869), p. 306.
[22] H. M. C., *Salisbury MSS.*, VIII, p. 296.
[23] Great Britain, *C. S. P. D.*, V (London, 1869), p. 83.
[24] *Ibid.*, p. 84.
[25] Great Britain, *C. S. P., Ireland*, VII (London, 1895), p. 345.
[26] *Ibid.*, Nov., 1600-31; July, 1601, p. 249.

army had been hastily assembled, commanded by the Lord Admiral as General, and employing Maynard as secretary.[27] Maynard wrote Hickes from camp urging him to quiet the fears of the ladies, for with such as he to guard them, all would be well.[28]

Events continued to enhance Maynard's prestige. The Queen died and a more liberal-handed monarch made his way to London. While enroute, at Theobalds, on May 7, 1603, Maynard knelt and rose at the King's direction to become Sir Henry Maynard, knight.[29] At the King's coronation, Maynard claimed as his right, as seised of Eston manor, the privilege of being Caterer and Larderer.[30] When the Earl of Sussex became Lord Lieutenant of Essex in August, 1603, Maynard was named one of his deputies. That same year he served Essex as Sheriff.[31] Probably the high water mark in his career was reached in 1604 when he was sent to France as England's ambassador.[32] His preparation had been excellent. He had for over twenty years been privy to diplomatic correspondence. It was a natural appointment to hand to a man of capability. Barring the obvious patronage of the Cecils, this might be considered an appointment from the ranks of career diplomats.

After direct connection with the Cecils had ended, Maynard continued on good terms with members of the family. On more than one occasion, he was asked to assist the suit of a granddaughter of the late Lord Treasurer. Once he was asked to assist a family chaplain and again to cause Robert Cecil to intervene in a family dispute.[33] Then in July, 1599, Maynard was to be seen entertaining Robert Cecil's son, William, at Eston Lodge.[34] The favors were evidently returned. In 1600, William Maynard, Henry's eldest son and probably Burghley's namesake and godson, wrote Sir Robert Cecil that "I can neither recount, nor render adequate thanks for the benefits you have conferred upon me for the father's sake."[35] On many occasions there must have been exchanges of courtesies as when Maynard sent Lord Cecil the first apricots and cherries that ripened in his garden.[36]

Without question a very real sense of gratitude bound Maynard to the House of Cecil. Equipped only lightly with inheritance by his famliy, he became a rich man. How did he do it? It is fairly certain that he received no salary for none is recorded. Likely he was first among those

[27] McClure, *Chamberlain*, I, p. 80.
[28] B. M., *Lansdowne MSS.*, v. 87, item 58, f. 164.
[29] Gabriel, "Commons," p. 515.
[30] Great Britain, *C. S. P. D., James I*, I (London, 1857), p. 24.
[31] Gabriel, "Commons," p. 515.
[32] Great Britain, *C. S. P. D., James I*, VIII (London, 1857), p. 181.
[33] Great Britain, *C. S. P. D.*, V (London, 1869), p. 182.
[34] H. M. C., *Salisbury MSS.*, IX, p. 248.
[35] *Ibid.*, p. 461.
[36] *Ibid.*, XV, p. 187.

gentlemen who drew no salary but whose service placed them in the way of considerable reward. These were the men to whom Burghley left pieces of plate worth £3-4. The sole consideration beyond this was the stipulation that Maynard was to have "an estate" in the tenement he occupied in Westminster for his life and three years beyond, at the accustomed rents.[37] These were mere tokens in comparison with what fell his way as secretary. When in 1593 a syndicate sought to outbid Sir Horatio Palavicino for the purchase from the Queen of a captured cargo of pepper for which the Queen wanted £100,000, the syndicate got the pepper but not without paying out £1,333.6.8 as gratuities to politicians who got them the contract. Of this sum, £100 went to Maynard as Burghley's secretary.[38] This example may safely be multiplied many times over.

Other grants came directly through the intervention of Lord Burghley. On August 18, 1585, Maynard was granted the office of writing the writ of *Diem Clausit Extremum,* a writ which started the process of an Inquisition *Post Mortem.*[39] Maynard admitted receipt of many earlier favors in his letter of defense to Lord Burghley. Doubtless, some of these favors were sinecures. The next documented grant was of the office of surveyor of crown lands in Hertfordshire, with an annual fee of £13.6.8, granted during good behaviour in 1594. Two years later the same office in Essex was conferred on Maynard, this also to be held during good behaviour and carrying with it a fee of £20 annually.[40] James I confirmed the latter grant with the same fee.[41]

In the same year that Maynard got the Essex job, Burghley showed that he was eager to undo the impression of hard usage of Maynard. Burghley dipped into the Court of Wards and found a one year old ward, Judith Witherwicke, for Maynard.[42] For payment of £33.6.8, Maynard was to receive £3.6.8 which should continue for twenty years if the child lived.[43] Maynard also received the lease of the ward's land, valued at £7.4.8 annually, for payment of only £6.13.4.[44]

It is more than frustrating to have so little evidence to account for Maynard's rise to wealth, while there is so much evidence of Maynard's possession and use of wealth. His lands, for instance, represented an investment of several thousand pounds. In 1571 Maynard came into possession of the messuage of St. Mary Magdalene in St. Albans upon

[37] Collins, *Burghley,* p. 96.
[38] Lawrence Stone, *An Elizabethan: Sir Horatio Palavicino* (Oxford, 1956), p. 222.
[39] Gabriel, "Commons," p. 515.
[40] P. R. O., E. 315/309.
[41] P. R. O., E. 315/320.
[42] P. R. O., Cal. and Index, Pat. Rolls, 38-43 Eliz., p. 22.
[43] P. R. O., Wards 9/159.

the death of his stepfather, Francis Rogers.[45] This likely formed part of his mother's dower rights. Maynard obtained a twenty-one year lease of lands called Selhurst in October 1584. The lands belonged to the archbishopric of Canterbury and were worth £12.13.4 annually. The lease was renewed in 1593 for twenty-one years on the same conditions.[46] In 1587 Maynard secured a twenty-one year lease on several properties in Warwickshire which had belonged to Francis Englefield.[47] By 1588 Maynard was able to pay £5,000 to purchase Tilty Abbey in Essex from Thomas Howard. The following year he received the grant of Little Easton, Essex, from Queen Elizabeth. With Robert Wright he paid £1874.9.7 in March, 1590, to round out his Tilty Abbey lands and secure others in Warwick.[48]

Other rather considerable purchases of lands appear to have involved some questionable collusion on the part of the guarantors of the will of Sir Horatio Palavicino, the wealthy money-lender. Lady Anne Palavicino, sole executrix of the estate of her husband, placed the administration of her functions as executrix in the hands of a committee of four, consisting of Lord Thomas Howard, Sir Thomas Knyvett, Sir Henry Maynard and a lawyer, Francis Brakin. Shortly after Palavicino's death in 1600, a marriage was arranged between the Lady Anne and the debt-ridden Sir Oliver Cromwell who thereupon gained access to the large Palavicino fortune, contrary to the will of Sir Horatio.[49] Just three years earlier Maynard had purchased the 1,100 acre manor of Great Easton from Sir Oliver Cromwell to round off his property in the adjoining village of Little Easton. Six months later, the manors of Newhall and Claybury, also belonging to Cromwell, went to Maynard, presumably at very favourable prices.[50] The marriage seems strikingly like a pay-off.

Maynard died seised of the manor and great park of Thaxted, Essex; the manor and woods of Great Braxted, Essex; a rectory, a marsh and five other messuages in addition to those already mentioned. The Inquisition *Post Mortem* indicated that the most substantial of his purchases were bought to create a landed family property rather than for speculative purposes.[51]

Stone's investigation in depth of the affairs of Sir Horatio Palavicino reveals his friend Maynard's capability. He was, in fact, able to lend £5,000 as early as 1593. Here indeed was affluence for which the surviving evidence cannot account. Palavicino actually used the prof-

[44] P. R. O., Wards 9/188.
[45] William Page, ed., *Victoria County History of Hertfordshire*, 4 volumes (London, 1902-1914), II, p. 401.
[46] Great Britain, *C. S. P. D.*, V (London, 1869), p. 526.
[47] P. R. O., Cal. Pat. Rolls, 17-30 Eliz.
[48] Gabriel, "Commons," p. 515.
[49] Stone, *Palavicino*, p. 298.
[50] *Ibid.*, p. 302.
[51] P. R. O., C 142/319/195, I. P. M.

fered loan to him by his friend, Maynard, as a ruse to get the Earl of Shrewsbury's manor of Kingston, one he was anxious to acquire. This was supposed to be the only acceptable surety to Maynard who was to supply Palavicino the money. And even then the loan was only for three months.[52] Whether or not Maynard provided Palavicino with the money is neither known nor important. What is important is that in 1593 no one doubted that Maynard was capable of lending so large a sum. Very likely the two men, Maynard and Palavicino, had many business dealings. Maynard's financial ability was even sufficient to commend him to the widow of a great financier.

Presumably both Hickes and Maynard had reputations as moneylenders when Francis Bacon wrote to his "good friends" in March, 1595, asking for a loan.[53] The above account of Maynard's financial involvement may make the recognizances for debt in which he participates more meaningful. In three separate instances, Maynard appeared either to lend or to stand bond to the extent of £5,000.[54] Likely Maynard's proven ability as a financial manipulator was one factor, outside their friendship as associates in Burghley's household, which persuaded Barnard Dewhurst to make Maynard the overseer of his estate which was to have over £2,000 out on loan for several years.[55]

Henry Maynard entered Middle Temple on May 26, 1581 at the special request of Sir John Popham, Treasurer of the Inn. He was called to the bar in 1594. He also served in the parliaments of 1584, 1586, 1588, and 1597 for St. Albans and in 1601 he sat for Essex. Maynard served as J. P. for Essex from 1594 until 1610.[56] While in London, Maynard was a communicant of St. Martin's-in-the-Fields where in 1597 he contributed 10s. toward a building program.[57] There, too, his son Henry was buried in 1574.[58] We see a note of respect and affection in Maynard's gift of several pieces of plate to St. John's College, Cambridge, Burghley's old school. The plate eventually went to aid the cause of Charles I during the Civil War.[59]

Maynard died May 11, 1610, very likely not much above sixty years of age. His will contains a rich expression of devout protestant conviction. To the poor he bequeathed £45, spreading this among several parishes. Of the eight sons and two daughters born to the Maynards, three sons and the girls survived their father. The girls were handsomely endowed for females of their station, each receiving £2,000. Son Charles

[52] Stone, *Palavicino*, p. 197.
[53] B. M., *Lansdowne MSS.*, v. 80, item 71, p. 176.
[54] P. R. O., L. C. 4/193, f. 185; L. C. 4/194, f. 14, f. 98.
[55] P. C. C., 7 Cobham.
[56] Gabriel, "Commons," p. 515.
[57] Kitto, *Accounts*, p. 502.
[58] *Ibid.*, p. 278.
[59] Thomas Baker, *History of the College of St. John the Evangelist, Cambridge*, 2 parts (Cambridge, 1869), II, p. 633.

got all the houses situated in London. Francis was given £500 with which to buy lands, plus leases of lands in Warwickshire. To Sir William went the house called Easton Lodge with all its furnishings. Lady Susan, the widow, received 400 ounces of plate. The rest of the plate and leases were bequeathed to Sir William. The executors received the body of Robert Joceylin, a ward, with the leases of his lands and the marriage, all to be used for the portions of Maynard's daughters. Lady Susan and William were executors while Lord Cavendish was the overseer.[60]

The Maynards succeeded not only to the Bourchier estates but to their burial place as well. Henry was entombed magnificently in marble and alabaster in the Maynard Chapel in the parish church of Little Easton. Over the tomb is a mural monument on which appears the following:

> Whence, who, and what I was, how held in Court,
> My prince, the peers, my countrie can report.
> Aske those of me (good reader) not theise stones.
> They knew my lyfe, theise do but hold my bones.[61]

The three surviving sons of Henry and Susan, daughter and coheir of Thomas Pearson, Gentleman Usher of the Court of Star Chamber, each achieved a measure of success. The eldest subsequently became knight, baronet, then Baron Maynard of Wicklow in Ireland and finally Baron Maynard of Estains in England. The second son, John, was a distinguished courtier, Knight of the Bath, and leading Presbyterian during the Civil War.[62] The youngest, Charles, was an Auditor of the Exchequer.[63]

Joseph Mayne

Mayne does not appear until the last two years of Burghley's life. He apparently always acted the presumptuous fellow, pushing beyond his station when chance permitted. When first mentioned, he was concerned lest another got the lease of lands belonging to a ward already committed to his custody. Mayne lamented that he would do well to come out to the good with both the wardship and the lease, so much had he already laid out to get the wardship. He urged Robert Cecil to answer the other fellow "absolutely that you have passed all your interest in the lease of the lands to me."[1]

---

[60] P. C. C., 43 Wingfield.
[61] Chancellor, *Monuments*, p. 84.
[62] *Concise D. N. B.*, p. 862.
[63] Demain-Saunders, *Maynards*, p. 640.

---

[1] H. M. C., *Salisbury MSS.*, VII, p. 223.

A complaint was lodged against Mayne, described as a yeoman of Lord Burghley's, by Renald Smith, another servant who, by his own admission, was so dedicated to Burghley's service that he had in effect lost the freedom and liberty of a gentleman. Smith charged that Mayne, enjoying the support of Robert Cecil, had constantly provoked him. The papers he had sent to Cecil's secretary, Mr. Willis, would indicate as much. After sending the papers, Smith learned of an affray between Mayne and Edward Bowker, Burghley's bottleman, which took place in Burghley's pallet chamber. Further, Smith insinuated that Mayne was meddling in matters inappropriate for his concern, matters in which Mayne opposed Cecil. Smith asked for half an hour in which to remove certain objections mutteringly or openly made against himself.[2]

Cecil very probably found both at fault, both too troublesome to continue in places of service. This impression stems from Cecil's rejection of Mayne's offer to be of service after Burghley's death. Mayne wanted to wear Cecil's cloth and to have his countenance in good causes, not to be burdensome as an ordinary household servant.[3] Not cast down by one rejection, Mayne wrote again, anxious to clear himself of the offence conceived against him, unable to bear being abandoned altogether by the Cecils.[4]

A Joseph Mayne, probably the same Mayne who served Burghley, received an office from the crown in July, 1595. To be held during good behaviour, it paid 60s.8d. annually.[5] It is not difficult to imagine the eager fellow importuning his aged master for a reward. In the year Mayne engaged Cecil in anxious correspondence, a Joseph Mayne, gentleman, of Creslowe, Buckinghamshire, was engaged in several land transactions. In 1598 he purchased the manor of Walton in Staffordshire from William Keymer.[6] In a recognizance for debt, dated October, 1598, Mayne acknowledged that he owed Keyner £2,000.[7] The following month Mayne went to Henry Best of London and borrowed £80.[8] He may well have borrowed from the funds Barnard Dewhurst had entrusted to his scrivener friend, Henry Best.[9]

In 1601 Mayne secured a license to alienate the manor of Walton to George Onslowe.[10] Onslowe thereupon signed a recognizance for debt acknowledging that he owed Joseph Mayne of Creslowe, Buckingham-

[2] *Ibid.*, p. 444.
[3] H. M. C., *Salisbury MSS.*, VIII, p. 324.
[4] *Ibid.*, p. 322.
[5] P. R. O., E. 315/309.
[6] P. R. O., Cal. and Index, Pat. Rolls, 38-43 Eliz., p. 42.
[7] P. R. O., L. C. 4/193, f. 288.
[8] *Ibid.*, f. 303.
[9] P. C. C., 7 Cobham.
[10] P. R. O., Cal. and Index, Patent Rolls, 38-43 Eliz., p. 14r.

shire, £5,000.[11] If the sums represented are correct, Mayne made a handsome profit on the transaction.

Possibly Cecil did overcome his scruples about Mayne and become again his support as Renald Smith said he had been during Burghley's last days. In 1604 Mayne was granted a lease in reversion of Creslowe pastures, in Buckinghamshire, with allowance for hedging and ditching.[12] In 1607 Mayne was given the benefit of the recusancy of Henry Hast and John Mayne of Buckinghamshire.[13] Mayne capped his career by becoming receiver of Buckinghamshire in 1609, a position within the gift of the Lord Treasurer, at that time the Earl of Salisbury whom Mayne had known as Sir Robert Cecil.[14]

Nothing further is known about Mayne.

James Morrice

It is possible that the Maurice who served as clerk of the kitchen when the Queen visited Theobalds in 1581 was James Morrice.[1] This James Morrice was likely the M. P. for Wareham in 1563 and for Colchester in 1584, 1586, 1588 and 1593.[2] He served as clerk of the great kitchen on the occasion of the dinner honoring the French Commissioners in 1581.[3] He must have been acquainted with the Cecil household and with Sir William Cecil for he married Elizabeth Medley, a cousin of Lady Cecil. Elizabeth's brother, William, was a servant of the Cecils. In 1579 Morrice became attorney of the Court of Wards for life.[4]

Son of William Morrice, he succeeded to his father's lands in 1561 at the age of twenty-one, residing in Chipping Ongar, Essex. He was admitted to Middle Temple in 1558, was made Master of the Bench in 1578, Treasurer in 1596. James became an Essex J. P. in 1580. A puritan, he spoke strongly against Whitgift's anti-puritan measures in the parliament of 1593 and was imprisoned. Lord Essex failed to get him the appointment of Attorney General. He died in 1597, aged fifty-nine.[5] Clearly this person could not have been an ordinary servant yet it is not unlikely that he did assist on extraordinary occasions. Certainly he may be considered a follower of Burghley's.

[11] P. R. O., L. C. 4/194, f. 77.
[12] Great Britain, C. S. P. D., James I, VIII (London, 1857), p. 84.
[13] Ibid., p. 379.
[14] Ibid., p. 565.

[1] Cecil Papers, v. 140, p. 25.
[2] Fuidge, "Commons," p. 245.
[3] B. M., Lansdowne MSS., v. 33, f. 70, p. 175.
[4] Fuidge, "Commons," p. 245.
[5] Ibid.

Robert Napper

Robert Napper's name appeared on the four complete household lists extant from the time of Lord Burghley. From the position of his name on the lists, it is apparent that he was a gentleman.[1] Our only other source of information is his will.

The will of Robert Napper of Newington, Surrey must be that of the servant for he makes bequests to three fellow members of Burghley's staff. He had loaned £100 to his brother John, a London grocer, to whom it was forgiven. The parents of his wife, Anne Sugdon, were fondly remembered. To a cousin Nashe of London, also a grocer, went a Dutch cloak of fine black cloth. Thomas Bellot, Burghley's steward, got a plain white "corselet" with all the furniture belonging to it. Burghley's servant Richard Bradshaw owed him 20s. which was remitted, as was the 10s. debt of Philip Knight, another servant. The remainder of his property went to his loving wife Anne who was appointed sole executrix with her father as overseer. She was asked to give his children what they should have. The will was written in 1581.[2]

Another Robert Napper, son of James Napper of Punknall, Dorset, had a more distinguished career at Oxford, the Middle Temple, in parliament, and finally in Ireland. No relationship between the two can be established.[3]

Richard Neile

Probably the most completely documented service of any one of Burghley's numerous chaplains was that of Richard Neile. He was born in 1562 and christened at St. Margaret's, Westminster.[1] His father, a tallow chandler, had died poor and the son, though of no mean ability, was not a good grammarian. After completing his education at Westminster School, he failed or was ineligible for election to either of the universities.[2] Fortunately Dean Goodman, in spite of the schoolmaster's suggestion to the widowed Mrs. Neile that her son be apprenticed to some bookseller in Paul's Churchyard, pointed Neile out to Lady Burghley who herself sent him to St. John's College, Cambridge. Neile, to show his gratitude, when he became Dean of Westminster, regularly sent

[1] Cecil Papers, v. 140, p. 25.
[2] P. C. C., 36 Sainberbe.
[3] Gabriel, "Commons," pp. 535-536.

---

[1] Arthur Meredyth Burke, ed., *Memorials of St. Margaret's Church, Westminster, The Parish Registers,* 1539-1660 (London, 1914), p. 20.
[2] Sargeaunt, *Westminster School,* p. 25.

Richard Neile

two such scholars who had missed election to the university. He also acknowledged his debt to Lady Burghley whom he called his foundress and patroness, and to her husband and son, his masters, to whom he attributed whatever he had become.³

Neile became Vicar of St. Mary's, Cheshunt, November 4, 1590, on the death of the incumbent.⁴ While there he served as Burghley's chaplain for Theobalds was just outside the village of Cheshunt. He did not miss the opportunity to cultivate his contemporary, Sir Robert Cecil. When Cecil prepared to go on a mission to France in 1598, Neile wrote desiring to go along, explaining that as his waiting quarter had expired and Mr. Thompson had come up to wait, he would have sufficient leisure.⁵ This valuable letter throws light on the routine of service and may suggest why there were so many chaplains. It is tempting to assume that the same quarterly waiting system prevailed for all the principal officers, arising possibly from the division of the year into four legal terms. Evidence for such an assumption is slight, however.

Neile learned how a servant or follower of the great should behave while in their service and passed the advice on to all in a little book he wrote against the Archbishop of Spalato, called *Spalato's Shiftings in Religion*. In it he said:

> It was a rule given me by a discreet friend, when I first became domesticall to that right honorable and worthy servant to the state, the late Lord Burghley Lord Treasurer of England, neither to pry into Business not appertaining to my service, nor to be an intelligencer to my friends abroad, of such passages as I might observe in the course of that my service.⁶

Burghley would undoubtedly have approved.

Neile continued as Vicar of St. Mary's Cheshunt until he resigned in 1605 to accept appointment as Dean of Westminster. His successor in the vicarage was his half brother, Robert Newell. Newell was Neile's chaplain and succeeded Cuthbert Bellot as prebend of Westminster.⁷

Neile's promotions came fairly rapidly. From the deanery of Westminster he moved, in 1608, to the bishropic of Rochester; in 1610 to Lichfield; to Lincoln in 1614; to Durham, 1617; Winchester, 1628; and finally to the Archbishropic of York in 1631, where he remained until his death in 1640. It was Neile who discovered and preferred Laud. Neile became a privy councillor in 1627, sitting regularly on the Court of High Commission and in the Court of Star Chamber.⁸

---

³ Tanner, *Westminster School*, p. 26.
⁴ John E. Cussans, *History of Hertfordshire*, 3 volumes (London, 1870-1881), II, part 2, p. 243.
⁵ H. M. C., *Salisbury MSS.*, VIII, p. 35.
⁶ Peck, *Curiosa*, Liber I, note on page 30.
⁷ Clutterbuck, *Hertford*, II, p. 111.
⁸ *Concise DNB*, p. 933.

Evidently Neile was popular not only with Robert Cecil but with other members of the household. Thomas Bellot, when he wrote his will, asked to be burried in St. Clement Danes in London but hoped that, if possible, Dr. Neile could preach the sermon.[9] It seems a little strange that this devout man, whose extravagantly long and florid discourse on religion bears the almost unmistakable markings of extreme protestantism, should desire the sponsor of Laud to preach his funeral sermon. Neile's closeness to the Cecils does, in fact, suggest that the young Neile and the old Laud would not have been compatible.

Thomas Ogle

Ogle was another relative, Lady Cecil's first cousin, who was employed in some capacity by Cecil, perhaps as an estate agent. He was the son of Richard Ogle, who died in 1555, and Beatrix, daughter of John Cooke of Gidea Hall, Essex. Beatrix was therefore the sister of Lady Burghley's father, Sir Anthony Cooke. Thomas was the brother of Audrey Ogle, wife of Vincent Skinner, one of Cecil's secretaries. Thomas married Jane, daughter of Adelard Welby of Gedney, Lincolnshire.[1] In 1556 Ogle wrote to Cecil about estate business, concluding his note with his mother's request concerning the remainder of her jointure which was in the keeping of Sir Anthony Cooke. She prepared a letter instructing Cooke to deliver the money to Cecil who was asked to bring the money to Mrs. Ogle when he could.[2]

Four years later, after Elizabeth's accession, Thomas continued to handle some of Cecil's business. It is not clear whether he served Cecil privately or Cecil the Principal Secretary. Perhaps the distinction was not clear to him either. He appears reporting on the horses which had been selected, possibly to be used for carrying provisions to court or to transport the Queen on progress.[3] In February, 1562, Ogle appeared on the commission of peace for Lincolnshire as one of the quorum.[4] His only reward seems to have been the lease of Gedney and Pawlett manors in Lincolnshire for twenty-one years.[5] Ogle died in 1574, leaving behind ten children, of whom only two sons, Richard and Thomas, are mentioned in his brief will. Five-year old John would become a noted military commander.[6] The Skinners were remembered with gold rings. Son Richard

[9] P. C. C., 81 Wood.

[1] Maddison, *Lincolnshire Pedigrees*, pp. 730-733.
[2] Great Britain, *C. S. P. D.*, I (London, 1856), p. 84.
[3] *Ibid.*, p. 439.
[4] Great Britain, *Cal. Pat. Rolls,* Elizabeth, II (London, 1948), 439.
[5] P. R. O., Cal. Pat. Rolls, 1-16 Eliz., p. 231r.
[6] Concise DNB, p. 968.

and his wife were to be the executors. That part of his estate, disposable by will, was not large.⁷

John Parlor

Parlor is a nebulous character who was associated with Lord Burghley only once in history, in 1591 when he appeared on a list of those to serve the Queen during her visit to Theobalds in that year.¹ This may be the son of Nicholas Parlar of Kirby Stephen, Westmoreland who married Alice, daughter of Rafe Sarocole of Manchester, Lancashire. They lived in Westminster and their son Hugh married Margaret, daughter and coheir of William Billesby, an exchequer official originally from Lincolnshire.²

On March 24, 1561 a John Parloure received the lease of the keepership of the Gate House prison from Dean Bill and the Chapter of Westminster, the lease to run for twenty-one years at a rental of 12d. per year. The grant was accompanied by a list of charges that might be made on prisoners in the Gate House by the keeper.³ Dean Goodman confirmed the grant on May 4, 1563, to run for a period of forty-one years at 12d. a year.⁴ In 1566, a John Parlour was made bailiff for life of the manor of East Greenwich, a royal manor.⁵

It is possible that we are dealing with at least two John Parlors, the Gate House Keeper and the gentleman who served Lord Burghley.

Boniface Pickering

The pedigree which would explain this servant's connections is completely confused. John Bridges, the eighteenth century historian of Northamptonshire, presents the pedigree of a Gilbert Pickering in the most awkward English imaginable. It is not clear who had whom and by whom. What does emerge, however, is that the Pickerings of Northamptonshire were descended from the fourteenth century speaker of the House of Commons, Sir James Pickering of Westmoreland. And a Gilbert Pickering begat a Boniface. One of them—it is not clear which—possessed, ac-

---

⁷ P. C. C., 29 Martyn.

¹ Cecil Papers, v. 140, p. 37.
² George J. Armytage, ed., *Middlesex Pedigrees*, Harleian Society Publications, LXV (1914), p. 27.
³ Westminster Abbey Library, Register Book V, p. 8, ff. 35-36.
⁴ *Ibid.*, p. 20, f. 88r.
⁵ P. R. O., Cal. Pat. Rolls, 1-16, Eliz., p. 153.

cording to Bridges, employments of trust and credit under Lord Burghley by which he considerably improved his fortune.[1]

A Pickering was placed in charge of the ewery during the dinner at Burghley House for the French Commissioners in 1581.[2] When the Queen visited Theobalds on another occasion, Boniface Pickering was appointed as servitor for the second table.[3] The Boniface Pickering who was patron of All Saint's Church, Aldwiche, Northamptonshire in 1568 and who most likely served in Burghley's household, died in 1585.[4] To his eldest son Gilbert, he left the manor of Tichmersh and several other messuages and tenements, some of which had been purchased from Sir Thomas Cecil.[5] This Gilbert was likely the one who was knighted in 1611 as reward for the dangerous wound his young son acquired in the capture of some Jesuits who resisted arrest.[6]

This Gilbert may also have been the Mr. Pickering of Westminster to whom Thomas Bellot, Burghley's steward, bequeathed 15s. when he died in 1611.[7]

John Purvey

Sometime after the death of Lawrence Eresby in 1561, John Purvey married his widow, Magdalen, sister of Mary Cheke, first wife of Sir William Cecil. As a brother-in-law, it would not be unnatural to find him employed by Cecil. Purvey, who must have been about Cecil's age, likely got his start at the hands of another. He and Walter Mildmay were named the two principal auditors of the Duchy of Lancaster in 1546, Mildmay for the division known as the North Parts, Purvey for that known as the South Parts. The job was for life.[1] He had first served as clerk to Robert Heneage, duchy auditor, whose father had got his foot in the door as gentleman usher to Cardinal Wolsey.[2]

Purvey's first wife was Anne, daughter of William Woodliff, a London mercer who held the manor of Wormley, Hertfordshire. Another daughter of Woodliff married Walter Tooke. Anne and John had a son, William, born about 1560, who in 1587 succeeded his father as auditor of the South Parts for life.[3]

[1] John Bridges, *The History and Antiquities of Northamptonshire*, 2 volumes (Oxford, 1791), II, p. 383.
[2] B. M., *Lansdowne MSS.*, v. 33, f. 70, p. 175.
[3] Cecil Papers, v. 140, p. 37.
[4] P. C. C., 10 Windsor.
[5] Bridges, *Northamptonshire*, II, p. 385.
[6] McClure, *Chamberlain*, I, p. 313.
[7] P. C. C., 81 Wood.

---

[1] Somerville, *Duchy of Lancaster*, p. 443.
[2] *Concise DNB*, p. 599.
[3] Somerville, *Duchy of Lancaster*, pp. 443-444.

In 1561 Purvey was granted custody of the manors of Base Giddings, Priers, and Hoddesdon in Hertfordshire with a fee of 66s.8d.[4] In the same year he was made feodary of Hertfordshire for the Court of Wards, receiving as his deputy in 1567 his brother-in-law, Walter Tooke. Purvey served in this capacity until he died in 1583.[5] In 1562 he appeared on the commission of the peace for Hertfordshire and was of the quorum.[6]

Purvey also had a career in parliament, representing Huntingdon in 1553; Horsham, 1554; Hertfordshire, 1558; and Higham Ferrers, 1559 and 1563.[7]

As a member of the family, Purvey's visits to Theobalds for meals were noted in the margins of the accounts, along with the names of some rather distinguished guests. As the household accounts are relatively complete for 1575-1578, a glance at them reveals Purvey's appearance there in the fall, winter and spring of 1575-1576. Mr. and Mrs. Purvey joined a gala throng of 125 for Sunday dinner with the Cecils on December 18, 1575. On February 9, 1576, three of Purvey's servants dined there. As a hospitable gesture, on Tuesday, April 3, 1576, Purvey sent over eleven chickens for the Cecils' pleasure. Perhaps they were served on Tuesday evening, April 17, two weeks later, when Purvey took supper at Theobalds. On Friday, June 8, 1576, Purvey joined the Earl of Northumberland at a meal in Theobalds.[8]

Purvey's regular employment with Cecil concerned the management of the Cecil estates. Thomas Bellot, steward, on February 7, 1571, acknowledged receipt of £20 from Purvey for wood sales.[9] In April, 1572, Bellot took from Purvey £46.13s. for his rent collections of Base, Priers, and Hoddesdon and for certain wood sales.[10] This indicates that he served as an estate bailiff. On extraordinary occasions, both Purvey and his son might be found in domestic service, as when Burghley mustered a giant staff to wait upon the French Commissioners who dined in great style at Burghley House, the Strand, in 1581.[11]

Purvey died in 1583 or 1584 and his will was filed in 1585. He held property at Wormley, Hoddesdon, Broxborne and Amwell, Hertfordshire; Louthe, Fanthorpe and Marblethorpe, Lincolnshire; and in Norfolk. Most of the "stuffs" on the Lincolnshire properties went to his wife Magdalen, as well as all his goods and cattle at Hoddesdon, Hertfordshire that had belonged to her first husband, Eresby. Son William

[4] P. R. O., E. 315/309.
[5] Unpublished list of officers of C. of Wards, compiled by Professor Joel Hurstfield.
[6] Great Britain, *Cal. Pat. Rolls, Eliz.*, II (London, 1948), p. 438.
[7] Fuidge, "Commons," p. 278.
[8] Cecil Papers, v. 226.
[9] P. R. O., S. P. 12/v. XCI/f. 6.
[10] *Ibid.*, f. 7.
[11] B. M., *Lansdowne MSS.*, v. 33, f. 70, p. 175.

received all goods, corn, hay, cattle, woods and all other movables in his fields, barns, or houses at Wormley, Broxborne, Cheshunt or anywhere in England. William was given, as well, the lease of the mansion house of Saint Lawrence Jewry, London, with its goods, provided his wife might live there. Lord Burghley was given his best gelding. Magdalen received £200 above the stated legacies. William was made sole executor while Walter Tooke, Robert Hayes and Peter Osborne were named overseers.[12] The latter, Osborne, married to a niece of Magdalen's, had been an executor of Eresby's will, as well, and was highly regarded by all.[13]

Robert Ramsden

The evidence does not make clear whether Lord Burghley or Gabriel Goodman first preferred Robert Ramsden. But on June 20, 1571, a royal mandate was issued appointing him to the prebend of Westminster vacated by the resignation of William Wickham.[1] He held his post until 1576.[2] Having secured this income producing position, Ramsden was ready for marriage. In 1572, described as a clerk of St. Clement Danes, he obtained a marriage license to marry Rose Foxley, spinster, of Enfield, Middlesex.[3]

Ramsden also held the parsonage of Spofford in the archdiocese of York. When he came down to his living, presumably after his waiting quarter with Lord Burghley, he carried letters to Archbishop Grindal of York. When he returned to Burghley, he carried letters from Grindal to Burghley. Strype records that just as Burghley was anxious for his honest dependents to be raised, the same mind he bore toward his chaplain. The Archbishop, aware of this, declared in 1575 his own high esteem for Ramsden and his intention to "help him to an archdeaconry." The one Grindal had in mind was held by a pluralist, Dr. Chaderton, president of Queen's College, Cambridge, who, as an absentee, could not perform his duties. The Lord Treasurer responded warmly to this plan, yet he wanted the determination of Ramsden's qualifications to rest with Grindal, or so he said: "If your grace shall dispose this archdeaconry upon Mr. Ramsden for my sake, I have cause to thank your Grace; but yet, except he seem meet for such a charge; as, if he were not able for it, my name and credit would suffer." And therefore Burghley left it to the Archbishop, "not being able of himself to discern what is requisite in a

[12] P. C. C., 19 Butts.
[13] *Ibid.*, 5 Streat.

---

[1] Westminster Abbey Library, Register Book VI, p. 4, f. 22.
[2] *Ibid.*, unpublished list of officers.
[3] *London Marriage Licenses*, p. 53.

man to occupy such an office as had large jurisdiction, and was called *oculus Episcopi....*"[4]

Lord Burghley could afford to write in such a fashion certain that his meaning was clear. And Grindal, aspiring to a higher dignity, was not about to omit this gesture of friendship to the man who in the next year secured for him the Archbishopric of Canterbury itself.[5] As for Ramsden, he undoubtedly became Archdeacon of York. His son Richard, requesting to be employed as Cecil's chaplain in 1598, related that his father, late Archdeacon of York, was Chaplain to Lord Burghley and tutor to his children.[6]

Sir William Reede

Reede was a professional soldier with a lifelong experience on the northern border. Perhaps that was his home country. As early as 1560, Cecil's attention was drawn to the valor and distinction of Captain Reede as a fighter.[1] In view of the relationship between them, it does not seem presumptuous to assume an earlier more personal association. By 1569, Reede had already been appointed Captain of Holy Island, Northumberland. In that year he wrote to Cecil that the fort was badly in need of repair.[2] Cecil must have found him a worthy addition to the Cecil partisans, especially valuable on the border.

When Reede applied for a lease, his suit was granted. In 1579 a draft warrant was issued in favor of William Reede, Captain of Holy Island, Northumberland, for a lease in reversion of the cell and rectory there, in consideration of his good service and the charges bestowed by him in building there, " 'and to encourage him and others to whom he may lease it, to do the like, for the better defence thereof against foreign attempts.' " It was granted in reversion for thirty years.[3] An undated request from William Reede to Lord Burghley asked for a lease, without fine, of lands of which Reede was already tenant, formerly belonging to Sir John Parrott.[4]

In 1587, Burghley must have questioned Lord Hunsdon's complaint about the lack of good captains on the border. Hunsdon replied that he knew Reede was a good captain, but that there were some captains left in Berwick who were captains when Reede was a private soldier, and who

[4] John Strype, *Life of Edmund Grindal* (Oxford, 1821), pp. 280-281.
[5] *Concise DNB*, p. 540.
[6] H. M. C., *Salisbury MSS.*, XIV, p. 78.

---

[1] H. M. C., *Salisbury MSS.*, I, p. 211.
[2] *Ibid.*, p. 405.
[3] H. M. C., *Salisbury MSS.*, II, p. 239.
[4] *Ibid.*, V, p. 76.

were not inferior to him in knowledge, experience and courage.[5] This may also have been an argument against Reede's promotion over so many others just as worthy. But promoted he was, and when next we meet him in 1591 he is Sir William Reede.

However in that year he had to defend himself for determining on his own authority how to disburse the £6,000 he brought to the Earl of Huntingdon, Lord President of the Council of the North. Reede wrote to Burghley, detailing the needs and his defence of his expenditures. He went on to acknowledge Burghley to be the best friend he had in England, a fact he could never forget. He reminded Burghley that it was his influence that had obtained a lease for Reede, and afterward his patent for Holy Island. More recently, Burghley had secured it for Reede's son. Thus Reede offered himself unreservedly in Burghley's service as recompence and went on to exculpate himself a second time.[6] Reede had reason to defend his position which paid him £72 annually.[7]

Reede came out of this scrape with Burghley's confidence in him undiminished. In August 1593, Reede wrote thanking Burghley for accepting his son, also named William, into Burghley's service. And he said that as he had been directed, he had represented Burghley at the christening of Burghley's godson, William, son of Ralph Gray, and had dealt liberally with the nurse and midwife.[8]

Lawrence Robinson, alias Baker

Robinson probably entered the service of Sir William Cecil in 1553.[1] By 1556 he had become bailiff of Maxey in Lincolnshire and was one of those given a livery at Whitsuntide, 1556.[2] He does not appear to have drawn a salary in this capacity. Perhaps he enjoyed an allowance out of his collections or some special privilege derived from his responsibilities. Only when an extraordinarily large staff was needed to serve the French commissioners in 1581 was Robinson called upon to shoulder his share of the domestic duties. What he did on that occasion is not indicated.[3] If he ever appeared regularly in attendance upon the Cecils, it was probably with Sir Thomas Cecil, once Sir Thomas had married and settled in the ancestral mansion at Stamford. From Robinson's will it is evident that his daughter, Amy, served Sir Thomas' wife, Lady Cecil.[4]

---

[5] Great Britain, *C. S. P., Borders,* I (London, 1894), p. 275.
[6] *Ibid.,* pp. 386-387.
[7] *Ibid.,* p. 443.
[8] *Ibid.,* p. 485.

---

[1] B. M., *Lansdowne MSS.,* v. 118, p. 35.
[2] *Ibid.,* p. 45.
[3] *Ibid.,* v. 33, f. 70, p. 175.
[4] P. C. C., 16 Carewe.

Robinson received his share of his master's rewards to faithful servants. In May, 1562, he received a lease for twenty-one years of lands in Aldikefilde, Lincolnshire, late of St. Mary's chantry in Quadringe, Lincolnshire, for which Robinson paid a fine of £30.8s. A further part of the same grant covered lands of the chantry in Ardenkirke, Lincolnshire. The total annual rent was set at £7.12s[5].

In 1571 Robinson received the wardship of John Traves, paying a fine of over £15.[6] Ten years later Robinson obtained a twenty-one year lease of certain pasture in Aldisfeild and elsewhere in Lincolnshire.[7]

By 1584, three years after his last recorded grant, Robinson was dead. He was survived by his wife, Alice, and nine children. The three daughters were to have £200 each on the day of their marriage. Each of the five youngest sons got 100 marks. In addition, Thomas received some leases; Adam, a house, Richard, eleven acres and some other lands. Matthew, joined with his mother as executor, probably received the bulk of the estate by use.[8]

Sir Thomas Cecil and Robinson's cousin, Richard Stevenson of Peterborough, were to settle any questions about the will outside courts of law. Lord Burghley was left forty fat wethers, and Lady Burghley was given a gold ring set with a ruby. Sir Thomas got twenty fat wethers, his wife the best milk cow she could find. Robert Cecil received twenty lambs, the same bequest being made to Sir Thomas' son, William. Mrs. Jane Cecil received twenty ewes. Relatives got an ambling mare, a milk cow and certain lesser bequests. Several servants were remembered. Sir Thomas Cecil and Richard Stevenson were supervisors of the will. The most striking feature of the will is the amplitude of the bequests to the Cecils, suggesting even that these favors were more numerous and more considerable than the records reveal.[9]

Andrew Scarre

Important as he was in the early period of Cecil's development of extensive landed estates, Andrew Scarre is nonetheless almost lost to history. In 1556 he was described as bailiff general of the Cecil estates.[1] He was obviously a fairly large operator, a man of parts, for he could afford to pay Cecil £20 rent and considerable substance in kind when Cecil made a lease to him in 1555 of Sheldingthorp pastures and the

[5] Great Britain, *Cal. Pat. Rolls*, Elizabeth, II (London, 1948), pp. 357-358.
[6] P. R. O., Wards 9/380.
[7] P. R. O., Cal. Pat. Rolls, 17-30 Eliz., p. 16r.
[8] P. C. C., 16 Carewe.
[9] *Ibid.*

[1] B. M., *Lansdowne MSS.*, v. 118, p. 45.

stock in them.² Several of his accounts are preserved in the *State Papers*. He was living in 1572 when a subsidy roll for Kesteven, Lincolnshire lists him as of St. Martin's parish, Stamford. He paid 12s. on £12 of goods.³

Nothing further is known about him. In 1594 a William Scarre of Stamford Baron, possibly a son, died, leaving behind a very firm protestant statement of faith and a modest estate in trust for his wife, Anne. As there were no children, most of the residue was bequeathed to friends or cousins. Among the friends was Richard Shute, one of Burghley's servants and a person who appears frequently in the wills of others who likely served Burghley.⁴

William Seres

William Seres, a stationer by trade, early became a trusted servant of William Cecil. They may have been friends in 1549 when Seres was printing books at Peter College and Cecil was a twenty-eight year old clerical worker. In that year John Cheke, the king's schoolmaster and Cecil's brother-in-law, published a book against the late rebellion, entitled *The Hurt of Sedition, How Grievous It Is to a Commonwealth*, which was printed by John Day and William Seres, Seres being then at Peter College.¹ Peter College then or a few years later, was held by Cecil in fee simple and rented by William Seres for £33.6.8 annually.² The Company of Stationers eventually acquired this property and established its headquarters there.³

The evidence suggests that Seres served as an under bailiff for Cecil, perhaps also as a purchasing agent. In 1556 Seres purchased cloth for liveries for Cecil's household.⁴ At other times he collected money for Andrew Scarre, bailiff general of the Cecil estates in the 1550's.⁵ Each of these duties was performed, according to the accounts, more than once. Seres was himself leasee of a tenement in London, and collector of the rents of others. Eventually he received the lease of Cecil's houses in Paul's Churchyard, the annual return of which was £29.6.8. This lease included the privilege of buying his own dwelling house over a period of years.⁶

² *Ibid.*, p. 21.
³ P. R. O., E. 179/138/548.
⁴ P. C. C., 87 Dixy.

---

¹ John Strype, *Ecclesiastical Memorials*, 3 volumes (Oxford, 1820-1840), I, pt. 2, p. 305.
² B. M., *Lansdowne MSS.*, v. 118, f. 12, f. 57.
³ Cyprian Blagden, *The Stationers Company, A History, 1403-1957* (London, 1960), p. 50.
⁴ B. M., *Lansdowne MSS.*, v. 118, p. 45.
⁵ P. R. O., S. P. 11/107-108.
⁶ B. M., *Lansdowne MSS.*, v. 118.

That he was a trusted servant is shown by the confidence placed in his integrity in 1553 when Cecil, troubled by the plot to make Lady Jane Grey Queen, was preparing to flee. Cecil distributed his papers and plate between the homes of one Willson and Seres, his servant, both men living in London.[7] They were not left long, for Cecil did not in fact leave the country.

Probably the two Seres, father and son, also William, served in the domestic household only on special occasions. William Seres of London first appeared in such capacity in a list of servants and retainers compiled in the 1550's.[8] During the Queen's visit to Theobalds in 1572 a Seres was assigned some form of service.[9] It is quite probable that this was the son, William. The son, who was admitted to the livery of the Company of Stationers in 1578 during the last year of his father's mastership, was not actually a printer.[10]

Cecil was able to use his influence twice on behalf of Seres to secure for him royal patents of monopoly. The first patent, dating from the reign of Edward VI, is mentioned in the second, dating from the reign of Elizabeth. William Seres, Junior, acknowledged after his father's death that Burghley had been the means to these patents.[11] On July 3, 1559 the licence was issued to William Seres to print all authorized books of private prayers, called primers and psalters. No others were allowed to print such books on pain of forfeiture.[12] The patent reveals that under Mary, Seres was not only deprived of a similar privilege but was imprisoned for a considerable time, suffering great loss from confiscation of a large number of primers.[13] The second patent was granted to Seres and to his heirs.

This privilege made Seres one of the biggest printers of the day and one of the most influential members of the Company of Stationers. Seres, with the Queen's Printers and John Day, enjoyed the three largest monopolies granted in Elizabethan times to printers. They did not enjoy them untroubled, for the poorer members of the company continuously challenged their right to these monopolies.[14]

The Stationers received their charter of incorporation in 1557. It has been termed a master-stroke of Tudor politics. The effect was to concentrate the craft of printing books, and to a considerable extent their distribution, in the hands of a single company in London. The exception was the authorized printers of the universities. The government

---

[7] B. M., *Cotton MSS.*, Titus B. II, No. 175, f. 374.
[8] B. M., *Lansdowne MSS.*, v. 118, p. 36.
[9] Cecil Papers, v. 140, p. 20.
[10] Edward Arber, ed., *A Transcript of the Register of the Company of Stationers of London;* 1554-1640, 5 volumes (London, 1875-1894), II, p. 415.
[11] Arber, *Transcripts,* II, p. 383.
[12] Great Britain, *Cal. Pat. Rolls,* Elizabeth, I (London, 1939), pp. 54-55.
[13] Arber, *Transcripts,* II, p. 60.
[14] Blagden, *Stationers Company,* p. 50.

thereby secured the surveillance and control of the nation's reading matter while the company acquired a monopoly valuable to its members.[15] As a result of their incorporation, the Company's rules needed changing. This was done in 1562 and approved by the Lord Treasurer and the two chief justices. William Seres and Richard Tottell paid the law charges necessitated by the changes.[16] The decree of 1566, which provided the Company with the authority to search and seize books violating the laws, is clear evidence of the use of the company as an executive tool of the government.[17]

In view of the amazing authority granted the stationers' company in a vital area of public life, it is instructive to note the prominence of William Seres, trusted servant of the crown's first minister, in the company. Seres was continously a generous benefactor. Whenever a benevolence was taken for the company, Seres performed his share. He gave 20s. upon the incorporation of the society, 20s. for wainscoting in the council chamber.[18] He maintained for some years a cellar chamber in the Stationers' Hall for Dr. William May, deprived Dean of Saint Paul's, paying a 4s. annual rent. He presented the hall with gifts of furniture for several of the rooms.[19] Nor did his generosity cease with his death for he left the company an annuity of £3.[20] But more important, he served as Master of the Company for five years, serving five annual terms, three of them consecutive.

In 1570, 1571, then again in 1575, 1576, and 1577, Seres held the Mastership, an office which, while an honor, was not always a welcome one. Though there were no limits on the number of terms that could be served, it involved some expenses and most stationers were content to serve twice. The Master was expected to provide either a dinner or a piece of plate.[21] No other Elizabethan stationer served as long in the Mastership as did William Seres, Burghley's servant.

Cecil found other ways to reward Seres' service after he had secured a printing monopoly for him. One was a very practical method. Cecil sent a good bit of business to Seres. Some of Cecil's friends, like Walter Haddon, the Latinist, had several of their books published by Seres.[22] Cecil himself made extensive purchases from him as a 1556 bill for £6 worth of books suggests.[23] Furthermore, Cecil caused John Hart to pur-

[15] W. W. Greg and E. Boswell, editors, *Records of the Court of the Stationers' Company*, 1576-1602 (London, 1930), p. LX.
[16] Blagden, *Stationers' Company*, pp. 38-39.
[17] *Ibid.*, p. 70.
[18] Arber, *Transcripts*, I, pp. 50, 62.
[19] *Ibid.*, pp. 130-141.
[20] *Ibid.*, p. 245.
[21] Greg, *Records*, p. XXIX.
[22] Lawrence V. Ryan, "Walter Haddon: Elizabethan Latinist," *Huntington Library Quarterly*, XVII (February, 1954), pp. 118-124.
[23] Cecil Papers, v. 143/92.

chase from Seres most of the ink, paper and books used by royal wards remaining in the custody of the Court of Wards.[24]

In 1570 Cecil granted Seres the custody of a ward, one John Frelove, for which Seres paid £8. The same year Seres obtained a Court of Wards' lease of a Yorkshire ward's lands for a fine of £8.13.4.[25] In 1576, for a fine of £8 paid in one sum, Seres obtained the lease of Kirklington manor, in Notting, part of another ward's lands.[26] The last gift, a royal office, must have come either in the last year of the life of the senior Seres or as a gift to his son. In either case, a William Seres was made keeper of Dayton Wood, in Somerset, for twenty-one years.[27]

Young Seres wrote to Burghley in 1582, requesting his aid in continuing the printing privilege. Somewhat under a cloud at the time, the monopoly was nonetheless the only means Seres had of honoring his father's request to pay his mother £20 annually for life, and to relieve his brothers and sisters.[28] Probably Burghley assisted the young man, who had acted as his messenger in 1576.[29] And Seres also found favor with Robert Cecil who employed him in 1601 to help execute his farm of silks, a position for which a Thomas Cawood said Seres was the fittest man in London.[30]

Nothing is known about the elder Seres' estate or lands as he apparently left no record. The only account of a lease, outside Cecil's sale of a tenement in Paul's Churchyard to Seres, is in Westminster Abbey Library. In 1571, Dean Goodman, who undoubtedly knew Seres well from their simultaneous service to the Cecils, and the chapter of Westminster leased to Seres a vacant piece of ground in Bello Alley, in St. Martins-le-Grand, for twenty-one years. The space indicating the rent is blank in the record.[31] An estate in Hertfordshire is said to have been obtained by William Seres, printer of the 1549 Bible, in 1585 and sold in 1590.[32] This William Seres must have been the son, for the elder Seres was dead when his wife caused Robert Robinson to be admitted a freeman of the Stationers Company in June, 1580.[33] The only augmentation of the estate of William Seres by legacy during his lifetime was the bequest of £6.13s. left him by Cecil's brother-in-law, Lawrence Eresby, who died in 1561. The children of Seres received £4 from Eresby.[34]

We discover from the will of William Seres the younger, that his

[24] P. R. O., S. P. 15/19/89, 89r.
[25] P. R. O., Wards 9/373; Wards 9/380.
[26] P. R. O., Wards 9/381.
[27] P. R. O., Cal. Pat. Rolls, 17-30 Eliz., p. 9.
[28] Arber, *Transcripts*, II, p. 383.
[29] Strype, *Reformation*, II, part 2, p. 48.
[30] H. M. C., *Salisbury MSS.*, XI, p. 112.
[31] Westminster Abbey Library, Register Book VI, p. 4, f. 19r.
[32] Page, *Hertfordshire*, II, p. 153.
[33] Arber, *Transcripts*, II, p. 323.
[34] P. C. C., 5 Streat.

father had several children; a daughter who married a Mr. Disney; a daughter named Sarah who married a Mr. Harrington and had numerous children including a son James; and finally, a son John who predeceased his brother William. William the younger died in 1607, leaving his wife Alice £100 annually. They had no living children.[35]

Seres the elder, in his later years unable to follow his business, assigned his privilege, with all his presses, letters, stocks and copies to Henry Denham, for a yearly rent.[36] It is therefore estimated that Seres' period of activity spanned the years from 1546 to 1577.[37]

Marmaduke Servant

Servant's chief association with Lord Burghley was as Usher in the Court of Wards, in which position he succeeded William Pratt in 1579 and continued to serve through the reign of Elizabeth.[1] Although nothing is known of William Pratt, his predecessor was one Quentin Sneynton, known to have served in the Cecil household in the Marian period. Servant also served domestically on occasion and was well known to some of the servants. Thomas Bellot, Burghley's steward, left Servant a bequest of 30s. and to Mrs. Servant, a legacy of 15s.[2]

Nothing is known about Servant's origins or early career. He can be traced no further back than his marriage in 1566 to Jane Pennyman, spinster, of St. Sepulchre's, London.[3] Very likely, if not a resident of London by birth, he had at least been in the city some time before 1566. It may be assumed that Servant was employed by Burghley prior to his appointment as Usher in 1579, for as early as 1574 he was receiving particulars of leases from an exchequer office for Lord Burghley. Apparently the name gave the clerk some trouble for at one point he appears as Marmaduke, servant to the Lord Treasurer, again, and usually, as Marmaduke Servant.[4]

As Usher in the Court of Wards, Servant was responsible for the maintenance and equipment of the room in the Palace of Westminster in which the Court met.[5] He would also likely be used, as Sneynton was, to carry money to royal officials in distant parts of the realm. On April 26, 1584, Burghley and Walsingham signified to Sir John Forster, on

[35] *Ibid.*, 84 Huddleston.
[36] Arber, *Transcripts*, I, 81.
[37] *Ibid.*, V, p. CIV.

[1] Unpublished list of officers of the Court of Wards, compiled by Prof. Joel Hurstfield.
[2] P. C. C., 81 Wood.
[3] *London Marriage Licenses*, p. 33.
[4] P. R. O., E. 315/202, pp. 79r, 88r.
[5] Hurstfield, *The Queen's Wards*, p. 229.

the border, that they had sent to him, by Marmaduke Servant, the sum of £2,000. The money was to be disposed of as Mr. Davison, envoy to the King of Scots, should order.[6]

Already Servant had rendered personal service in his master's house. When the French Commissioners were entertained in Burghley's London mansion in 1581, Servant kept the cellar, a position calling for a sober man.[7] In 1585, Servant was chosen one of the first assistant burgesses of Westminster under the statute of that year constituting Westminster a municipality.[8] Appointed by the Dean of Westminster, the assistant burgesses would likely also have been approved by the High Steward, Lord Burghley.[9] By 1601 Servant had become a burgess.[10] In these capacities, Servant was required to be present for the sermon in Westminster Abbey each Sunday morning, or forfeit 4d. for each absence.[11]

Burghley found remuneration for Servant outside his own bailiwick. In 1578 he was appointed bailiff of Newington with a fee of 50s. Five years later he became bailiff and collector of the rents of the royal tenements in the city of Westminster and the parish of St. Martins, with a fee of 46s.8d.[12]

Even more substantial reward was obtained from the two wardships Burghley conferred upon Servant. In 1588 Robert Lacy of York died, leaving lands worth £24.8.8 annually and an unborn child as heir. The child, a boy named John, was just six weeks old when the office was held in 1589. By 1591 the wardship had been granted to Servant for £30.[13] Servant was to receive £3.6.8 annually until the child reached the age of seven; thereafter he would get £5.[14] A further favor was obtained by Servant who was granted a lease of the ward's lands, worth £7 annually, for a fine of £8 paid in cash.[15] A second wardship was a rather peculiar case and probably of limited value. Lancelot Backhouse of Westmoreland died in September, 1592. The office was not held until May, 1593. By the latter date his heir, a brother named Robert, was twenty-one years old. However, the custody, wardship and marriage of Robert Backhouse was sold to Servant for £6 cash and without exhibition.[16] Presumably Servant's opportunity for profit would come

[6] Great Britain, *C. S. P., Borders,* I (London, 1894), p. 133.
[7] B. M., *Lansdowne MSS.,* v. 33, f. 70, p. 175.
[8] Manchee, *Westminster,* p. 212.
[9] *Ibid.,* p. 6.
[10] *Ibid.,* p. 210.
[11] *Ibid.,* p. 220.
[12] P. R. O., E. 315/309.
[13] P. R. O., Wards 9/158.
[14] P. R. O., Wards 9/221.
[15] P. R. O., Wards 9/188.
[16] P. R. O., Wards 9/158.

when he bargained with the legally mature Robert for his freedom to marry as he chose.

Dean Goodman and the chapter of Westminster obliged Servant by permitting the purchase of two leases. In December, 1599, Servant obtained from them a forty-one year lease of two little messuages on the south side of Tothill Street, at a rent of 16s. per year.[17] In April, 1600, the Dean and chapter granted him a forty-year lease of a tenement next to the Falcon tenement at 20s. a year.[18]

In 1605 Servant died, apparently having been a strong protestant and a good husband. Joan, his wife, was to see to his burial in St. Margaret's, Westminster, and to serve as his sole executrix. Sixty poor widows were to have 12d. each and the two chief burgesses of Westminster were to have a dinner on election day for their pains in delivering the money to the widows. Joan was to get the house and shop in Paul's Churchyard held of the Dean and chapter of St. Paul's, all the houses on Lambert Hill in London which were held of the Bishop of Hertford, two tenements in Westminster, held of the Dean and chapter; and a pension of 12d. a day granted by Queen Elizabeth to Servant's son-in-law, John Greene, formerly Her Majesty's "coser" maker, but purchased from Greene by Servant for £160. It seems likely that John Greene had fallen upon evil days for his shop and annuity had been purchased by Servant. Nor was Greene mentioned either in the body of the will or as an executor though he had married Servant's only child, Susan, and there were at least four grandchildren. One of these, the only daughter, Joan Greene, was bequeathed £100 and Servant asked that the wardship of Haselrige, granted him by Lord Salisbury, might be granted to Joan toward her preferment. Five friends, including Thomas Bellot's brother, George, and William Pitt, Barnard Dewhurst's scrivener-money-lender friend, were made supervisors and overseers. Others were Sir Cuthbert Pepper, who received the picture of the Right Honorable Lord Cecil "with the curtain belonging;" William Man, who got a piece of gold worth 20s.; and Stephen Thurgar, whose reward was also a 20s. gold piece. Pitt received a similar gold piece plus a French pistol, inlaid with bone, with its case. George Bellot got a gold ring with a death's head on it.[19]

Henry Sheffield

Henry Sheffield, an old servant of Lord Burghley's, is a rather obscure figure. There is no background information, nothing to document his service beyond a name on a list. In 1572 Sheffield served as a carver

---

[17] Westminster Abbey Library, Register Book VIII, p. 10.
[18] *Ibid.*, p. 14.
[19] P. C. C., 57 Hayes.

for the second meal when the Queen visited Burghley at Theobalds.[1] He was appointed to serve again, in an unknown position, during another royal visit.[2] From a letter of Sir George Carew to Sir Robert Cecil in 1594 or 1597, we learn that Sheffield would like to be a captain in Ireland if men were to be sent over. During the Earl of Desmond's rebellion he had been Sergeant Major of the army. He had also been preferred to the Queen by Lord Burghley. And if he obtained his desire, the Queen would for the time be relieved of his pension of 4s. a day which he held, probably as a gentleman pensioner.[3]

Various correspondence in the *Calendars of State Papers, Ireland*, fills in the details of the summary of his career contained in Carew's letter. Sheffield was in Ireland in 1579, at the beginning of the rebellion led by Desmond. At that time he was recommended to the Privy Council as one who ought to be commissioned to train men.[4] In 1580 Sheffield asked Lord Burghley for a letter of recommendation to Lord Grey. He also mentioned his appointment as Sergeant-Major.[5] Sheffield acted as agent in the payment of Alderman Martin's money to Robert Napper in 1581.[6] Sheffield thanked Lord Burghley in 1586 for his letters to the Lord Deputy and offered to take employment under Sir Thomas Cecil.[7] By 1587, Sheffield had returned to England.[8] He returned to Fener's Court, his home in county Carlow, Ireland, sometime in 1591.[9] Sheffield was in Ireland when the next rebellion broke out, serving as captain, Sergeant-Major, and leader of one hundred foot soldiers.[10]

Nothing further is known about Henry Sheffield. He enjoyed a close relationship with Lord Burghley and seemed to benefit from Burghley's patronage.

Richard Shute

The first record of Shute appears in the accounts of the Court of Wards. In two instances, money was paid to feodaries of the Court by Richard Shute. In each case the lands involved were either in Lincolnshire or Northamptonshire. In the first instance, the sum paid the feodary was for part of an arrearage of a ward's lands "charged upon

---

[1] Cecil Papers, v. 140, p. 20.
[2] *Ibid.*, p. 37.
[3] *Ibid.*, v. 170, p. 135.
[4] Great Britain, *C. S. P., Ireland*, II (London, 1867), p. 183.
[5] Great Britain, *C. S. P., Ireland*, II (London, 1867), p. 240.
[6] *Ibid.*, p. 289.
[7] *Ibid.*, III (London, 1880), p. 43.
[8] *Ibid.*, p. 396.
[9] *Ibid.*, IV (London, 1885), p. 425.
[10] *Ibid.*, VII (London, 1895), p. 323.

Peter Kemp, gentleman."[1] Whether or not Peter Kemp held the ward or was associated with the Court of Wards, the implication is clear that Shute was affiliated with Wards in 1576. Nothing further is known about Shute until the beginning of his correspondence with Lord Burghley in 1578. Since 1578 was the year of Peter Kemp's death and since Shute's letters to Burghley are very similar in content to Kemp's letters, it seems a reasonable assumption that Shute was Kemp's successor as Burghley's Lincolnshire factor and estate steward. Yet like most of the others who occasionally found themselves waiting tables, Shute had his turn in domestic service on the occasion of the 1581 banquet honoring the French marriage commissioners.[2]

The year following his assumption of Kemp's duties, Shute was rewarded with the feodaryship of Lincolnshire for the Court of Wards. He retained this lucrative post until ousted from office in 1595.[3] We have Shute's own word for the fact that this appointment was his pay, his only salary, for service to Lord Burghley.[4]

The facts in the story just related require elaboration. Shute's service to Burghley included supervision of the workmen constructing the great mansion which still stands in Stamford, inhabited today by a descendant of Lord Burghley. Any writer from Stamford knew to include a word about the health of Jane Cecil, as Kemp regularly did and as Shute continued to do. The sale of timber and legal matters pertaining to the estate were also discussed in the first surviving correspondence between Shute and Burghley.[5]

Two years later Shute reported the outcome of a case before the Lincolnshire assizes involving the validity of Burghley's lease of Armitree manor. The question was whether the lease covered merely the site of the manor, or the manor and farms. The case was an interesting one. If we accept the facts at face value, the arrival at justice came about in spite of the touring judge who could adjudicate from the facts but who could not appreciate that the facts, while true in themselves, did not tell the whole story. It must have been an amusing scene. The judge was for voiding the lease, reported Shute. And when the jury gave the verdict to Burghley, understanding, as the judge did not, how manor and farms had always passed as one entity, the judge rose angrily as if to leave the court. At that moment "one Neale the foreman of the jury stoutly answered the court saying they knew better what they did than the court understood the cause. . . ." And so, it seemed, they did. To assuage the judge's choler, Shute accepted only 10s. of the £10 awarded for damages.[6]

[1] P. R. O., Wards 9/381.
[2] B. M., *Lansdowne MSS.*, v. 33, f. 70, p. 175.
[3] Unpublished list of Wards' officers, compiled by J. Hurstfield.
[4] Cecil Papers, v. 63, f. 31.
[5] Great Britain, *C. S. P. D.*, I (London, 1856), p. 597.
[6] Cecil Papers, v. 162, p. 4.

Shute's unpopularity became apparent in 1588 when he was appointed to a commission to bring order out of the Rutland estates, confused by the rapid deaths of two Earls of Rutland.[7] The Dowager Countess did not like the idea of any commission, but especially one on which Shute sat, a man she knew to be more curious than all the rest. She was assured, however, by a relative that she should not dislike the commission as it then stood for Shute had gone up to London.[8]

In 1589 Shute went to the Star Chamber with a case against some of his neighbors at Stamford, especially one Edward Heron, who defamed Shute by alledging that he brought about the dismissal of John Backhouse as a Burgess of Stamford, and so ought to be removed himself as a Burgess. Actually, Shute maintained, all twelve Burgesses, meeting together on May 18, 1585, dismissed Backhouse "for notorious bad causes shown."[9] Whether the case was heard and, if so, what verdict was given, are facts which did not survive. In any case, Shute's standing in the community, or Burghley's influence, was sufficient to enable Shute to be selected to represent Stamford in the parliament of 1593.[10]

Shute evidently intended to keep Burghley supplied with information he thought would be of interest about the area and its people. In 1591 we learn as Burghley did that the unfortunate Arthur Hall had broken up his home and let his grounds in order to supply money for his daughter's marriage. Shute went on to advise Lord Burghley about placing cattle on one of his manors. Some of his land in the Wildmore fens was still subject to overflowing and Shute did not hesitate to blame Burghley for not compelling Heron to repair a bank. He accompanied this letter with a separate note devoted to a recommendation of Richard Symes of Stareton, Northamptonshire to Burghley as a retainer. Shute assured Burghley that Symes was ". . . a sufficient wise and honest man and of great government every way and of good livelihood. . . ." Shute modestly added that he had sold Symes lands worth £20 annually. One wonders how much this glowing recommendation cost Symes and whether Burghley judged him worthy.[11]

By 1597 Shute must have been ousted from all his offices, likely even cut off from the performance of any kind of service upon the Cecil family. Perhaps it was to regain their favor that Shute struck out at people who had succeeded him. One of these, John Browne, wrote in 1597 to Robert Cecil to answer the malicious complaints made to Burghley against himself for alledged abuses in Essendine Park. Shute charged Browne with felling timber and spoiling the woods. Browne denied the charges, maintaining that the woods were better preserved since he had charge.

---

[7] H. M. C., *Rutland MSS.*, p. 261.
[8] Hurstfield, *Wards*, p. 51.
[9] P. R. O., Star Chamber 5/5-62/10.
[10] History of Parliament Trust, Members of Parl., 1559-1601, p. 95.
[11] P. R. O., S. P. 12/ff. 272, 272r.

Browne countercharged Shute with spoiling the wood with his horses and by allowing bullocks, kine and sheep to enter. Furthermore, Shute sold twice as much wood as the forest would bear, to benefit his deputy who kept two of Shute's bastards.[12]

In one of the most interesting of Shute's letters, written to Robert Cecil a few days after Burghley's death, it is apparent that Shute's campaign for re-instatement was getting nowhere. He made quite clear that his exemplary service was without fee, wage or other reward beyond the office of feodary which was taken from him even though the grant appeared under the Great Seal. Shute said, "How otherwise my service hath been rewarded, I will not dig into the grave, or give out in writing, but leave it to your honorable knowledge." He hoped to persuade Cecil himself to review his case. If he would not, then, in veiled language, Shute suggested the possibility of recourse to other means of obtaining justice, presumably the courts. Probably Shute hoped to pressure Cecil to handle the matter favorably rather than permit a public spectacle of his father's ways and means of doing business. The whole argument was couched in terms eloquent with humility and excessive deference.[13]

In his efforts to receive justice, Shute apparently did try legal means to get his post back, only to be called a shameless fellow in court. He tried to destroy his deputy feodary, referring to him as " 'a base fellow who could both whine and bite.' "[14] A year later Shute had got no further with Sir Robert even though Shute pitifully reviewed his case, how he had been imprisoned for debt and publicly disgraced. Finally, he desired rather to have Cecil's favor without the office, than to have the office or other preferment without Cecil's favor.[15] What determination was finally made of his case is not known. At this point, he drops from sight.

With other evidence at hand, it seems questionable that, strictly speaking, Shute enjoyed only the single though substantial reward of a feodaryship. It is unthinkable that Shute obtained the twenty-one year lease of certain privileges in Newington, Kent without the aid of some powerful figure in the government. As he was Burghley's man by that time, it is equally unlikely that someone else would have been helping him to such good things.[16] It is equally unlikely that in 1585 Shute came by the office of bailiff for certain lands in Pinchbeck, Lincolnshire, with a £6.13.3 annual fee, without Burghley's help, particularly as the gift was within the jurisdiction of Burghley as Lord Treasurer.[17] It is somewhat surprising that no wardships can be traced to Shute who, as

[12] Cecil Papers, v. 51, f. 48.
[13] *Ibid.*, v. 63, f. 31.
[14] Hurstfield, *Wards*, p. 210.
[15] Great Britain, *Salisbury MSS.*, IX, p. 223.
[16] P. R. O., Cal. Pat. Rolls, 17-30 Eliz.
[17] P. R. O., E 315/309.

feodary, must have uncovered some very choice ones. Perhaps Burghley understood that he had a very good thing in the office itself. Shute did join with Thomas Olney and William Spencer in an obligation of £50 to assure payment of £25 for the wardship of Edward Olney, son of the former sheriff of Northampton. However, in this case, it appears that Olney got the wardship.[18]

It is worth noting that Shute, despite his host of enemies, was the valued friend of two Lincolnshire yeomen who served Lord Burghley and Sir Thomas Cecil. Thomas Tampon, who died in 1584, asked his good friends Richard Shute, gentleman, and William Atkinson, to whom he left rings worth 40s. and 30s. respectively, to serve as the supervisors of his will.[19] When the same William Atkinson died in 1590, he remembered his "very loving and trusty" friend Richard Shute with a cushion of needlework and asked him to aid his brother in performing his last will and testament.[20] Finally, when a William Scarre, possibly a son of Andrew Scarre, William Cecil's bailiff general, died in 1594, he bequeathed to his "worshipful good friend" Shute his filly.[21] A man with firm friends and equally convinced enemies, Shute was perhaps typical of his age.

Vincent Skinner

Vincent Skinner was a Lincolnshire man, a grandson of Robert Skynner, a mercer of Lincoln, and the son and heir of John Skinner and Elizabeth, daughter of John Fairfax of Swarby, Lincolnshire. Vincent's father inherited lands in Thorpe and Wainfleet, Lincolnshire, though Vincent is described as of Thornton College in the same county.[1] When first heard from, he was at Trinity College, Cambridge, entering at Easter in 1557. He received his B. A. in 1561, becoming a Fellow the same year.[2] We know that among his fellow students were Michael Hickes and George Blyth, the latter probably a tutor by this time. Both these men became Burghley's secretaries. Skinner continued his education in the accepted fashion of the day. He was admitted to Lincoln's Inn on January 14, 1565 for training in law.[3] Thomas Windebank, an early secretary, and George Blyth were already there, and Michael Hickes

[18] P. R. O., Wards 9/221.
[19] P. C. C., 13 Watson.
[20] *Ibid.*, 12 Sainberbe.
[21] *Ibid.*, 87 Dixy.

[1] Cecil Papers, Marriage Settlement of the Earl of Salisbury with the daughter of Lord Cobham, 1589, pp. 33-34.
[2] *Alumni Cantabrigiensis*, IV, p. 85.
[3] *The Records of the Honorable Society of Lincoln's Inn: Admissions, 1420 1893*, 4 volumes. (London, 1896), I, p. 73.

joined them within two months. Amidst such tangled relationships it is impossible to explain or to guess who introduced one to the other and so to Cecil. Actually the question is superfluous for in each case there is reason to believe that Cecil knew his man quite apart from the others, probably also knew their families.

The Skinners were well connected and prosperous, among the more influential gentry. They had succeeded in tapping the fountain of honor, the central government, and enjoyed several valuable grants as a consequence. Vincent and his brother were mentioned as kinsmen in the will of Sir Henry Fairfax, the last prior of Kyme, Lincolnshire.[4] A John Skinner of Lincoln, likely Vincent's uncle, served in 1548 with William Cecil on a commission for *Inquisitions Post Mortem* in the county and city of Lincoln.[5] More important was the position held by Vincent's father as receiver of the honor of Bolingbroke, from 1547 onwards. This meant that he was in effect receiver for the Duchy of Lancaster lands in Lincolnshire.[6] In 1575 Vincent was given the reversion after his father who was still in office in 1581, though Vincent had succeeded by February, 1588. In 1560, John Man, the first husband of Skinner's first wife, became John Skinner's deputy receiver.[7]

Vincent began a career with the Duchy which was to widen with the passing years. Since 1573 he had served as escheator for Lincolnshire. In 1579 he was made "Lincolnshire Chantries Receiver."[8] In 1582, he became feodary, succeeding his wife's late brother, Nicholas Ogle, first cousin of Lady Cecil. The following year he was made Constable of Bolingbroke Castle for life, also Constable of Lincoln Castle, an office he farmed out in 1586.[9] This recitation provides insight into the closeness of English society, demonstrates the interrelatedness of families. In such a close society it would be folly to insist upon any one means of introduction to Burghley's service against the many obvious possibilities.

Two years before his marriage, Skinner published the first edition of a translation from Latin of the history of the inquisition which he called *A Discovery and Plain Declaration of Sundry Subtile Practices of the Holy Inquisition of Spain,* the original the work of Reginald Gonsalvo Montanus. When a second edition was published in 1569, he dedicated it to Matthew Parker, Archbishop of Canterbury, with a preface exhorting the English nation to pray for the deliverance of its enemies, to be strong in faith and courageous in deed.[10] This corresponds with the puritan interests of so many of the fellows of Lincoln's Inn. It explains,

[4] Cecil Papers, Marriage Settlement, p. 34.
[5] Great Britain, *Cal. of Pat. Rolls,* Edwards VI, II (London, 1924), p. 136.
[6] Somerville, *Lancaster,* p. 579.
[7] *Ibid.,* p. 580.
[8] *Ibid.*
[9] *Ibid.,* p. 583.
[10] Strype, *Reformation,* I, part II, p. 305.

as well, why Skinner might be addressed in favor of a puritan as permanent preacher to the Inn. The man so favored, a Mr. Clark, got the job.[11]

John Man of Bolingbroke died in 1569 and on January 16, 1570 Skinner married his widow, Audrey, daughter of Richard Ogle of Pinchbeck.[12] Audrey may have been the same person who entered Cecil's service in 1544 though it is difficult to imagine how a child, presumably a very young one, might have served.[13] It is possible that, as Lady Cecil's cousin, she spent some of her youth in the Cecil household. Cecil considerately arranged the wardship of Richard Man for Skinner and his wife so that the value of the marriage might be realized for Skinner, so that Audrey might enjoy her former husband's income unimpaired, and perhaps most important, so that she might have the responsibility of bringing up her own son.[14]

That this marriage brought Skinner and Cecil together cannot be doubted. When Skinner began working for Cecil is open to speculation. In June 1571, Skinner wrote to Hickes, at Lincoln's Inn, that he was laid up with leg trouble, at Bolingbroke, presumably his wife's home. Acknowledging help from Hickes in the past, Skinner admitted he was beset with financial troubles and asked Hickes for money to tide him over.[15] It is possible that neither man was in Cecil's employ at this time. However, in a list of officers connected with the Court of the Exchequer for 1575-1576, Vincent Skynner is listed as secretary to the Lord Treasurer.[16] How many secretaries the great statesman had at any one time is unknown. There must have been more than one, or clerks who could substitute, when in 1578 Skinner requested leave to spend the month of September in Lincolnshire on business.[17] He did not get away until later for he delivered to Sir Thomas Cecil at Burghley House a letter from Burghley on September 11, 1578, probably only then making his way homeward.[18]

Michael Hickes and Skinner, long-time friends, worked closely together as secretaries. Unfortunately, as it is the Hickes collection of letters which has been preserved, only the incoming letters are extant. Thus, with only Skinner's word for it, we reconstruct a rather intimate friendship between the two men. So great was Skinner's regard for Hickes that when he desired to further the suit of a Mr. Wheler he would not use Hickes as a means for fear of hurting him or his chances for

---

[11] *Ibid.*, III, part I, p. 80.
[12] Cecil Papers, Marriage Settlement, pp. 33-34.
[13] B. M., *Lansdowne MSS.*, v. 118, p. 35.
[14] P. R. O., Privy Seal Office, Index 6743, Docket Book.
[15] B. M., *Lansdowne MSS.*, v. 13, f. 39, p. 116.
[16] P. R. O., E. 101/336/26.
[17] B. M., *Salisbury MSS.*, XIII, p. 158.
[18] *Ibid.*, p. 200.

advancement.[19] Skinner revealed another facet of their relationship when he spoke mystically and piously to the equally devout Hickes concerning a mutual friend who suffered an ill fortune.[20] If this friend was Stubbs, the puritan pamphleteer, then it is quite likely that Skinner assisted Hickes in moving Burghley to arrange his freedom. In a bantering letter to Hickes in 1586, Skinner again alluded to Hickes' preferment, after which he requested Hickes to arrange for a Dr. Bright to see Burghley about a new system of shorthand which Bright would gladly teach young Robert Cecil.[21] The two men had also stood together behind the center table at the banquet for the French commissioners in 1581 as translators.[22]

It seems likely that at one point Skinner outranked the other secretaries. This is suggested in the indenture by which the conveyance of lands by Lord Burghley to Robert Cecil was guaranteed by Lord Cobham, Sir Thomas Cecil, Edward Wotton, Anthony Cooke, Francis Bacon, Vincent Skinner and Barnard Dewhurst. All the guarantors of the conveyance were related to the Cecils in some way, thus giving them a status above mere servants who were only employed on this occasion to witness the signing and sealing.[23] It was Skinner, too, who seemed to be the real channel of the annual appointment of escheators, no doubt a golden privilege. The office, with its fees and opportunities for unofficial rewards, was in theory assigned by the Lord Treasurer on the advice of the justices of assize.[24]

Skinner's faithful service was rewarded in 1593 by promotion to the Exchequer staff itself where he became Writer of Tallies and Counter Tallies for life.[25] This was an excellent advance, one paying over £90 official salary, plus fees and tips. Besides, he received £9 annual allowance for a clerk to assist him in the writing.[26] In July, 1599, however, Skinner wanted to retire. As he wrote Robert Cecil, "the quarrel I have had about my place has hindered and so utterly discouraged me, that I could not do the service I intended."[27] Skinner went on to speak of the nature of his office. He said, "My office is a place serviceable in State causes,—inasmuch as the matter of the finances in all States is one part thereof,—but chiefly in the matter of issues, no way being so open for overture of the actions of princes, or for discovering of their secret intentions, as by the issues of treasure."[28] He went on to explain the trouble,

[19] B. M., *Lansdowne MSS.*, v. 51, item 1, f. 2.
[20] *Ibid.*, v. 33, f. 79, p. 193.
[21] *Ibid.*, v. 51, item 27, f. 55.
[22] *Ibid.*, v. 33, f. 70, p. 175.
[23] Cecil Papers, Legal 22/5, f. 1.
[24] Hurstfield, *Wards*, p. 231.
[25] H. M. C., *Salisbury MSS.*, IV, p. 377.
[26] P. R. O., E. 403/2282.
[27] Great Britain, *C. S. P. D.*, V (London, 1869), pp. 241-242.
[28] *Ibid.*

the re-erection of the pell of issues, and the consequent enlargement of the number of those privy to issues. Skinner indeed had a difficult time with the Clerk of the Pells, Chidioch Wardour, who waged a continuous battle to re-instate the pells. Skinner, tired though he was of the fray, was persuaded to remain.

Apparently the Queen, in her last days, was concerned about the number aware of royal business. She was assured by the Lord Treasurer, Lord Buckhurst, that we would keep the Privy Seal himself, and none should know it but himself, Mr. Chancellor, Mr. Skinner and Mr. Wardour. However, he could not pay Her Majesty's money without warrant of the Privy Seal unless an act of parliament be passed permitting it.[29]

Skinner confessed once that he had served in only one house.[30] Therefore all that came to him outside the Duchy of Lancaster offices, and perhaps even these, were secured in part by the Cecils and were intended as reward or payment for service. Certainly this was true of his Exchequer job. It was likely true of two other small offices. One, granted in 1575, made Skinner bailiff of the manor of Neward and provided an annual fee of £4.11.3. The other gave him custody of the lands of the former priory of St. John in Anglia, paying him annually £3.6.8.[31]

Two wardships can be traced to Skinner, both granted about the same time, early in his employment. The first, already mentioned, was the wardship of Richard Man, his stepson. The other, in 1573, was the wardship of one Anne Daynes.[32] The particulars are not available. Skinner joined with Barnard Dewhurst and Robert Cecil in a bond of £500 to guarantee payment of £250 for the wardship of Giles Allington in 1587, the annual worth of which was £66.13.4. As Robert Cecil is the first named, it is likely that he got the wardship.[33] After Burghley's death, in April, 1604, one other grant fell Skinner's way, the keeping of Kirkly Park, Lincolnshire, with the survivorship going to his son William.[34] Then, too, the Cecils included Skinner in their allotment of knighthoods when the bountiful James came to Theobalds on May 7, 1603.[35]

In some measure, a number of leases which were handed to Skinner may have been a part of his reward. On July 5, 1574, a patent was issued to him for a third part of the rectory of Barwick in Cardiganshire for twenty-one years.[36] A very interesting deed exists complete, so far

[29] Great Britain, *C. S. P. D.*, VI (London, 1870), p. 167.
[30] Great Britain, *C. S. P. D.*, V (London, 1869), pp. 241-242.
[31] P. R. O., E. 315/309.
[32] P. R. O., Wards 9/380.
[33] P. R. O., Wards 9/221.
[34] Great Britain, *C. S. P. D.*, VIII (London, 1857), p. 99.
[35] Gabriel, "Commons," p. 599.
[36] P. R. O., Cal. Pat. Rolls, 1-16 Eliz., p. 341.

as I can tell, among the Cecil Papers by which Vincent Skinner in 1588 secured the lease of Chesthunt Nunnery for 1,000 years. The witnesses included such stalwart fellow servants as Barnard Dewhurst, Thomas Bellot, and Michael Hickes.[37] In April, 1592, St. John's College, Cambridge, Burghley's old school, leased Dounchorte manor and Bleane woods to Skinner for twenty years, at an annual rent of £8.17.6, thirteen quarters of wheat and one-half quarter of malt.[38] Finally, in March, 1607, he received the grant, in fee-farm, of the manor of Thornton in Lincolnshire.[39]

None of these gifts or grants succeeded in staving off a kind of chronic indebtedness which plagued Skinner all his life. We noted him seeking a loan from Hickes in 1571, just after marriage to a well-to-do widow. Maynard wrote Hickes in 1596 about a certain matter, declaring that Skinner would have to trouble his memory, "for that he pretendeth that he knoweth that a debt now demanded of him by Her Majesty was remitted (in 1573), being now twenty-three years past. . . ."[40] Matters did not improve so that when Skinner died on February 29, 1611, it was in debtor's prison.[41] Outside lands worth £10 a year, Skinner's Inquisition *Post Mortem* reveals ownership of Thornton manor only.[42] He did not leave a will.

Skinner, a J. P. by 1594, also enjoyed a fairly long career as a member of Parliament. He sat for Truro in 1571, Barnstaple in 1572, Boston in 1584, 1586, and 1588; Boroughbridge in 1593; St. Ives, 1597; and Preston, 1604. After Audrey died, Skinner married Elizabeth, daughter of Robert Fowkes, and widow of Edward Middlemore of Enfield, Middlesex.[43] They had one son, William, born in 1597, died in 1627. His wife was Bridget, second daughter of Sir Edward Coke, Lord Chief Justice.[44] Skinner shared a chamber in Lincoln's Inn with his son at the time of his death.[45]

Quentin Sneynton

Sneynton joined the Cecil household service in 1554, in the same year that Gabriel Goodman, future Dean of Westminster, came as a school-

[37] Cecil Papers, Deeds 191/5.
[38] Baker, *St. John's,* Part I, pp. 435-436.
[39] Great Britain, *C. S. P. D.,* VIII (London, 1857), p. 351.
[40] B. M., *Lansdowne MSS.,* v. 80, item 67, f. 168.
[41] Maddison, *Lincolnshire Pedigrees,* p. 288.
[42] P. R. O., C 142/356/134.
[43] Gabriel, "Commons," p. 599.
[44] Maddison, *Lincolnshire Pedigrees,* p. 288.
[45] J. D. Walker and W. P. Baildon, editors, *The Records of the Honorable Society of Lincoln's Inn: The Black Books, 1422-1845,* 4 volumes. (London, 1897-1902), II, p. 181.

master.¹ It is difficult to determine what he did from the entries in William Cayworth's accounts. He appears to have acted as a messenger, delivering money, passing between the Wimbledon and Canon Row homes of the Cecils, or as a purchasing agent. He may well have been a gentleman usher. In 1556 he delivered 12d. to Cecil "to play," probably at dice.² When Cayworth accounts for 14d. for the boat hire of Sir William and Lady Cecil to Canon Row on May 15, 1557, he indicates that Sneynton was along and paid the fare. In the same week, on Wednesday, May 19, Sneynton disbursed 25s. for wagon wheels. When on Friday, May 21, Cecil went down to London by boat, Sneynton paid the 3d. fare.³ On Wednesday of the following week Sneynton paid 3d. for cards; on Friday he went to Wimbledon, paying 1d. for his boat hire. It must have been an exciting time. Cecil journeyed almost daily to the Earl of Bedford's house and messengers were frequently being sent to Hatfield where the Princess Elizabeth awaited her change of fortune.⁴

For such work Sneynton, one of thirty-five servants, drew a quarterly salary of 10s., or £2 annually.⁵ He very likely continued this service, possibly for the same salary, until he became usher in the Court of Wards in 1564, a lifetime appointment carrying with it a £5 annual salary.⁶ This seems in practice never to have been less than £6.⁷ A new court house had just been built for the Court of Wards, adjacent to Westminster Hall. It was Sneynton's duty to keep this chamber. Actually he employed a Mrs. Adnes Brinknell, a widow, for this task.⁸ Perhaps she prepared the two or three dinners provided the Court each term. Sneynton was responsible for them as well as for providing all supplies, as rushes, sand, coal and wood. He had also to see to such repairs as replacing glass in the windows or restoring and oiling locks. His disbursements during 1565 came to £308.14.9.⁹

In his capacity as a crown officer, Sneynton was called upon to transport money during the rebellion of the northern earls. He and John Hart, Chester Herald, were granted £26.14.4 for their extraordinary expenses involved in the carriage of £4,000. At a later date, a £23.10. fee was added by the Privy Council in full payment of their expenses.¹⁰ Such a journey came at an awkward time for Sneynton who had just been married. A licence was granted to him on July 9, 1568 to marry Agnes

[1] B. M., *Lansdowne MSS.*, v. 118, p. 35.
[2] Cecil Papers, General 139/f. 4.
[3] *Ibid.*, v. 143/82.
[4] *Ibid.*, v. 143/81.
[5] *Ibid.*, v. 143/79.
[6] P. R. O., Cal. Pat. Rolls, 1-16 Eliz., p. 175r.
[7] P. R. O., Wards 9/373.
[8] P. C. C., 27 Pyckering.
[9] P. R. O., Wards 9/373.
[10] P. R. O., E. 403/2259.

or Anne Hall of Westminster at St. Margaret's, Westminster.[11] She may have been a sister of Arthur Hall, Burghley's ward, or certainly a cousin, since she and Arthur shared an uncle, Edmond Hall.[12]

That Cecil used the Court of Wards as a means of rewarding Sneynton for services performed in domestic service and as a crown officer should not be surprising. In 1563 Sneynton was granted the wardship and marriage of Anne and Catherine Read, coheirs of Richard Read of Lincolnshire, with an exhibition of 43s.4d. The purchase price was £26.13.4.[13] The most impressive grant, so favorable to the purchaser that the Court felt impelled to explain it, was given Sneynton sometime between 1570 and 1575. For a fine of 40s. Sneynton obtained a lease of lands valued at £12.13.1 annually, in consideration, it was explained, for his service in the Court of Wards. Coming from the estate of Her Majesty's ward, William Riggs of Lincolnshire, this was more than twice Sneynton's annual salary from the Court.[14] In spite of this, Sneynton was only asked to pay 6s. on £6 income, said to be in goods rather than lands, when the second payment of a subsidy was due the Queen in 1572.[15] Unfortunately, Sneynton did not long survive his good fortune. He died in 1575.

Sneynton and his wife Anne did not have surviving children. He left her 100 marks, the dwelling and household stuff at Hamonesstreet, Cheshunt, plus Stook's pasture with three kyne. The remainder of the estate went to various persons. Sneynton's next concern, after his wife, was for his master: "And whereas I am most bound to my good Lord Burghley . . . and to my good lady and mistress his wife by whom I have received all that good that God hath sent, In consideration thereof my most bounden duty is not to forget the same with some small token expressing the same." The token was a bequest to Robert Cecil of the leases of Sneynton's tenement in Hamonestreet, and grounds called Peeks. Twenty pounds were designated for the making of a foot bridge. The poor of Cheshunt were given 20s., the church 13s.4d. for repairs. Other bequests were made to St. Margaret's, Westminster for the parish poor and for repairs. The sum of £5 was left to the widow who kept the Court of Wards, and small bequests to several godsons and servants. Sneynton's sister Mary got certain Lincolnshire lands. Three small endowments were set up from other Lincolnshire lands; one to send a poor scholar to the free school of Neward; another to aid a poor body,

[11] George J. Armytage, ed., *Marriage Licences Issued by the Dean and Chapter of Westminster, 1558-1699*, Harleian Society Publications, XXIII (1886), p. 2.
[12] P. C. C., 27 Pyckering.
[13] P. R. O., Wards 9/156.
[14] *Ibid.*, Wards 9/190.
[15] *Ibid.*, E 179/121/223, f. 3.

lame, blind or sick; the last to the Cheshunt church and to St. Margaret's for two small sermons to be made twice a year.[16]

The supervisors were John Conyers and his wife's uncle, Edmond Hall. It seems likely that Sneynton lived in the Court of Wards for Conyers was left Sneynton's great joined bedstead standing within the parlor of the Court of Wards, together with the new bolster and the curtains, in consideration of their old friendship and his pains in the performance of the will. Hall received £2 for his pains.[17]

Thomas Speed, alias Lewkenor

Here is a servant for whom there is scarcely any evidence beyond his reward to tell us how he served Burghley or even why he changed his name. We know that he was a servant by August 14, 1577 when the Bishop of Durham wrote to Burghley that he would be happy to accede to Burghley's request and grant to the bearer of the letter, Thomas Speed, the office of Keeper of Burtley Woods.[1] We also know that Speed was available for household duty on two extraordinary occasions in 1581. When Burghley entertained the French commissioners on April 30, 1581, Speed shared charge of the plate house with one other.[2] He was again present when in October the Queen visited Theobalds, though his duty station, on this occasion, is not given.[3]

In the same year that Burghley arranged for the Bishop of Durham to give Speed an office, Burghley himself conferred upon Speed the wardship of George Gunter.[4] Then sometime between 1570 and 1581, Speed was allowed to purchase for 13s.4d. a lease of the lands of John Sych, a ward, yielding 10s.8d. annually.[5] Further favor came in 1582 when Speed was made a royal bailiff with an annual fee of 5s. To this was added five years later another royal bailiwick carrying with it an annual stipend of £5.[6] At the same time, on December 4, 1587, Dean Goodman and the Chapter of Westminster leased to "Thomas Speed, gentleman of Westminster and servant to the Lord Treasurer of England," two little messuages on the south side of Tothill Street, for a term of forty years at 16s. a year.[7] The very same lease later went to Marmaduke Servant, another Burghley employee and one of Speed's executors.[8]

---

[16] P. C. C., 27 Pyckering.
[17] *Ibid.*

---

[1] B. M., *Lansdowne MSS.*, v. 25, f. 32, p. 68.
[2] *Ibid.*, v. 33, f. 70, p. 175.
[3] Cecil Papers, v. 140, p. 25.
[4] P. R. O., Wards 9/381.
[5] *Ibid.*, Wards 9/190.
[6] *Ibid.*, E. 315/309.
[7] Westminster Abbey Library, Register Book VII, p. 7, f. 41.
[8] *Ibid.*, Register Book VIII, p. 10, f. 74.

When Thomas Speed, alias Lewkenor, died in 1599 he left a will in which he incorporated an almost passionate statement of religious faith, unmistakably protestant. Without wife or children, he left his estate entirely to relatives and friends. Born in Durham, Speed was living in the Strand at the time of death. He stated, too, that such goods as he left he gained by true and painful service. To his sister Ann Hunt went £20 and all such linen, pewter, brass and household stuff that Speed left at his departure from Enfield House, Hertfordshire. From a tenement in Croxdell there was sufficient income to leave small annuities to several relatives. He left £5 to "poor John Momford my chamber drudge." The Servants were well remembered, Marmaduke receiving a white bowl worth £4, his wife an emerald ring and his daughter a ruby ring. To Mr. and Mrs. Houghton went £3 worth of gifts. Marmaduke Servant, a Mr. Mason and Miles White each received £5 for serving as executors. Over £267 was distributed by the will.[9]

Richard Spencer

Richard Spencer was a son of a "rising" Northamptonshire knight who was a clever landlord and a shrewd marriage broker. The family's eldest son was to be ancestor of the Earls of Sunderland and Dukes of Marlborough. Three of the six daughters married peers, the second Lord Hunsdon, the third Lord Monteagle and the fifth Earl of Derby. Richard was the fourth of five sons, born about 1553 to Sir John Spencer of Althorpe and to Katherine, his wife, daughter of Sir Thomas Kitson of Hengrave, Suffolk.[1]

Richard took a B. A. at Oxford in 1572, an M. A. at Cambridge in 1575, at the age of 22, and in the same year was admitted to Caius College, Cambridge.[2] Considerably after the usual age of admission, Lord Burghley obtained his entrance into Gray's Inn in March 1585.[3] He had already appeared in Burghley's household on the visit of Elizabeth to Theobalds in 1572, assuming the Spencer mentioned to be Richard Spencer, the only Spencer on record as serving Lord Burghley.[4] In 1577 he received the manors of Offley and Cockernhoo in Hertfordshire from his father and settled at Offley, building there in 1600 the mansion known as Offley Place. His wife, Helen, was a native of the county, the fourth daughter and coheir of Sir John Brockett of Brockett

[9] P. C. C., 53 Kidd.

[1] Finch, *Families*, Pedigree II, Spencer of Althorp.
[2] *Alumni Cantabrigiensis*, v. IV, p. 133.
[3] *Register of Admissions to Gray's Inn*, 1521-1889, p. 67.
[4] Cecil Papers, v. 140, p. 20.

Hall, and Helen, daughter and coheir of Sir Robert Lytton of Knebworth.[5]

Richard's training was in politics and diplomacy. As early as 1577, he was observing events in Paris. In 1582, he sent a newsletter from Augsburg to Lord Burghley. In 1588 Robert Cecil asked his father for permission to accompany the Earl of Derby on his embassy to Ostend. He hoped also that his cousin Spencer might be permitted to accompany them if Burghley could give him leave even though his absence would be inconvenient. Robert thought Spencer would be a good companion, and he assured his father that in their idle hours they could study civil law together. The Earl, father-in-law of Spencer's sister, was pleased to have Spencer's company and offered to deal with Burghley for leave.[6] Spencer, incidentally, was a fourth cousin once removed to Robert Cecil, the relationship deriving from Robert's mother's family.[7] The extent of the awareness of kinship in Elizabethan England is an amazing phenomenon to us today. And no one was more alive to it than Lord Burghley, a genealogical buff of talent and considerable practice.

Spencer had been in Scotland and the Low Countries in 1583.[8] He was attending Lord Burghley in 1585 when William Herlle, who wished to spread scandalous information about a servant of Burghley's, was told by Mr. Spencer that Burghley, having taken physic, was not available.[9] He was also present in the household when the Queen visited Theobalds in May, 1591.[10] He had, at the same time, a career in politics. It began in 1588 when he was elected M. P. for Berealston. He served in 1594 for East Looe and in 1604 for Brackley.[11]

Robert Cecil, in an undated letter to the Lord Keeper of the Great Seal, written sometime after 1594, continued his interest in "my cosin Richard Spencer" whom he wished to be in a certain commission.[12] He was a man of sufficient parts for almost any commission, being called upon in 1597 to serve as Sheriff of Hertfordshire.[13] With the coming of the new monarch in 1603, Spencer was one of that host of gentlemen who became knights in the first year of the reign.[14] In the next year it was rumored that Spencer was to be appointed ambassador to Spain. But Spencer pleaded weakness both of body and estate and was excused.[15] The estate was immediately strengthened by giving the office

[5] Clutterbuck, *Hertfordshire*, III, p. 96.
[6] P. R. O., S. P. 12/v. CCVIII/f. 158, r, 159.
[7] Unpublished genealogical chart, compiled by H. V. Jones.
[8] Matthews, "Parliament," Section 3, p. 210.
[9] Great Britain, *C. S. P. D.*, II (London, 1865), p. 263.
[10] Cecil Papers, v. 140, p. 37.
[11] Matthews, "Parliament," p. 210.
[12] B. M., *Harleian MSS.*, 6997, f. 162.
[13] Matthews, "Parliament," p. 210.
[14] *Ibid.*
[15] McClure, *Chamberlain's Letters*, I, pp. 198, 201.

of *Custos Brevium* in the Common Pleas jointly to Richard and his brother, Thomas.[16] By 1609 both body and estate were mended for Spencer was sent as ambassador in charge of the treaty between Spain and the Low Countries. He died in 1624.[17]

John Stileman

We know nothing of John Stileman until 1572 when he was appointed a server for the first table during the Queen's visit.[1] In April, 1581, he was present to wait upon the French commissioners as they dined in Burghley House.[2] In the fall he was on hand to serve during another royal visit to Theobalds.[3] On one other occasion, for which the date is missing, Stileman was similarly engaged.[4] He therefore appeared in the four surviving household lists of the Elizabethan period. Otherwise there is no correspondence or evidence to link Stileman to Cecil until 1597, with the exception of material in the records of the Court of Wards.

In 1597 Burghley was exceedingly generous to Stileman. He granted Stileman the wardship and marriage of John Shurland of Norfolk, thirteen years of age, with an annual "exhibition" of £5. Stileman paid £20 for the wardship.[5] Coupled with this was a separate grant of the ward's Suffolk lands, yielding an annual rent of £6.13.4. The fine for this lease was £6.13.4.[6] The custody of the body and the marriage of William Romney of Gloucestershire was likewise sold to Stileman for £6.13.4 paid in ready money.[7] The Court of Wards was last used to reward Stileman in April 1598 when he was given the wardship and marriage of Thomas Gynes of Essex, two years of age, whose lands were valued at £10.16.4 annually. While the first two grants do not clearly show that the J. Stileman mentioned is the same as the one in Burghley's service, the last speaks of him as of Theobalds in Hertfordshire.[8]

Apart from his correspondence with the Cecils, the only information available is a licence to marry granted to John Stileman, Gentleman, and Alice Hill, Spinster of St. Clement Danes, daughter of George Hill, a saddler, in 1586.[9]

[16] Finch, *Families*, p. 174.
[17] Matthews, "Parliament," p. 210.

---

[1] Cecil Papers, v. 140, p. 20.
[2] B. M., *Lansdowne MSS.*, v. 33, f. 70, p. 175.
[3] Cecil Papers, v. 140, p. 25.
[4] *Ibid.*, p. 37.
[5] P. R. O., Wards 9/157.
[6] *Ibid.*, Wards 9/190.
[7] *Ibid.*, Wards 9/221.
[8] P. R. O., Wards 9/158.
[9] *London Marriage Licences*, p. 152.

By 1597, when we have his first extant letter, he had become a keeper of the park at Theobalds.[10] In the following year he felt it his duty, when Lord Burghley could no longer be troubled over such matters, to acquaint Robert Cecil of the existence of a crew of "ill-designed fellows," who carry guns and cross bows and vow they will not leave any deer in Theobalds or Cheston Parks. Stileman described the measures he had taken to prevent them from carrying out their purpose and recommended others. Mrs. Stileman sent Cecil some raspberries, peas, and a fat pig. This letter was sent from Stileman's "poor lodge" in Cheston Park on July 29, 1598, a few days before Burghley's death.[11] The next letter, from December, 1598, indicates that Sir Robert Cecil kept Stileman on in his employ. Stileman wrote on estate business, then discussed the case of Jennings the gardener who wanted £4 more a year. The poor man was very needy but Thomas Bellot saw no reason why he should get more as Cecil had given him the benefit of the garden.[12]

Stileman was apparently not without his faults, certainly not lacking in critics. He found it necessary to write Cecil to vindicate himself from certain charges which caused him to offer to retire from his place. The note is undated, though said to be in the time of Elizabeth, likely after Burghley's death.[13]

Nothing further is heard from Stileman after a note to Robert Cecil in January, 1600, reporting abuses which were daily committed in Cecil's woods.[14]

Morris Thompson

Thompson was the son of Robert Thompson who is said to have come out of the North. Morris, who gave Cheshunt, Hertfordshire as his residence, married Katherine, daughter of John Harvey of Potterells, Hertfordshire. They had one son, Robert of Wooton, Hertfordshire.[1] If the sons of Robert are an indication of the direction in which the family was progressing, it may aptly be described as a rising family. Robert's son Morris was the father of the first Lord Haversham; George was a London merchant; and Sir William was a merchant who reportedly left his son, Sir Samuel, £1,800 annually and £40,000 in cash.[2] Unfortunate-

[10] H. M. C., *Salisbury MSS.*, VII, p. 321.
[11] *Ibid.*, VIII, p. 281.
[12] Great Britain, *C. S. P. D.*, V (London, 1869), p. 137.
[13] Cecil Papers, General 29/17-18.
[14] Great Britain, *C. S. P. D.*, V (London, 1869), p. 376.

[1] Walter C. Metcalfe, ed., *Visitations of Hertfordshire, 1572 and 1634*, Harleian Society Publications, XXII (1886), p. 97.
[2] George W. Marshall, ed., *Le Neve's Pedigrees of Knights*, Harleian Society Publications, VIII (1873), p. 45.

ly evidence is lacking which would connect the prosperity of the fourth generation with their great-grandfather's service under Burghley.

Morris Thompson appeared in the roster of Burghley's servants at Theobalds for the Queen's visit in 1572, when he was delegated the custodianship of the plate.[3] No earlier record of service has been found. A Maurice, who very possibly was Morris Thompson, was assigned to the great kitchen as clerk of the kitchen for the French Commissioner's dinner in May, 1581.[4] He performed the same service when Elizabeth visited Theobalds in October, 1581.[5] He was again present though the date is in dispute.[6] Nothing further is known about him.

Richard Troughton

A Richard Troughton entered Cecil's service in 1547.[1] While he is not among those who received a salary, he did receive livery as indicated in a list prepared of liveries bought at Whitsuntide, 1555.[2] He also appeared in an undated list of fifty-six servants and retainers in Cecil's service in the 1550's, as bailiff of Witham.[3] In 1554, Thomas Sklater, alias Thomson, writing Cecil from Grantham, reported charges alledged against Troughton, bailiff of South Witham, by one Wymberley. Enclosed was a note from Thomas Wymberley to Cecil in which he complained of vexations and tyrannical proceedings in the manor court of Witham.[4]

Nothing further is known about Troughton until he appears in 1562 in Star Chamber. It is apparent that he had been preferred by Cecil to the Queen's service, having become porter at the court gates. It is likewise evident that he had been granted the parsonage at South Witham, Lincolnshire, which he sold for debts.[5]

Service to the Queen did not prevent Richard Troughton from appearing regularly throughout the reign in Burghley's service. He was present at Theobalds as a carver or ewery keeper during the Queen's 1572 visit.[6] While he did not appear during either the Queen's visit or the dinner for the French Commissioners in 1581, he was again present, possibly in 1591.[7]

[3] Cecil Papers, v. 140, p. 20.
[4] B. M., *Lansdowne MSS.*, v. 33, f. 70, p. 175.
[5] Cecil Papers, v. 140, p. 25.
[6] *Ibid.*, v. 140, p. 37.

---

[1] B. M., *Lansdowne MSS.*, v. 118, p. 35.
[2] *Ibid.*, p. 43r.
[3] *Ibid.*, p. 36.
[4] Great Britain, *C. S. P. D.*, I (London, 1856), p. 63.
[5] P. R. O., Star Chamber 5/T/6/10.
[6] Cecil Papers, v. 140, p. 20.
[7] Cecil Papers, v. 140, p. 37.

We find him once again in Star Chamber at an undetermined time toward the end of the reign when Troughton was "your Majesty's eldest yeoman porter at the court gates." There was a dispute between him and his wife's son-in-law. Troughton, in his presentation, spoke of the debts of his wife's first husband, then explained that while he was away at Stamford prior to the last feast of St. John the Baptist, his "mansion house" was entered by force and some £200 worth of goods stolen, including the evidences of John Obbins. John Obbins, the son-in-law, told a different tale. He said that Troughton had used up the £200 worth of goods his wife had at marriage, that she was originally worth £40 a year and that Troughton had wasted her money. Furthermore, she, fearing Troughton, fled to the home of her son-in-law. Troughton's rebuttal seems to be the irrelevant complaint that he couldn't afford to serve the Queen. If he had got a certain parsonage at £4 a year he would have become a minister. One wonders whether the court laughed or rebuked him.[8] Evidence as to the conclusion is missing. What exists is sufficient to reveal a fellow contsantly engaged in litigation.

Two other scraps of information have been found. One is a grant from the Court of Wards in 1568 of a lease to Troughton of a part of one Luke's lands in Bedfordshire or 26s.8d. paid in ready money.[9] It is quite possible, even likely, that he also got the wardship though the evidence is not available. The other information concerns a lease in reversion to Richard Troughton, the tenant, for thirty years, of the demesne lands of Hanstope manor, Buckinghamshire with a rent of £28.10s. Troughton secured this on August 8, 1598 for a fine of £40.[10] This may or may not be our Richard Troughton who has not previously been linked with Buckinghamshire. The Troughton of the lease was there in 1596 when he was party to a recognizance for debt.[11]

Matthew Twiford

It seems highly likely that the Matthew Twiford who appeared in Burghley's household in 1572 as an usher of the hall during the Queen's visit, may well be the same to whom a wardship was granted in 1563.[1] The grant was to Mr. Twiford, yeoman, and carried an annuity of £3.6.8.[2] The ward was Dorothy Daniel, next heir of Peter Daniel of Chester who died during the last year of the reign of Queen Mary. Twiford paid £9 for the wardship and would have been almost im-

[8] P. R. O., Star Chamber 5/T/30/25.
[9] P. R. O., Wards 9/373.
[10] Great Britain, *C. S. P. D.*, V. (London, 1869), p. 79.
[11] P. R. O., L. C. 4/193.

[1] Cecil Papers, v. 140, p. 20.
[2] Great Britain, *Cal. Pat. Rolls, Eliz.*, II (London, 1948), p. 618.

mediately repaid, for the annuity was to begin when Peter died. The child was then about four years old.³

Nothing further has been found concerning Twiford.

William Waad

Waad was born in 1546 to Armigil Waade, a native of Yorkshire who was styled the English Columbus for his voyage to Cape Breton and Newfoundland in 1536.¹ William was the younger son though apparently singled out by his father as the abler. When his father died in 1568, it appears from the will that twenty-two year old William, not the older Thomas, was the principal heir. William was also the sole executor, indicating that he possessed already a sense of responsibility as well as, perhaps, ability.² William resided at Battles Hall, Essex, and at Belseys House, Hampstead, Middlesex to which he succeeded his father in 1568.³ In 1571, at the age of twenty-five, he was admitted to Gray's Inn.⁴

In the next year Waad appeared in the household of his father's good friend, the newly created Baron Burghley, acting as servitor for the second meal during the Queen's visit.⁵ Evidently he commended himself to Burghley for he was collecting news for him in Paris in 1576, in Italy in 1578 and 1579, at Strasburg and Paris in 1580. In the latter year he was sent as ambassador to Portugal, returning to England in 1581.⁶ He was likely too late to assist Burghley during the two state occasions when Burghley entertained in the grand manner. Burghley must have had something to do with Waad's promotion, on October 7, 1584, to the lifetime office of Clerk of the Privy Council.⁷ In the same year he sat in parliament for Aldborough.⁸

Waad continued to be employed on foreign missions until 1585. Back in England, it was he who seized Mary Stuart's papers in 1586. He resumed the role of ambassador in 1587 to go as envoy to France. Returning in 1588, he sat in the parliament of that year for Thetford, serving for Preston in 1601 and West Looe in 1605.⁹ In spite of a busy

---

³ P. R. O., Wards 9/156.

¹ *Concise DNB*, p. 1349.
² P. C. C., 6 Lyon.
³ Mort, "Commons," p. 324.
⁴ *Register of Admissions to Gray's Inn*, 1521-1889, p. 42.
⁵ Cecil Papers, v. 140, p. 20.
⁶ *Concise DNB*, p. 1349.
⁷ P. R. O., Cal. Pat. Rolls, 17-30 Eliz., p. 13r.
⁸ History of Parliament Trust, Members of Commons, p. 108.
⁹ *Concise DNB*, p. 1349.

career, Waad found time, possibly in 1591, to assist in the household at Theobalds which was swollen for the Queen's almost routine visit.[10]

Waad joined the throng of knights created by James I in 1603. In 1605 he became Lieutenant of the Tower, a post from which he was dismissed in 1613 on the complaint of Lady Arabella Stuart who charged that he had embezzled her jewels.[11] He joined the Virginia Company in 1609.[12] Immediately after the death of Robert Cecil, Lord Salisbury, it was rumored that Waad was one of the competitors for the secretaryship.[13] But a year later his public career ended in disgrace. Perhaps he would not have been dismissed from his post had Salisbury been alive for the Cecils, father and son, seem to have been his chief props.

Burghley does not appear to have used the Court of Wards as a means of reward for Waad. However, he got some leases to which Burghley may have helped him. In May 1590, Waad secured a twenty-one year lease of St. John's Wood, adjacent to his home in Hampstead, Middlesex.[14] Three years later, in May, 1593, he was granted the farm of several manors in Huntingdon, Nottingham, Buckingham, Kent, Derby, Hertfordshire, and Surrey for forty years.[15] In 1601 he held a patent for making sulphur, brimstone and oil.[16]

Waad survived his disgrace by ten years. He married twice, the first time to Anne, daughter of Owen Walker, of St. Alban's, Wood Street, London, in 1586.[17] The second wife, who survived him, was another Anne, daughter of Humphrey Brown.[18] Waad's will contains a fervent religious statement full of the author's sense of sinfulness and of his repentance. Only one child, a minor named James, godson of the King, succeeded him. James was to have £50 a year until fifteen years of age, then £100 until his majority. Waad, describing himself as the most ancient servitor of the kingdom, requested that the Privy Council, which he had served for thirty years, and his father before him, would favor his family in any difficulties they might have.[19]

Gilbert Wakering

The Wakering family resided in the fourteenth century in the parish of Great Wakering in Essex, from which it took its name. In the time

[10] Cecil Papers, v. 140, p. 37.
[11] Mort, "Commons," p. 324.
[12] *Concise DNB*, p. 1349.
[13] McClure, *Chamberlain's Letters*, II, p. 355.
[14] P. R. O., Cal. and Index, Pat. Rolls, 31-37 Eliz., p. 29.
[15] *Ibid.*, p. 24.
[16] Mort, "Commons," p. 324.
[17] *London Marriage Licenses*, p. 145.
[18] Mort, "Commons," p. 324.
[19] P. C. C., 116 Swann.

of Edward III and Richard II, a John Wakering served as Chancellor of the Duchy of Lancaster. Another Wakering served under Henry V as Master of the Rolls and Keeper of the Privy Seal. In 1416 one John Wakering was Bishop of Norwich. It was from this family that Gilbert descended. He was the son of Edmund Wakering by his first wife, Margaret, daughter of John Archer, and was probably born in Essex.[1] Gilbert, the second son, married Elizabeth, eldest daughter of Sir Robert Hampson, knight, Alderman of London, who also possessed property at Bloxwich, Staffordshire and Rickmansworth, Hertfordshire.[2] As a younger son of gentry who appear to have been declining rather than rising, it is not surprising to find him seeking his fortune in London.

We hear nothing of him until 1581 when the Queen visited Theobalds and Burghley gave his splendid dinner for the French Commissioners, at both of which functions Wakering served.[3] Very likely he had already been in Burghley's service some years. It must have been by Burghley's influence as Lord Treasurer that in 1576 he was made bailiff of three royal manors in Sussex with a fee of 53s.4d.[4] Likewise must Burghley have been responsible for securing him the position of woodward of Staffordshire sometime between 1583 and 1587.[5] In 1592 Burghley granted him the more lucrative office of Surveyor of the County of Norfolk and the City of Norwich which carried with it a fee of £13.6.8.[6]

At the same time, Burghley was using the Court of Wards as a source of reward for Wakering. On August 7, 1587, he was given custody of John Butler, a natural idiot, whose lands were worth £10 annually.[7] When Wakering served as escheator of Norfolk and Suffolk for the first time in 1594, he had opportunity to uncover wardships rightfully belonging to the crown.[8] Wakering wrote to Burghley that he thought the family of Francis Jenny of Suffolk was going to conceal a ward. If Burghley would grant the wardship to him, he hoped to be able to find a tenure for Her Majesty.[9] Whether or not this plea proved successful, he did get a small wardship in April, 1596. The custody of three-year-old Margaret Vernon of Staffordshire was given to Wakering for a fee of £13.6.8. It would only pay him 33s.3d. annually.[10] However, he also got, for an additional fine of £6.13.4, the least of her lands, valued at

[1] Wright, *Essex*, II, p. 616.
[2] Walter C. Metcalfe, ed., *Visitations of Essex*, 2 parts, Harleian Society Publications, XIII (1878), II, p. 513.
[3] Cecil Papers, v. 140, p. 25; B. M., *Lansdowne MSS.*, f. 33, f. 70, p. 175.
[4] P. R. O., E. 315/309.
[5] P. R. O., E. 101/336/26.
[6] P. R. O., E. 315/309.
[7] P. R. O., Wards 9/157.
[8] P. R. O., List of Escheators, unpublished, p. 92.
[9] Hurstfield, *Wards*, p. 61.
[10] P. R. O., Wards 9/158.

£5.15.1 annually.[11] A revealing epilogue, in conjunction with this grant, helps explain how the grantee might not come to enjoy his grant. Wakering wrote to Robert Cecil on April 30, 1600 to request that the Court of Wards censure Walter Leveson and others who had intruded on a part of Margaret Vernon's lands in order that her inheritance might be established and Wakering enjoy his grant.[12]

A final honor and favor was conferred upon Wakering by Burghley before the latter's death in 1598. Burghley appointed Wakering to another term as escheator of Norfolk and Suffolk in 1597.[13] When a Thomas Browne wrote Robert Cecil in 1599 requesting employment under him, he said that the only grant he ever had for his service under Burghley was a wardship which, however, cost him £200 as was well known to Gilbert Wakering, escheator of the same county last year, and which he could not get possession of for lack of help from the Court of Wards.[14] Wakering probably got his share of the £200.

Wakering was another upon whom King James bestowed knighthood in 1603. As Sir Gilbert, Wakering continued to cultivate the Cecil's, sending Sir Robert sweetmeats for which Wakering's own servants received 2s.6d. in reward from Cecil.[15] The policy probably paid off, for Wakering had yet need of a valuable patron. Perhaps Cecil supported his request for a lease of a messuage called Holbeach, in Kingswinford, Stafford.[16]

Wakering probably was serving as a justice of the peace when the Privy Council wrote to him from Theobalds requesting that he settle the differences between himself and a Mr. Cox by arbitration rather than by arresting Cox.[17] By 1610 Wakering was sickly and aged, he told Lord Salisbury, and ready to surrender his Surveyorship of Norfolk and Norwich. He recommended a James Pitts as his successor.[18] He was fortunate to have survived so long for in 1605 certain papists conspired to set fire to his home, among others, because they disliked his religion.[19] It can safely be assumed that he was a man of markedly protestant convictions. Nor is this surprising in a man so closely connected with Lord Burghley.

Wakering lived seven years after his retirement, dying in 1617 at Rickmansworth, Hertfordshire, one of the manors brought him by his

[11] P. R. O., Wards 9/188.
[12] H. M. C., *Salisbury MSS.*, X, p. 131.
[13] P. R. O., List of Escheators, unpublished, p. 92.
[14] H. M. C., *Salisbury MSS.*, IX, p. 63.
[15] *Ibid.*, XV, p. 74.
[16] Great Britain. *C. S. P. D.*, VIII (London, 1857), p. 375.
[17] Great Britain, *C. S. P. D.*, VIII (London, 1857), p. 448.
[18] *Ibid.*, p. 644.
[19] B. M., *Salisbury MSS.*, XXIII, p. 529.

wife. Leaving no sons, he made his wife, Elizabeth, who survived him, his sole executor.[20]

Thomas Windebank

Thomas Windebank was the son of Sir Richard Windebank, officer of Calais, and Margaret, daughter and coheir of Griffith ap Henry whose name suggests Welsh ancestry.[1] Margaret Windebank's only sister, Oriscian, also married a Calais man, George Ridisdale, a merchant of the Staple of Calais. They had two daughters, Honor, who married John Cotton, and Margaret, who married Raphael Throckmorton. When George died in 1555, he left Thomas Windebank £6.13.4.[2] Nothing is known about the birthplace of Thomas though it was very likely Calais. Nor can a Windebank family be traced further than Sir Richard.

Richard was a professional soldier whose career was largely devoted to the defense of England's French possessions. Prior to 1533 he was a spear in the garrison at Calais, a gentleman soldier entitled to 18d. a day and 6d. for his man.[3] As a deputy commissioner of war for Henry VIII, he recruited troops in Germany in 1544, already wearing one of the signs of age, a white beard.[4] His mission must have been successful, or his work generally effective, for on September 30, 1544 the King knighted Windebank and four others at Boulogne.[5] This was accompanied by promotion to the position of under marshal of Boulogne whereupon his place as a spear was given to his eldest son, Richard.[6] One of his fellows in the administration of Boulogne was Sir Edward Dymock whose daughter would one day marry the senior Richard's son, Thomas. Sir Richard played a strategic role at the accession of Mary when the chief captain of Guisnes, Lord Grey of Wilton, who had promoted Queen Jane, would not proclaim the new Tudor Queen. His deputy, Sir Richard Windebank, rallied to the new Queen, carrying the garrison with him. At the same time, Sir Richard proclaimed the unswerving loyalty of his superior, Lord Grey.[7]

In April 1554, Lord Wentworth, the governor, wrote from Calais to

[20] P. C. C., 6 Weldon.

[1] Sir George J. Armytage, ed., *Middlesex Pedigrees,* Harleian Society Publications, LXV (1914), p. 123.
[2] P. C. C., 12 Ketchyn.
[3] John G. Nichols, ed., *The Chronicle of Calais to 1540,* Camden Society, XXXV (1846), pp. 136-137.
[4] Great Britain, *Letters and Papers, Foreign and Domestic,* Henry VIII, XIX, part I (London, 1903), pp. 434, 475.
[5] *Ibid.,* part II (London, 1905), p. 174.
[6] *Ibid.,* p. 175.
[7] Strype, *Memorials,* III, part I, p. 22.

the Queen to recommend Sir Richard Windebank, an old servant of her father "who has very honestly and painfully served in the wars, and is both sage and discreet in peace," for the vacant post of knight porter.[8] Whether or not he got the place matters little. The dislocation resulting from the loss of Calais must have come as a severe shock to one whose fortune and career had been rooted there. Richard did not long survive it. Weak and sick, on August 8, 1558, he made his will, leaving everything to his wife, Dame Margaret. He spoke of himself as a recent inhabitant of Calais.[9] Dame Margaret, perhaps crushed by the double loss of home and husband, did not long survive. She made her will on October 13, 1558, making Thomas her principal heir and sole executor, and was buried in mid-December, 1558.[10] Richard, presumably the eldest son and a professional soldier like his father, was not mentioned in either will.

A Richard Windebank was still in the military service in 1562 when he received and mustered the soldiers at Rye.[11] The Richard Windebank who in 1566 was made captain and custodian of Sandowne Castle in Kent, with an annuity of £20, was surely a relative of Thomas who collected Richard's pay occasionally.[12] In 1568 Richard received the grant of the site of Mary de Downe Barton in Kent.[13] Six years later Richard received an annuity of £20.17.6 for life.[14] This was increased to £27.7.6 in 1576.[15] Richard was succeeded as captain of Sandowne Castle by an Aaron Windebank, possibly his son.[16]

Thomas, who served Cecil, was admitted to Lincoln's Inn on March 21, 1558, just a few months before the deaths of both his parents.[17] He may have come directly from a university to the Inn. As Windebank wrote to Lord Willoughby in 1599 that his old master, the late Lord Treasurer, some forty-one years ago had given him certain good advice about holding confidential the affairs he was privy to, it can be asserted that he entered Cecil's about 1558.[18] He may very well have followed in the footsteps of Roger Alford, Cecil's clerk who had been promoted to the Exchequer. Certainly Windebank seemed to perform the functions of a clerk or secretary. On May 25, 1560, he wrote from Greenwich to Oseley, Clerk of the Privy Seal, that as he was commanded by his master

[8] Great Britain, *C. S. P., Foreign,* Mary (London, 1861), p. 70.
[9] P. C. C., 37 Noodes.
[10] P. C. C., 16 Wells; Strype, *Reformation,* I, part I, p. 46.
[11] Great Britain, *C. S. P. D.,* I (London, 1856), p. 207.
[12] P. R. O., E. 403/2452; E. 403/2259.
[13] P. R. O., Cal. Pat. Rolls, 1-16 Eliz., p. 239.
[14] *Ibid.,* p. 338r.
[15] P. R. O., Cal. Pat. Rolls, 17-30, Eliz., p. 6r.
[16] P. R. O., E. 403/2275.
[17] *The Records of the Honorable Society of Lincoln's Inn,* v. I, Admissions from 1420 to 1799, p. 64.
[18] Great Britain, *C. S. P., Borders,* II (London, 1896), pp. 615-616.

to be ready to go north, "both to do him honor and myself honesty, I think it not amiss to see to provide myself of some chain." As Windebank didn't have time to provide himself with one, he sought to buy or borrow one of Oseley's upon which he would be willing to spend £30 or £36. Otherwise he would have to buy one on the market and risk being deceived.[19] He did not have much time for Cecil was sent on May 28, 1560 with Dr. Wotton into Scotland to expel the French.[20] Windebank also drew funds to pay someone who may have brought information from the French in 1560, the money being an assignment made from royal household expenses.[21]

Probably the most difficult assignment given Windebank by Cecil was that of guiding Cecil's eldest son Thomas, a lively nineteen year old youth, along the road of continental adventure and travel in the hope that it might be a real educational experience. Windebank very well knew that his own future rested somewhat on how he succeeded in the venture begun about June 1, 1561 and destined to last two years.

It was an arduous period in Windebank's life. He had not only to cope with the vagaries of an active youth who found sport more compelling than his father's scholarly interests, but with the fretful anxieties of a father who feared the outcome of his son's inclinations. There were even periods when it seemed that a great fever or the plague would deprive the father and the mentor of their youthful tribulation. However near wars and disease came, they left intact the vigor of young Thomas who finally returned home to seek maturity in marriage. That, in brief, is what happened between June, 1561 and their return in the spring of 1563.[22]

Cecil chose wisely the man who would accompany his heir. Cecil obviously hoped that Windebank, probably not many years older than Thomas, would prove a congenial companion, a good example and a careful guardian. It is not clear what Windebank was actually supposed to do beyond the general supervision of Thomas. Hugh Allington, writing to Windebank on February 5, 1562, sent him news of the promotion of Mr. Day to the provostship of Eton.[23] Allington termed Day, who later became Bishop of Winchester, Windebank's predecessor.[24] What Day did in Cecil's household is not known. He may have served as secretary, schoolmaster or chaplain, though likely not the latter for his successor, Windebank, had no obvious qualification for the chaplaincy. Regardless of what he did, Day was clearly an able fellow whose superior qualities his successor must to some degree have shared. When we learn

[19] P. R. O., S. P. 15/63/144.
[20] H. M. C., *Salisbury MSS.*, V, p. 69.
[21] P. R. O., E. 101/429/11-11r.
[22] B. M., *Harleian MSS.*, part V, p. 69.
[23] P. R. O., S. P. 12/21/84.
[24] *Concise DNB*, p. 528.

that Windebank was succeeded by Hugh Allington, a nephew by marriage and subsequently brother-in-law of Cecil, we have some idea of the kind of man Cecil chose to guide and guard his son.[25]

Windebank was probably allowed to select the other adult companion who seemed to combine the functions of tutor and gentleman servant. His choice fell upon Thomas Kendall, possibly somewhat older than Windebank, but an honored friend of the Windebank family and a witness of Margaret Windebank's will in 1558.[26] In 1575, when he described himself as richer in years and diseases than in anything else, he kept a school in Norwich and could write with facility in Latin, French and Italian as well as in English.[27] Kendall was considered almost on a par with Windebank and Thomas Cecil if cost of lodgings is a useful index. Kendall's lodging cost 7 crowns a month while Windebank and Thomas each paid 8 crowns. Two crowns were paid for a fourth person, a servant to be secured in France.[28]

The experience of travel through France, the Low Countries and Germany was an invaluable asset for a person like Windebank whose principal service was to Lord Burghley and then the Queen. Though the more immediate objective was not achieved with the distinction hoped, Thomas Cecil was not a disgrace to his father, as Cecil, in his more pessimistic moments, feared he would be.

In the same year the travellers returned to England, Windebank left Cecil's service and was succeeded by Hugh Allington.[29] Cecil, whose note dates Windebank's departure, does not tell us what work he undertook. Whatever it was, it must have been provided by Cecil who had promised Windebank promotion for faithful service with Thomas Cecil.[30] Possibly Windebank went directly into the signet office where four years later, in 1567, he was given lifetime employment as a Clerk of the Signet.[31] His superior continued to be William Cecil, Principal Secretary of State.

By 1565 Windebank had begun to receive benefits from Cecil's control of the Court of Wards. In that year Windebank was granted the wardship of Thomas Allott.[32] In 1567, for a fine of £10, Windebank was given a lease of the lands of one Madison of Devonshire.[33] A year later, the wardship of Thomas Garneyes was given Windebank.[34] Though the surviving wardship records are incomplete, there is evidence that between 1590 and 1597, Windebank again profited from the Court of Wards, receiving for

[25] H. M. C., *Salisbury MSS.*, V, p. 69.
[26] P. C. C., 16 Wells.
[27] P. R. O., S. P. 12/103/66.
[28] P. R. O., S. P. 12/18/30.
[29] H. M. C., *Salisbury MSS.*, V, p. 69.
[30] P. R. O., S. P., 12/18/35.
[31] P. R. O., Cal. Pat. Rolls, 1-16 Eliz., p. 217r.
[32] P. R. O., Wards 9/373.
[33] *Ibid.*
[34] P. R. O., Cal. Pat. Rolls, 1-16 Eliz., p. 235r.

a fine of £30 a lease of the Lincolnshire lands of Humfrey Lytleberry, worth £24.4.8 annually.[35] Even this partial record offers proof that Cecil did not forget Windebank. And it suggests that Windebank had sufficient reason to maintain a strong sense of loyalty to the House of Cecil.

The Cecils probably helped Windebank to some of the other choice plums that fell into his lap. Lands in York and Lancashire were conferred upon him in 1578.[36] In 1584, he was given additional lands in Somerset and Northampton on a thirty-year lease.[37] John Astley was joined with Windebank in 1589 in the grant of a monopoly in which they were to have all forfeitures and penalties incurred in the burning of timber to make iron contrary to the statute of 1 Elizabeth.[38] In 1596 Windebank and Thomas Lake were granted a joint patent for writing letters patent.[39]

As one of the Clerks of the Signet, serving under the Principal Secretary, one would expect Windebank to be considered one of the Queen's secretaries in a general way. But Windebank seemed to have occupied the position of a confidential, private secretary to the Queen.[40] What a strategic location for a Cecil follower to occupy! And there is no doubt that it worked to the advantage of the Cecils. Windebank wrote in 1594, for instance, that he had just secured the Queen's signature on three important letters which he inclosed unsealed for Lord Burghley and Robert Cecil to examine. The letters might then be sealed with the signet in Lord Burghley's custody even though it was the greater signet.[41] Windebank was the man on the scene, the man who could tell Robert Cecil in 1594 that though his letter, sent from the Strand at 4:00 p.m. did not arrive until 1:00 a.m., due probably to the negligence of the London post, he would nonetheless show it to the Queen first thing next morning.[42] Next day Windebank wrote Cecil again, explaining how the Queen herself read the letter, taking it out of Windebank's hands. She was "half angry that I was not with her two hours sooner, which I could not be by reason her Majesty was not then stirring. Glad I was when her Highness slipped over the date of your letter, to the other contents. . . ."[43]

This close working relationship between Windebank and Robert Cecil continued after Burghley's death. As the Queen aged, Principal Secretary Robert Cecil relied upon Windebank to use his judgment in presenting matters to her. Sometimes he instructed Windebank in the

[35] P. R. O., Wards 9/188.
[36] P. R. O., Cal. Pat. Rolls, 17-30 Eliz., p. 22.
[37] *Ibid.*, p. 19.
[38] Price, *Patents of Monopoly*, p. 146.
[39] *Ibid.*, p. 144.
[40] Great Britain, *C. S. P. D.*, I (London, 1856), preface, p. xii.
[41] *Ibid.*, III (London, 1867), pp. 443-444.
[42] Great Britain, *C. S. P. D.*, III (London, 1867), p. 443.
[43] H. M. C., *Salisbury MSS.*, IV, p. 486.

little deceits they used with the Queen. In July, 1601, for example, Cecil wrote Windebank: "I pray you read this advisedly first, and then let the Queen see it, as a letter written merrily to you from me, if you find her well disposed."[44] Another deception was arranged in 1602 when Cecil was ill. He wrote to Windebank: "Upon some intelligence received, I have directed a longer letter to the Queen than is fit for her fair eyes to read. Pray deliver it, and crave liberty to read it to her, but read it yourself first, to be perfect, and then seal it up with my seal which I send you." In a postscript, he suggested selecting a time to offer it when Elizabeth was not disposed to sleep.[45]

Windebank not only had the confidence of the Cecils but enjoyed the Queen's trust, as well as her reward. While there is not much evidence of her bounty, in 1591 a warrant was issued to deliver to Thomas Windebank £300 as Her Majesty's free gift, being the fine paid for a lease in reversion of the Deanery of Auckland.[46]

Some evidence remains of the flow of patronage correspondence to Windebank whose double entree, with the Queen and the Cecils, must have attracted many place and favor seekers. One very interesting letter came from Windebank's cousin, J. Throckmorton, who asked him "to deliver my letter to Secretary Cecil and to favor my cause with him, and get him to accept my offer of service. . . . He is the first to whom I ever offered such service, and I hope I shall not be refused." With utter candor, Throckmorton continued: "I know these things cannot be well compassed without gratifying some of his near followers, or others employed. None but you must know it, but I will give £20 a year to whomever he appoints, as long as I continue in employment either of captain in this cautionary town of Flushing, or serjeant-major of the garrison." He therefore sought the name of one of Cecil's honest fellows.[47]

There were others like Thomas Clerke who thanked Windebank for favors to his nephew, Norton, in 1588.[48] Bishop Aylmer wrote Windebank on behalf of a Mr. Sparkes whose anticipated prebend in Southwell was stopped in the processing stage when he was confused with a Puritan of the same name. Windebank immediately wrote to Walsingham asking him to present the bill again to the Queen.[49] The most interesting of the examples left to us is the one in which Secretary Robert Cecil himself asked Windebank to urge Her Majesty to appoint Dr. Jegon of Cambridge to the Deanery of Norwich. Cecil gave as his reasons "both for her service, his [Jegon's] desert, and my credit, as I have used him in divers public places and will in more, for he is capable of direction and in

[44] Great Britain, *C. S. P. D.*, VI (London, 1870), p. 154.
[45] Great Britain, *C. S. P. D.*, VI (London, 1870), p. 154.
[46] *Ibid.*, p. 8.
[47] Great Britain, *C. S. P. D.*, VI (London, 1870), p. 41.
[48] Great Britain, *C. S. P. D.*, II (London, 1865), p. 559.
[49] *Ibid.*, p. 609.

that place may do good service."⁵⁰ Finally, Andreas de Loo, an Italian, wrote in the language of his country desiring Windebank to secure the Queen's approval of an extension of his license from twelve years to sixteen years.⁵¹ In none of these cases is there any mention of reward though we can be pretty certain it was offered and accepted.

Very little of Windebank's own personal correspondence survives beyond a few corrected copies of letters kept by their author. One such letter reflects its kinship to an earlier Windebank, eager to provide for his future. It was written in 1599, the year following Burghley's death. Addressed to Lord Willoughby at Berwick, it contains the offer of Windebank's service whenever it would prove useful. Subtly Willoughby was reminded of Windebank's past efforts on his behalf and then regaled with the Queen's flattering remarks about him. Windebank concluded the letter with an equally discreet demonstration of his own trustworthiness.⁵² It is a remarkable document, characteristic of the ability which maintained Windebank in the midst of government service for so long a time. One had to calculate the road ahead carefully in Windebank's time. Cultivating Lord Willoughby was simply adding another signature on the insurance policy.

Thomas Windebank's domestic life, or as much as we know about it, was not particularly happy during the last decade of his life. He married Frances, daughter of the prominent Sir Edward Dymock of Lincolnshire.⁵³ Sir Edward served with Sir Richard Windebank at Calais and the youngsters may have grown up together. The marriage took place sometime after 1563, when Windebank was certainly still a bachelor, and 1575, when Thomas Kendall referred to Windebank's wife.⁵⁴ There were four children from this union: Francis, who was twenty-four years old in 1607 and who became Secretary of State to Charles I; Anne and Mildred who married brothers, Henry and Robert Reade; and Margaret.⁵⁵

Frances Dymock Windebank must have died prior to 1596 for in that year Mary, the second Mrs. Windebank, appears, constantly nagging and unhappy. It is difficult to avoid the impression that she was something of a shrew, an unhappy second mate for Windebank. Her life at Haynes Hill, the Windebank estate in Wiltshire, must have been lonely during Windebank's frequent sojourns at Court. In 1596, Mary brought her unhappiness to the attention of Robert Cecil, her husband's superior, and asked for Cecil's intercession. She complained that Windebank's married daughter caused strife between her and her husband and so

⁵⁰ *Ibid.*, VI (London, 1870), p. 55.
⁵¹ *Ibid.*, II (London, 1865), p. 658.
⁵² Great Britain, *C. S. P., Borders*, II (London, 1896), pp. 615-616.
⁵³ Armytage, *Middlesex Pedigrees*, p. 123.
⁵⁴ P. R. O., S. P. 12/103/66.
⁵⁵ Armytage, *Middlesex Pedigrees*, p. 123.

should be sent to her own home. If not, then Mary desired Cecil's aid to secure her portion so she, Mary, might leave. Furthermore, Windebank did not like her friends and had grown tired of her. He left her without clothes, servants or money beyond £10 to pay her doctor and "poticary" and keep house for a month. Mary concluded: "Hoping your honor will pity my case and be a means under God to work my speedy delivery, I humbly take my leave. . . ."[56]

Cecil must have accepted the invitation to mediate for about a week after Mary's letter, Thomas Fowler, Windebank's cousin, sent regrets to Cecil that sickness prevented him from attending Cecil in the matter. This was a reply to a letter inviting Mary's friends to visit Cecil. Fowler urged Cecil to move swiftly to resolve the crisis for Mary appeared to need servants, money and apparel.[57]

Cecil must have succeeded for Windebank and Mary were still together in June, 1600. In that month it is clear that another crisis was brewing. Let Mary speak for herself as, writing from Haynes Hill to Windebank at Court, she said: "Let me remind you of the good agreement that has been between us since Mr. Read and his wife [Windebank's daugher, Anne] have been absent, and what slander and disquiet there always is when they come. . . ." Mary asked permission to visit friends when they came to stay with Windebank on his coming from Court for she insisted she could never forget the wrongs received from them. It would grieve her to be apart from him, but upon their departure she hoped they could come together with as great love as ever.[58]

Mary went on to speak specifically about Mildred's forthcoming wedding to Robert Reade which would bring old Mr. Reade, who wrote Mary "a most railing slanderous letter," and all their kin to Windebank's house. For Mary to be present would breed strife between them. She continued to complain: of the musty wheat which made the bread taste, of her sickliness, and of Windebank's sending the horses to graze, leaving her without transportation. In a postscript, Mary said: "If you will not yield to this reasonable request, it shall be the last breach between us, for my patience has been so much tried that I can endure it no longer."[59] We can only guess at the outcome. Nor can we know which was to blame. Mary's shrewishness may have resulted from genuine grievances, as suggested by Fowler's letter. The absence of Windebank's own correspondence renders judgment all the more difficult.

Windebank died in 1608 and was buried in the parish church of St. Martin's-in-the-Fields where he had worshipped, baptized his children and served as warden.[60] His will reveals his sound protestantism though

[56] H. M. C., *Salisbury MSS.,* VI, p. 400.
[57] *Ibid.,* p. 418.
[58] Great Britain, *C. S. P. D.,* V (London, 1869), p. 440.
[59] *Ibid.*
[60] Kitto, *Accounts,* pp. 335, 434, 502, 577.

his position with Sir William Cecil scarcely leaves this open to question. The will does not mention his wife who may either have died or have taken her portion and left. Windebank's daughter Margaret received £800, the largest single sum, as well as Windebank's gold chain and a ring. To each daughter went a house in St. Martin's parish. The lease of his dwelling house, with its furniture and household goods, was left to his son, Francis, who got lands in Berkshire and Wiltshire as well. Haynes Hall and its lands likewise passed to Francis as well as the reversion of Clare manor and Dorchett Ferry, both near Windsor and the gifts of Elizabth to Windebank. Francis and Henry Green, an old servant and friend, were executors. Green got £50 for his pains. Windebank's elder son-in-law, Henry Reade, was appointed overseer.[61]

Windebank, who sent his own son abroad for experience in language, travel and affairs, had the satisfaction of seeing him established in the succession to his own office before his death. Francis, on February 21, 1605, received a grant in reversion, after Levinus Monck and Francis Gale, of the clerkship of the signet.[62]

In three generations the Windebanks had moved from the third or fourth rank of government service to the first rank, when Francis served Charles I as Secretary of State.

Francis Yaxley

Yaxley is one of those fascinating characters the truth about whom may never be known. His *DNB* biography gives his profession as conspirator. It seems not unlikely that he was a double agent whose pose as a good Catholic and friend of Mary Stuart was pre-arranged with Sir William Cecil whose servant he had been. This cannot, of course, be proved. It may be deduced from the evidence. The Spanish Ambassador described him as a good Catholic who combined a love of intrigue with an inability to keep secrets. The same authority reported that in January, 1561, he was in prison for babbling about Elizabeth's proposed marriage to Robert Dudley.[1] This would hardly seem to be the kind of fellow Cecil would keep close by him for a number of years as a trusted servant. Indeed, A. F. Pollard tells us in his *DNB* article that Cecil introduced Yaxley at Court and that Yaxley was said to reverence Cecil as though he were his father, was even referred to as Cecil's Yaxley. He readily acknowledged his indebtedness to Cecil's godly counsel and fatherly admonitions.[2]

---

[61] P. C. C., 1 Windebank.
[62] Great Britain, *C. S. P. D.*, VIII (London, 1857), p. 198.

---

[1] Albert Frederick Pollard, "Francis Yaxley," *D.N.B.*, XXI, p. 1220.
[2] *Ibid.*

Yaxley was of gentle birth, the son of Richard Yaxley of Mellis, Suffolk. The family had long been settled at Yaxley Hall, near Eye, Suffolk. His uncle was one of Henry VIII's physicians.³ Cecil himself tells us that Francis Yaxley entered his household as a servant in 1545, the year Cecil married Mildred Cooke, only the third servant to appear after Cecil began his record in 1544. From the same chart and another undated list, it is possible to ascertain that until at least 1553 Yaxley was still considered a member of the household.⁴

Yaxley was also employed by the Privy Council, possibly in the signet office, in 1547, just when Cecil entered the confidential service of Protector Somerset. In 1547, Yaxley was engaged in hiring Italian mercenaries for service in England. In June, 1549, Yaxley sent Cecil extracts from four letters which suggest his employment in the signet office or as Cecil's secretary.⁵ From 1550 to 1552, he was in Italy. He became an M. P. for Dunwich in February, 1553 and was admitted a student of Gray's Inn. In April he was sent to join Nicholas Wotton, the English Ambassador in France. It should be remembered that after 1550 Yaxley's master, William Cecil, was a Privy Councillor and one of the Principal Secretaries of State.⁶

Returnnig to England early in Mary's reign, Yaxley was elected M. P. for Stamford in 1555. By March, 1557, he had become clerk of the signet and in January, 1558, returned to parliament for Saltash. He retained his clerkship under Elizabeth when Cecil again became his official superior. Pollard states that the numerous letters to him from prominent people requesting his aid indicate that he possessed some influence.⁷ Thus it seems that from 1545 until his imprisonment in 1561, a period of about sixteen years, he enjoyed the confidence of Cecil and benefited from his favor. And Cecil was content to resume a relationship which may not have been vitally broken, for Cecil must have used Yaxley in 1555 when he allowed Stamford to send him to parliament. It seems incredible that so satisfactory a servant should suddenly become an ungovernable intriguer and babbler.

Perhaps the need for information dictated the preparation of an agent whose situation would inspire the confidence of those to be spied upon. Thus, once in 1561, and again in 1562, Yaxley was sent to prison for misconduct in matters of state. It is said that he was in league with the Countess of Lennox who employed him to obtain information from the Spanish Ambassador and to further the project of marriage between the Countess' son, Darnley, and Mary, Queen of Scots. In July, 1565, Yaxley went to Scotland, by way of Flanders. In Scotland, he at once

³ *Ibid.*
⁴ B. M., *Lansdowne MSS.*, v. 118, ff. 35, 36.
⁵ H. M. C., *Salisbury MSS.*, I, p. 74.
⁶ Pollard, "Yaxley," p. 1220.
⁷ *Ibid.*

became Darnley's confidant and secretary. Mary also told him all her secrets and sent him to plead her cause with Philip II of Spain. As Yaxley couldn't control his tongue, Pollard said, within a few days Randolph, the English Ambassador in Scotland, was able to describe the objects of his mission to the English government.[8]

Yaxley sailed for Spain on September 12, 1565, arrived October 20th, and was well received by Philip. Only five days later he left Spain with assurances of support and a considerable sum of money. En route, Yaxley was shipwrecked and drowned in the North Sea, his body being cast up on the Northumberland coast, complete with the money Philip sent which became the subject of a diplomatic dispute between Mary and Elizabeth.[9] If Yaxley was indeed one of Cecil's planted agents, his death was untimely as his usefulness was just beginning. Probably he would have "babbled" a good deal more for Ambassador Randolph and his master, William Cecil.

[8] Pollard, "Yaxley," p. 1220.
[9] *Ibid.*

APPENDIX

Appendix 159

NAME	CLASS*	ORIGIN	SETTLED	EDUCATION	WILL	RELIGION	EMPLOYMENT AND REWARD
Abraham, John	G		Stamford, Linc.				Steward, 1554-57
Alford, Roger	E	Denbighshire	Bucks		X	Protestant	Sec., 1547-1555; lease Crown lands; Teller of Receipts of Ex., 1555-1562; J. P. Bucks., 1564; ward, @15 Eliz.
Allington, Hugh	E	Worcester	Rutland	Cambridge	X	Protestant	Sec., 1561; 2 wards, 1562; reversion of Clerkship of C. of Requests for life, occupied, 1599; Clerk of Privy Seal for life, 1572; ward, 1573; crown lease, 1586.
Arisman, John	Y						Wardrobe, 1572, 1573, 1591.
Armestrong, Francis	?						Estate agent, 1546-1555
Arundell, John	G						Interpreter, 1581
Ashfield, ———	G						Usher, 1582
Atkinson, William	Y				X		Employed, 1556; keeper of Canon Row house
Audley, Henry	G						By 1590's, Exchequer receiver for Hamp., Wilts., Glouc.; crown lease, 1586.
Baldwin, Ralph	G						Employed, 1553, as an officer
Baynham, Edmund	G						Employed by 1572; ward

* E Esquire
G Gentleman
Y Yeoman
? Unknown

Appendix

NAME	CLASS*	ORIGIN	SETTLED	EDUCATION	WILL	RELIGION	EMPLOYMENT AND REWARD
Bellot, Robert	G	Cheshire	Denbigh				Gentleman servant, 1571; gentleman usher to Countess of Oxford; crown lease, 1574; woodward of Denbigh, 1576; farm of tolls of Wrexham, Denbigh, 1595; feodary of Denbigh, 1603.
Bellot, Thomas	G	Cheshire	London		X	Protestant	Steward, 1566-1598; Annuity from Burghley; ward, 1570; feodary of Benbigh, 1575; farm of tolls of Wrexham, Denb., and Mylcombe Wood, Cornwall
Bennet, ——	G						Chaplain
Blague, Thomas	G			Cambridge			Chaplain; Dean of Rochester
Blyth, George	E	Cambridge		Cambridge Lincoln's Inn	X		Clerk, sec., 1571; sec., Council of North, 1572; 2 crown leases; wardship, 1572
Bowker, Edward	Y						Footman
Bradshawe, Richard	G						Chamberlain to Lady Burghley
Brewer, Richard	?						Clerk
Brown, Edward	G	Linc.		Oxford	X	Protestant	Gentleman usher, 1572
Burden, George	G	Kent		Cambridge		Protestant	Schoolmaster, 1549; Deputy Receiver Gen. to Dean and Chapter of Westminster, 1564; Receiver and Solicitor to Dean and Chapt., 1576; ward (@1572-1581); Westminster leases, 1589

Appendix

NAME	CLASS*	ORIGIN	SETTLED	EDUCATION	WILL	RELIGION	EMPLOYMENT AND REWARD
Burrell, George	G						Gentleman servant, 1572; Servant-at-arms to Queen
Canfield, Thomas	Y						"One of his Lordship's yeomen"
Cave, William	G	Leicester					Servant, 1578-81; Sheriff of Leicestershire, 1588
Cayworth, William	G						Steward, 1544-57, possibly until 1566
Cheke, Henry	G			Cambridge		Protestant	Servant prior to 1576; Clerk of Privy Council, 1576; Sec. of Council of North, 1581
Cheke, John	G			Cambridge			Servant; military career, 1578 (d. 1580)
Clapham, John	G	London	London	Gray's Inn			Clerk and keeper of book of wards, 1591-1598; a Clerk of Chancery
Cole, Francis	Y		Hertford				Servant for 20 years
Constable, Robert	G		Ireland				Servant in 1577; Capt., English forces, Ire, 1597
Conyers, ———	G		Durham		X	Protestant	Servant; Exchequer auditor, 1586
Cooke, William	G		Glouc.				Servant, 1554; Clerk of Liveries, C. of Wards, 1561
Cooper, Thomas	?				X		Servant, 1550
Cope, Walter	G	Oxford	London		X	Protestant	Servant; Surveyor of Queen's possessions in Kent, 1579; Feodary of Oxfordshire, 1584; Crown lease, 1586; Feodary for Duchy of Lancaster, 1598

NAME	CLASS*	ORIGIN	SETTLED	EDUCATION	WILL	RELIGION	EMPLOYMENT AND REWARD
Coppin, George	G	Suffolk	London			X	Page, 1581; ward and lease, 1592; Clerk of Crown in Chancery, 1597
Curllewes,——	?		Hertford				Servant, 1572-1591
Dane, Richard	G						Servant for over 12 years
Dawson,——	?		Ripon				Servant, 1584
Dewhurst, Barnard	G	Lanc.	Hertford & London	Gray's Inn		X	Secretary, 1572-1596; Surveyor of royal manors and lands in Middlesex and London, 1577; ward, 1576; ward, @ 1570-1581; Crown lease, @ 17-30 Eliz.; Auditor of Westminster College, 1586; lease of tower from Westminster Abbey, 1588; Royal woodward of Hert., 1589; ward, 1591
Dudley, Amborse	G		Durham				Servant in 1597
Duringe, John	G		Linc.			X	Servant in 1597
Fades, Henry	G						Probably estate agent, 1572-1595; Surveyor of College of Westminster; 1595; Supervisor of works for Westminster Abbey, 1596-97
Fisher, William	?		Linc.				Receiver, 1552-1555
Floyde, John	G						Gentleman servant, 1571-1574; probably clerk Gentleman servant and clerk in 1575; ward, 1579

Appendix

NAME	CLASS*	ORIGIN	SETTLED	EDUCATION	WILL	RELIGION	EMPLOYMENT AND REWARD
Gilbert, Thomas	G						Clerk in 1581
Godman, John	G						
Gooch, Barnaby	G	Linc.	Linc.				Servant, 1558; ward; Gentleman Pensioner to Queen, 1563; service in Ireland, 1574
Goodman, Gabriel	G	Denbigh	London		X	Protestant	Schoolmaster, 1554; rector, 1558; rector, 1559; prebend of Cheswick, 1559; prebend of Westminster Abbey, 1560; Dean of Westminster, 1561; ward, 1576
Green, George	?						Servant, 1589
Gregory, John	?						Barber
Gresham, Thomas	G						Servant, 1576-1581; ward, 1595
Grey, Henry	E	North.					Servant
Grey, Ralph	G	North.	North.				Servant; Bailiff of Dunstanburgh Castle and lordship, 1571; Constable and steward of Dunstanburgh, 1578; ward, 1597
Haddon, William	G		Linc.				Estate officer, 1549; Woodward of Linc. & Rutland
Hall, Arthur	G	Linc.	Linc.	Cambridge			Servant; ward, 1562, '65; Queen's service
Hart, John	G						Sec. in court of Wards by 1563; Chester Herald, 1573

Appendix

NAME	CLASS*	ORIGIN	SETTLED	EDUCATION	WILL	RELIGION	EMPLOYMENT AND REWARD
Hickes, Michael	G	London	Essex	Cambridge Lincoln's Inn		Protestant	Secretary by 1581; feodary; ward, 1591; ward, 1596
Hoby, Postumous	G						Servant in training, his Mother paying 100 p.a. for privilege
Holcroft, Thomas	G	Cheshire		Gray's Inn			Employed 1550: ward, 1558-62, 1569, 1572; bailiff of Westminster
Hopton, Thomas	G						Servant; ward, 1572, 1573
Houghton, Roger	E	Lanc.		Gray's Inn	X	Protestant	Squire to Robert Cecil; Steward to Sir Robert Cecil
Jennings, ——	?						Gardner, 1581
Kemp, Peter	G		Stamford, North.				Lincolnshire factor and steward, 1560-1578; ward, 1567, 1569, 1570
Knight, Phillip							
Jesse, Richard	?						Clerk, 1575
Jones, Owen	?				X		Clerk, 1580; royal woodward in Denbigh, 1587
Lacy, Henry	G		Stamford, North.		X		Estate agent, 1550's
Lambert, Michell	?						Servant for 20 years
Langworthe, ——	G						Gentleman servant and clerk in 1583
Manners, George	E	Derbyshire					Servant, 1591

Appendix 165

NAME	CLASS*	ORIGIN	SETTLED	EDUCATION	WILL	RELIGION	EMPLOYMENT AND REWARD
Maynard, Henry	G	Hert.	Essex	Middle Temple	X	Protestant	Secretary by 1575; royal lease, 1584; office of writing writ of *Diem Clausit Extremum*, 1585; royal lease, 1587; royal manor, 1589; surveyor of crown lands in Herts., 1594; surveyor of crown lands in Essex, 1596; ward, 1596; Queen's service as general overseer of checks and musters in Ireland, 1597
Mayne, Joseph	Y						Servant in 1596
Medley, William	G						Servant; crown leases, @ 31-31 Eliz.
Morrice, James	G	Essex	Essex	Middle Temple		Puritan	Servant; attorney for C. of Wards, 1579
Napper, Robert	G		Surrey		X	Protestant	Servant, 1572-81
Neile, Richard	G	London	York	Cambridge			Chaplain, 1590; Vicarage of St. Mary's Cheshunt; eventually Archbishop of York
Nicholls, Degory	G			Cambridge			Chaplain, 1577; Master of Magdalen College, Camb., 1577-1582
Ogle, Thomas	G	Linc.	Linc.		X		Estate agent; lease of two Linc. manors, @ 1-16 Eliz.
Parlor, John	G	Westmorland	London				Servant; Keeper of Gate House Prison, Westminster 1561; bailiff of royal manor for life, 1566

Appendix

NAME	CLASS*	ORIGIN	SETTLED	EDUCATION	WILL	RELIGION	EMPLOYMENT AND REWARD
Pickering, Boniface	G	North.			X		Servant
Plommer, Richard	?						Coachman
Powell, Margaret	?						Servant
Powell, Thomas	?						Servant
Purvey, John	E		Hert.		X		Estate agent; custody of three royal manors, 1561; Wards feodary of Herts.
Ramsden, Robert	G						Chaplain, 1570's; prebend of Westminster, 1571; Archdeacon of York, c. 1575
Randall, William	?						Clerk, 1573
Reede, Sir William	G		Northumberland				Servant; lease in reversion of cell and rectory of Holy Island, Northumberland; later, patent for Holy Island proper
Robinson, Lawrence, alias Baker	G		Northamptonshire		X		Bailiff, 1553-1584; lease of chantry lands, 1562; ward, 1571; lease of pasture, 1581
Scarre, Andrew	G					Protestant	Bailiff-general, 1556
Sedon, John	?						Servant, 1589
Seres, William	Citizen		London			Protestant	Bailiff, 1550's; a royal Printing monopoly, c. 1547-1553; a royal printing monopoly, 1559; ward, 1570; ward's lands 1576; keeper of Dayton Wood, c. 1577-1580

Appendix

NAME	CLASS*	ORIGIN	SETTLED	EDUCATION	WILL	RELIGION	EMPLOYMENT AND REWARD
Servant, Marmaduke	G		London		X	Strong Protestant	Servant; usher, C. of Wards, 1579; bailiff of Newington, 1578; bailiff and collector of rents of royal tenements in borough and parish of St. Martin's, 1583; ward, c. 1588-1591, and 1593 assistant burgess of Westminster, 1585
Sheffield, Henry	G		Ireland				Servant, 1572-1594; gentleman pensioner to Queen; Captain in Ireland
Shute, Richard	G		Northamptonshire		X		Estate steward, 1578; feodary of Linc., 1579; lease of Newington, Kent, c. 17-30 Eliz.; bailiff of Pinchbeck, Linc, 1585
Skinner, Vincent	G	Linc.	Linc.	Cambridge Lincoln's Inn		Strong Protestant	Secretary by 1575; ward, 1573; royal lease, 1574; bailiff of manor of Neward, 1575; escheator for Linc. (Duchy of Lancaster), 1573; Linc. chantries receiver, feodary of Linc.,, 1582; constable of Bolingbroke Castle and Lincoln Castle; ward, c. 1570; royal lease, 1588; royal lease, 1592; writer of Tallies and Counter Tallies for life (Exch.)
Sneynton, Quentin	G		Hert.		X		Messenger and agent; 1554; usher in Co. of Wards, 1564; ward, 1563; Wards lease, c. 1570-1575

168	Appendix

NAME	CLASS*	ORIGIN	SETTLED	EDUCATION	WILL	RELIGION	EMPLOYMENT AND REWARD
Speed, Thomas alias Lewkenor	G	Durham	London		X	Strong Protestant	Clerk by 1577; keeper of Burtley Woods (from Bishop of Durham), 1577; ward, 1577; wards Lease, c. 1570-1581; royal bailiff, 1582; royal bailiff, 1587; Westminster lease, 1587
Spencer, Richard	G	Northamp.	Hert.	Oxford Cambridge Gray's Inn			Servant in 1572; government service in embassies
Stephenson, Henry	?						Chamber keeper, 1549; estate agent, 1556
Stileman, John	G		Hert.				Park keeper, 1572; wards, 1597, 1598
Tampon, Thomas	Y		Northamptonshire		X		Servant by 1581
Thomas, Owen	Y					Protestant	Kept chamber at Court, 1573-1585
Thompson,————	G						Chaplain, 1598
Thompson, Morris	G		Herts.				Keeper of plate, 1572
Tooke, Walter	G		Herts.				Estate agent; deputy feodary of Herts, 1567; feodary, 1583
Travers, Walter	G			Cambridge		Puritan	Chaplain and tutor; Provost of Trinity College, Dublin, 1595-1598
Troughton, Richard	G						Bailiff, 1547; parsonage prior to 1562; keeper of Queen's gates, by 1562; wards lease, 1568

Appendix

NAME	CLASS*	ORIGIN	SETTLED	EDUCATION	WILL	RELIGION	EMPLOYMENT AND REWARD
Tutt, Richard	?						Servant, 1572-1581; bailiff of manor of Christ Church 1582
Twiford, Matthew	Y						Usher in 1572; ward, 1563
Waad, William	E		Middlesex		X	Protestant	Servant in 1572; Amb. to Port., 1580; Clerk of Privy Council, 1584; Amb. to France, 1587; royal lease, 1590; farm of manors, 1593; patent
Wakering, Gilbert	G	Essex	Herts.			Protestant	Servant, bailiff of three royal manors, 1576; woodward of Staffordshire, 1583; ward, 1587; surveyor of Norfolk, 1592; ward, 1596; escheator for Norfolk and Suffolk, 1594 and 1597
Wheeler, Humfrey	?						Servant, 1591
White, Edward	?						Servant in 1576, identified as baker
Williams, George	?		Linc.				Bailiff, 1547-1554; chantry
Windebank, Thomas	G	Calais or Middl.	Wiltshire	Lincoln's Inn	X		Secretary, 1558-1563; ward, 1565; clerk of Signet, 1567; wards lease, 1567; ward, 1568; royal lease, 1578 and 1584; royal monopoly, 1589; free gift of £300 from Queen, 1591
Yaxley, Francis	G	Suffolk		Gray's Inn			Clerk, 1545; Clerk of Signet, 1557 (possibly by 1547)

INDEX

INDEX

A

Abbots' Kensington, 54
Abraham, Sir John, 23, 24, 45, 92
Aldford Castle, 27
Alencon, Duke of, 7
Alford, Anne, 25, 27
Alford, Edward, 26
Alford, Elizabeth, 27, 44
Alford, Francis, 17, 27, 40
Alford, Lancelot, 17, 27, 28
Alford, Robert, 27
Alford, Roger, family patron, 17; Teller of Exchequer, 19; employed, 24; grants to, 25; in parliament, 26; will of, 26; origins, 27; mentioned, 32, 40, 43, 44, 77, 147
Allington, George, 28
Allington, Giles, 28, 62, 131
Allington, Hugh, Clerk of Privy Seal, 20; career of, 28-32; Burghley's brother-in-law, 60; letter from, 148; succeeded Windebank, 149; mentioned, 77
Allott, Thomas, 149
Anderson, Henry, 55
Archer, John, 144
Armitree manor, 124
Arthington, William, 75
Arthur, William, 81
Arundell, 82
Ascham, Roger, 3, 77
Astley, John, 150
Atkinson, William, 127
Audeley, Henry, 95
Aylmer, Bishop, 151

B

Backhouse, John, 125
Backhouse, Lancelot, 121
Backhouse, Robert, 121
Bacon, Francis, 8, 14, 86, 102, 130
Barnard, Mr. *See* Dewhurst, Barnard
Barne, Thomas, 29
Barne, William, 29
Bateman, Thomas, 56, 57
Battles Hall, 142

Baynton, Anne, 29
Bedford, Countess of, 34
Bedford, Earl of, 133
Bedingfield, Christopher, 93
Bellot, Alice, 32
Bellot, Cuthbert, 39, 72, 107
Bellot, David, 18, 39
Bellot, Edward, 40
Bellot, George, 38, 39, 71, 72, 122
Bellot, Hugh, 39, 40, 72
Bellot, John, 18, 35, 39, 40
Bellot, Owen, 18, 39, 72
Bellot, Robert, 18, 40
Bellot, Thomas, firm protestant, 13, 38; unsalaried, 15; family patron, 17-18, 39, 40; household friends, 19, 38; Welsh patron, 20-21, brother of, 27; Cecil's steward, 32-33; reward, 34-36; patron of Bath Abbey, 36-37; receives annuity, 48; inventory by, 71; bequest of, 86, 91, 110, 120; bequest to, 106; funeral sermon of, 108; witnessed deed, 132; mentioned, 41, 42, 45, 57, 63, 72, 89, 90, 111, 139
Belseys House, 142
Best, Henry, 63, 104
Beverstone Castle, 87
Birkinshaw, Ralph, 98
Blake, William, 36
Blythe, George, secretary of Council of North, 22; career, 40-42; associated with Hickes, 81; mentioned, 46, 60, 96, 127
Blythe, John, 40
Bodley, Thomas, 58, 59
Bowes, William, 75
Bowker, Edward, 58, 104
Bowle, Dr. John, 58
Boydell, Thomas, 88
Bradshaw, Richard, 16, 106
Brakin, Francis, 101
Bridges, John, 94
Bright, Dr., 83, 130
Brinknell, Adnes, 133
Brockett, John, 136
Brokholes, Thomas, 88

Brown, Humphrey, 143
Browne, Anthony, 42
Browne, Edward, 42
Browne, John, 125
Browne, Thomas, 42, 145
Browne, Valentine, 43
Brydges, Edmund, 27
Budden, John, 35
Burden, George, 26, 43, 44, 69
Burghley, Lord. *See* Cecil, William
Burghley House, Stamford, 5, 6, 31, 45, 47, 110, 129, 138
Burghley House in the Strand, 7, 8, 64, 98, 111
Burton, Anthony, 92
Butler, John, 144

C

Caesar, Julius, 78
Cambridge University, 12, 22, 39, 40, 43, 46, 47, 64, 68, 70, 77, 79, 81, 83, 102, 106, 112, 127, 132, 136, 151
Camden, William, 44, 71
Camois, 57
Canfield, Thomas, 16
Cannon Row, 45, 133
Carew, Sir George, 123
Carey, John, 74, 75
Carleton, Dudley, 48, 52, 53, 86, 98
Carr, William, 73, 79
Cathornes, Elizabeth, 88
Cavendish, Lord, 103
Cawood, Thomas, 119
Cayworth, William, 45, 133
Cecil, Elizabeth, 31, 77
Cecil, Jane, Burghley's mother, 31, 42, 93, 115, 124
Cecil, Mary Cheke, Burghley's first wife, 3, 40, 59, 110
Cecil, Mildred Cooke, Burghley's second wife, 3; escort to Theobalds, 10; aids suitor, 16; loan fund of, 33; sobriety of, 38; cousins of, 45, 50, 77, 84, 105, 108, 128; charitable agent of, 70; aids Richard Neile, 106; mentioned, 13, 96, 155
Cecil, Richard, 9, 24, 25
Cecil, Robert, first Earl of Salisbury, Theobalds for, 6; Burghley's advice to, 11, 14; favors father's servants, 19; suitors of, 30, 43, 47; servants of, 51, 88, 89, 119; parliamentary patron, 55; purchases wardship, 62; correspondents of, 70, 78, 145; bosom friend, 86; grant to, 91; secretary of state, 97-99; lands conveyed to, 130; obtains wardship, 131; associates of, 137, 139; duplicity of, 150; seeks favor, 151; mediates domestic crisis, 152-53; mentioned, 35, 37, 48, 52, 54, 61, 64, 71, 75, 82, 83, 90, 103, 104, 105, 107, 122, 123, 143
Cecil, Robert, Marquess of Salisbury, 18
Cecil, Thomas, first Earl of Exeter, home of, 6; interpreter, 8; godfather, 26; seeks proof of gentility, 31; provides surety, 44; sells land, 54; inherits portraits, 71; book dedicated to, 78; obtains ward, 79; bequest to, 115; guarantor of conveyance, 130; foreign travel, 148-49; mentioned, 28, 77, 88, 93, 110, 114, 123, 127, 129
Cecil, William, first Lord Burghley, early life, 3; later career, 4; homes, 5-7; hospitality, 7-9; staff size, 9-11; profile of staff, 12-14; reward of staff, 15-19; influence of, 19-23; Burghley's stewards, 23, 27, 32, 37, 41, 45, 57, 86, 89; Burghley's secretaries, 25, 26, 29, 60, 81, 82, 85, 96, 130, 148, 155; escape plans of, 25, 117; parliamentary circle, 26, 42, 46, 55, 64, 78, 85, 88, 94, 102, 111, 125, 132, 137, 142; kinsmen of, 28, 41, 43, 46, 50, 59, 63, 66, 105, 108, 110, 128, 136; nephews of, 28, 41, 46, 59; brother-in-law, 31; property of, 31, 54; executors of, 33; bequests of, 35; gentleman usher to, 42; tutors, 43, 68, 127, 132-33; estate agents of, 45, 92, 115, 116, 124, 127, 139; clerks of, 47, 51; employees who published, 49, 67, 78, 80, 107, 128; footman to, 58; godfather, 75, 77; steward of St. Albans, 95; chaplains of, 106, 112; mentioned, 24, 28, 30, 34, 37, 38, 40, 44, 52, 55, 56, 59, 61, 65, 69, 70, 71, 72, 73, 74, 76, 79, 83, 84, 87, 90, 91, 93, 97, 98, 99, 100, 102, 103, 104, 109, 113, 114, 118, 119, 120, 121, 122, 123, 126, 129, 131, 135, 138, 140, 141, 143, 144, 145, 147, 148, 149, 150, 151, 152, 154, 156
Cecil House, 4, 5, 61, 90

Index

Chaderton, Dr., 112
Chamberlain, John, 48, 52, 53, 54, 56, 86, 87, 98
Charleton, Elizabeth, 34
Cheke, Alice, 41
Cheke, Anne, 28
Cheke, Henry, 20, 22, 46
Cheke, John, 3, 22, 46, 79, 116
Cheke, Sir John, 46
Cheshunt, 5, 32
Clapham, Anne, 48
Clapham, John, 19, 38, 47, 48, 49, 60, 96, 98
Clapham, Luke, 47, 48
Clare manor, 154
Clark, Mr., 129
Clarke, John, 27
Claybury, 101
Clement, John, 45
Clerke, Thomas, 151
Cleypool, Adam, 63
Cliff Park, 45
Cloke, John, 59
Cobham, Lord, 130
Coke, Sir Edward, 132
Collingwood, Robert, 75
Connock, Richard, 52
Conny, Henry, 51
Constable, Robert, 22, 49
Conye, Mary, 93
Conyers, John, 135
Conyers, Tristram, 61
Cooke, Sir Anthony, 50, 70, 94, 108, 130
Cooke, Elizabeth, 77
Cooke, John, 108
Cooke, William, 50
Cope, Sir Anthony, 54
Cope, Dorothy Greville, 50
Cope, Edward, 50
Cope, Sir Walter, 18, 35, 50, 51, 52, 53, 54, 55, 57, 66, 90
Cope Castle, 53
Coppin, George, 19, 38, 54, 55, 56, 57, 60, 90
Coppin, Robert, 55, 58
Coppins, Thomas, 58
Cotton, Honor, 146
Cotton, John, 146
Cox, 145
Cromwell, Oliver, 101

D

Dalton, James, 26

Dane, Richard, 58, 59
Daniel, Dorothy, 141
Daniel, Peter, 141
Darell, George, 67
Darell, Mary, 66
Darell, Thomas, 66
Darnley, 155
Day, John, 116, 117
Day, William, 20, 28, 29, 148
Daynes, Anne, 131
Denham, Henry, 120
Denys, Mary, 77
Derby, Earl of, 11, 136, 137
Derby House, 80
Desmond, Earl of, 123
Dethick, William, 80
Dewhurst, Anne, 59, 63
Dewhurst, Barnard, Burghley's secretary, 14; assists suitor, 16; estate of, 18; custodian of evidences, 47; career of, 59-63; appointed executor, 102; guarantor of conveyance, 130; witnessed will, 132; mentioned, 31, 83, 104, 131
Dewhurst, Robert, 63
Dewhurst, Thomas, 61, 62
Dorchett Ferry, 154
Dudley, Robert, 154
Durham, Bishop of, 135
Durninge, Elizabeth Cleypool, 63
Durninge, John, 63
Dymock, Edward, 146, 152

E

Earl's Court, 54
Edward VI, 25, 68
Egerton, Anne, 41
Egerton, Sir Thomas, 56
Elizabeth, Queen of England, first councilor of, 4; visits to Theobalds, 6, 8, 10, 40, 42, 51, 66, 80, 87, 89, 96, 97, 109, 110, 117, 136, 137, 138, 140, 142, 144; Queen's porter, chaplain, secretary, 20; gentleman pensioner of, 67; visits Hickes, 84; gift of, 151; mentioned, 7, 8, 11, 13, 15, 19, 22, 23, 26, 45, 52, 58, 59, 65, 72, 79, 82, 83, 90, 97, 98, 99, 100, 101, 108, 121, 123, 131, 133, 140, 150, 152, 155
Enfield House, 83, 136
Eresby, Lawrence, 110, 119
Essex, Earl of, 61, 63, 105
Eston Lodge, 84, 99, 103

Eston manor, 99
Eure, Lord, 75
Exchequer, 8, 19, 42, 51, 86, 130
Exchequer, Court of the, 129
Exeter, Earl of. *See* Cecil, Thomas
Eynns, Thomas, 41

F

Fades, Henry, 64
Fairfax, Henry, 128
Fairfax, John, 127
Fermor, Thomas, 60
Fitton, Edward, 88
Fitzwilliams, Sir William III, 84
Flamborough, 49
Floyde, John, 65
Fludd, Thomas, 65
Forster, John, 73, 74, 120
Fowkes, Elizabeth, 132
Fowler, Thomas, 71, 153
Foxley, Rose, 112
Frelove, John, 119
Freville, George, 48

G

Gale, Francis, 154
Gardiner, Thomas, 85
Garneyes, Thomas, 149
Gerard, John, 7
Gerrard, Sir Gilbert, 88, 89
Godolphin, Sir Francis, 52
Gooch, Barnaby, 22, 65, 66, 67
Gooch, Robert, 65
Godman, Cecily, 68
Goodman, Edward, 68
Goodman, Gabriel, Dean of Westminster, 18; patron of Welshmen, 32; executor of Burghley's will, 33; assists Bellots, 38-39; aids Cecil's servants, 43, 62, 64, 65, 106, 119, 122, 135; overseer of a will, 44; career of, 68-72; mentioned, 20, 21, 77, 112, 132
Goodman, Godfrey, 43, 72
Gorges, Arthur, 53
Gray, Ralph, 114
Gray's Inn, 13, 48, 58, 88, 90, 136, 142, 155
Great Braxted, 101
Great Easton, 101
Great Moreton, 32
Green, Francis, 154
Green, Henry, 154
Greene, John, 122

Gresham, Thomas, 72, 82
Greville, Richard, 50
Grey, Edward, 74
Grey, Henry, 73, 79
Grey, Isabel, 73
Grey, Lady Jane, 25, 75
Grey, Lord of Wark, 21, 75, 123
Grey, Sir Ralph, 21, 73, 74, 75
Grey, Thomas, second Marquis of Dorset, 50, 73, 79
Grey, William, 21
Grindal, Archbishop, 112, 113
Gunter, George, 135

H

Haddam, 63
Haddon, Walter, 118
Hall, Agnes, 133
Hall, Anne, 134
Hall, Arthur, 76, 77, 78, 125, 134
Hall, Cecil, 78
Hall, Edmund, 78, 134, 135
Hall, Francis, 76
Hall, Thomas, 76
Hall, Ursula, 76
Hampson, Robert, 144
Hardwyck, Frances, 62
Harrington, Mrs., mother of John, 92
Harrington, John, 92
Hart, John, 73, 79, 80, 118, 133
Hart, Mary, 80
Harvey, John, 139
Hast, Henry, 105
Hatfield, 4, 24, 45
Hatton, Sir Christopher, 7
Haversham, Lord, 139
Hawkins, John, 96
Hayes, Robert, 112
Haynes Hill, 152, 153, 154
Heneage, Robert, 110
Henry, Griffith ap, 146
Herlle, William, 137
Heron, Edward, 125
Hertford Castle, 51
Heydon, William, 49
Hickes, Baptist, 81, 87
Hickes, Clement, 81
Hickes, Elizabeth, 87
Hickes, Julian, 81
Hickes, Michael, outspoken protestant, 13; Burghley's secretary, 18; bequest to, 19, 38; correspondent of, 41; witnesses conveyance, 59; sells land,

Index

64; career of, 80-87; moneylender, 102; relations with Skinner, 129; mentioned, 25, 57, 60, 72, 96, 127, 132
Hickes, Robert, 80
Hickes, William, 18, 87
Hicks-Beach, Sir Michael, 18
High Commission, Court of, 107
Hill, Alice, 138
Hill, George, 138
Hoby, Thomas, 77
Hoby, Lady, 43
Hoby, Posthumous, 43
Holcroft, Elizabeth Fitton, 88
Holcroft, Elizabeth Reyner, 88
Holcroft, Juliana, 88
Holcroft, Thomas, 87, 88
Holdenby, 7
Holland, Earl of, 53
Holland House, 53
Houghton, Roger, 19, 35, 38, 89, 90, 91, 136
Houghton, Sheth, 91
Houghton, Thomas, 89
Howard, Thomas, 101
Hunsdon, Lord, 74, 75, 113, 136
Hunt, Ann, 136
Huntingdon, Earl of, 11, 114

I
Ireland, William, 46

J
James I, King of England, 19, 54, 57
Jegon, 151
Jennings, 61
Jennings, Nicholas, 88
Jenny, Francis, 144
Joceylin, Robert, 103

K
Kemp, Peter, 91, 92, 93, 124
Kempe, Sir Robert, 10
Kendall, Thomas, 149, 152
Kensington Palace, 57
Kidderminster, Edmund, 48
Killigrew, Henry, 8
Killigrew, Mary, 40
Kirkington Manor, 119
Kitson, Sir Thomas, 136
Knight, Philip, 106
Knotting Barns, 54
Knyvett, Thomas, 101

L
Lacy, Henry, 94
Lacy, Robert, 94, 121
Lacy, Thomas, 94
Lacy, William, 94
Lake, Thomas, 150
Lambart, Mr., 26
Lancaster, Duchy of, 128
Laud, 107
Lennard, Sampson, 66
Lennox, Countess of, 155
L'Estrange, Nicholas, 10
Leveson, Walter, 145
Lincoln's Inn, 13, 41, 81, 82, 94, 127, 128, 129, 132, 147
Little Easton, 101, 103
Loo, Andreas de, 152
Lowe, Thomas, 87
Lytleberry, Humfrey, 150
Lytton, Robert, 98, 137

M
MacWilliams, Henry, 46
Madison, 149
Man, John, 128, 129
Man, Richard, 129, 131
Man, William, 122
Manners, Roger, 7
Mantell, Margaret, 65
Mantell, Walter, 65
Marlborough, Dukes of, 136
Mary, Queen of England, 4
Mary, Queen of Scots, 155
Mason, Mr., 136
Maxey Castle, 64
May, Dr. William, 118
Maynard, Charles, 103
Maynard, Henry, Burghley's secretary, 13; receives gratuity, 16; bequest to, 19, 38; overseer of Dewhurst's will, 63; relations with Hickes, 84-85; career of, 94-103; mentioned, 18, 25, 59, 60, 72, 82, 83, 132
Maynard, John, 94, 95, 103
Maynard, Mary, 94
Maynard of Wicklow, Baron, 103
Mayne, John, 105
Mayne, Joseph, 103, 104
Medley, Elizabeth, 105
Medley, William, 105
Middlemore, Edward, 132
Middle Temple, 102, 105
Middleton, Robert, 16, 33, 48

Mildmay, Sir Walter, 45, 62, 110
Mills, Francis, 30
Minsterchamber, Francis, 29
Mitford, Margaret, 62
Mohun, Sir Raynald, 18, 39
Mohun, Walter, 50
Momford, John, 136
Monck, Levinus, 154
Montague, James, 37
Monteagle, Lord, 136
Morgan, William, 70
Morrice, James, 105
Morrice, William, 105

N

Napper, Robert, 106, 123
Neale, Richard. *See* Neile, Richard
Neile, Richard, 64, 82, 106, 107, 124
Nevil, Lady Katherine, 73
Newell, Robert, 107
Newhall, 101
Norfolk, Duke of, 4
Norris, Lord, 34, 39
North, Council of the, 41, 46
North, Lord, 11
Northumberland, Earl of, 9, 16, 25, 73, 111
Norton, Anne, 55
Norton, John, 63
Nottingham House, 57

O

Oatlands, 58
Obbins, John, 141
Offley Place, 136
Ogle, Audrey, 45, 108, 129
Ogle, Jane, 108
Ogle, John, 108
Ogle, Nicholas, 128
Ogle, Richard, 108, 129
Ogle, Thomas, 108
Olney, Edward, 127
Olney, Thomas, 127
Onslowe, George, 104
Ormonde, Earl of, 49
Osborne, Peter, 41, 42, 46, 47, 112
Oseley, Richard, 29, 30, 147
Oxford, Countess of, 40
Oxford, Earl of, 33, 34, 73, 80
Oxford University, 43
Oxley, Peter, 93

P

Palavicino, Lady Anne, 101
Palavicino, Horatio, 100, 101, 102
Palmer, Thomas, 5
Parker, Matthew, 66, 96, 128
Parker, Thomas, 30
Parker, William, 30
Parlor, John, 109
Parlor, Nicholas, 109
Parratt, Jane, 72
Parrot, Sir John. *See* Perrot, Sir John
Partheriche, William, 47
Parvis, Elizabeth Colston, 87
Parvis, Gabriel, 85
Pearson, Thomas, 103
Pembroke, Earl of, 86
Pennyman, Jane, 120
Pepper, Cuthbert, 122
Percival, Richard, 90
Peres, Peter, 93
Perrot, Sir John, 67, 113
Perrot, Robert, 94
Petre, Sir William, 3, 10
Philip II, 156
Philippes, Elizabeth, 43
Pickering, 19, 38
Pickering, Boniface, 109, 110
Pickering, Gilbert, 109
Pickering, Sir James, 109
Pitt, William, 63, 122
Pitts, James, 145
Popham, John, 102
Pratt, William, 120
Purvey, John, 110, 111
Purvey, Magdalene, 31, 59, 110, 112
Purvey, William, 110

R

Ramsden, Richard, 113
Ramsden, Robert, 112, 113
Rast, Roger, 49
Read, Anne and Catherine, 134, 153
Read, Richard, 134, 153
Reade, Henry, 152, 154
Reade, Robert, 152, 153
Reede, Sir William, 22, 75, 113
Reyner, Sir William, 88
Rich, Lord, 82
Rich, Sir Henry, 53
Richmansworth, 145
Ridisdale, George, 146
Ridisdale, Oriscian, 146
Riggs, William, 134

Index

Roberts, Francis, 90
Robinson, Amy, 114
Robinson, Lawrence, 114
Robinson, Robert, 119
Rogers, Francis, 101
Rowlett, Margery, 95
Rowlett, Ralph, 95
Roydon, William, 32
Ruckholt, 84, 86
Russell, John, 43, 77
Rutland, Earl of, 7, 18, 39, 67, 73, 79, 80, 88, 125

S

Sadler, Ralph, 80
St. Alban's House, 18, 62
Saint Lawrence Jewry, 112
Salisbury Court, 27
Salisbury, Earl of. *See* Cecil, Robert
Salisbury, Jane, 27
Salisbury, John, 27
Sandys, Archbishop of York, 96
Scarre, Andrew, 115, 116
Scarre, William, 127
Scudamore, Philip, 26
Seres, William, 22, 44, 116, 117, 118, 119
Servant, Marmaduke, 19, 38, 120, 121, 135, 136
Sewster, Giles, 25
Seymour, Edward, 3
Sheffield, Henry, 122, 123
Shirley, George, 60
Shrewsbury, Earl of, 102
Shute, Richard, 14, 93, 116, 123, 124, 125, 126, 127
Skinner, Bridget, 132
Skinner, John, 127, 128
Skinner, Vincent, outspoken protestant, 13; Writer of the Tallies, 19; Burghley's secretary, 60; letter to Hickes, 82; promoted, 83; kinsman of, 108; career of, 127-32; mentioned, 18, 62, 72, 81
Sklater, Thomas, 140
Skynner, Robert, 127
Smith, Renald, 104, 105
Smith, Thomas, 79
Sneynton, Quinten, 77, 80, 120, 132
Somerset, Protector, 77
Southwell, Frances, 62
Sparkes, 151
Speed, Thomas, 135

Spencer, Sir John, 136
Spencer, Richard, 136, 137
Spencer, William, 127
Stamford, 5, 6
Stamford Baron, 92
Stanhope, John, 77
Star Chamber, Court of, 107
Stationers, Company of, 22, 116, 117, 118
Stevenson, Richard, 115
Stileman, John, 138, 139
Stuart, Lady Arabella, 143
Stuart, Mary, 154
Stubbs, John, 82
Sturge, Thomas, 56
Suffolk, Duke of, 76
Sugdon, Anne, 106
Sunderland, Earls of, 136
Sussex, Earl of, 47, 99
Sych, John, 135
Symes, Richard, 125

T

Tampon, Thomas, 127
Taverner, Robert, 62
Thelwell, Edward, 68
Theobalds, building of, 6-7; Queen's visit to, 8-9; servants at, 10; steward of, 32; mentioned, 5, 40, 41, 42, 47, 51, 55, 60, 64, 65, 66, 80, 82, 84, 87, 89, 93, 96, 97, 99, 105, 107, 109, 110, 111, 117, 123, 131, 135, 136, 137, 138, 139, 140, 143, 144, 145
Thompson, Catherine, 139
Thompson, Robert, 139
Thornton manor, 132
Throckmorton, J., 151
Throckmorton, Margaret, 146
Throckmorton, Raphael, 146
Thrugar, Stephen, 122
Tichmersh, 110
Tilty Abbey, 101
Tompson, Morris, 80, 139, 140
Tooke, Walter, 110, 111, 112
Tottell, Richard, 118
Travers, Walter, 13
Traves, John, 115
Troughton, Richard, 20, 140, 141
Turner, Richard, 44
Tynwell, 31

V

Vale Royal, 88
Vaughan, William, 70
Vere, Lady Bridget, 34, 39
Vere, Edward de, 79
Vere, Elizabeth, 34
Vere, Lady Susan, 34
Vernon, Margaret, 144

W

Waad, Anne, 143
Waad, Anne Brown, 143
Waad, Armigil, 142
Waad, William, 20
Wakering, Edmund, 144
Wakering, Elizabeth, 144
Wakering, Gilbert, 19, 38, 60, 63, 143, 145
Wakering, John, 144
Wakering, Margaret, 144
Walker, Owen, 143
Walter, William, 26, 44, 69
Wardour, Chidioch, 131
Wards, Court of, 4, 8, 17, 19, 21, 34, 43, 54, 61, 62, 66, 73, 77, 80, 86, 100, 105, 111, 119, 120, 123, 124, 133, 134, 138, 141, 144, 149
Warwick, Earl of, 53
Waterhouse, Edward, 29
Welby, Adelard, 108
Wentworth, Lord, 146
Wentworth, Thomas, 33
Westminster School, 44
Westmoreland, Earl of, 73
Wheler, 129
White, Miles, 136
White, Nicholas, 29
Wickham, William, 112
Williams, George, 94
Williams, Richard, 71
Willis, Mr., 104
Willoughby, Lord, 147, 152
Willson, 117
Wimbledon, 25, 45, 77
Winchester, Marquess of, 4, 54
Windebank, Aaron, 17, 147
Windebank, Anne, 152
Windebank, Frances, 152
Windebank, Francis, 152, 154
Windebank, Margaret, 146, 149, 152, 154
Windebank, Mary, 152
Windebank, Mildred, 152
Windebank, Richard, 17, 146, 147, 152
Windebank, Thomas, Burghley's secretary, 17; estate of, 19; Queen's secretary, 20; letters from Allington, 28; grant to, 36; career of, 146-54; mentioned, 29, 72, 82, 127
Wingfield, Dorothy, 63
Wingfield, Elizabeth, 31, 76
Wingfield, Robert, 31, 63, 76, 77, 92
Witherwicke, Judith, 100
Wod, John, 29
Woodliff, William, 110
Woodrington, Hector, 74
Woodrington, Henry, 74
Wormley, 110
Wotton, Edward, 130
Wotton, Nicholas, 155
Wright, John, 58
Wymberley, Thomas, 140
Wyntershall, William, 41

Y

Yaxley, Francis, 20, 154
Yaxley, Richard, 155
Yaxley Hall, 155

Z

Zouch, Lord, 79

THE JAMES SPRUNT STUDIES IN HISTORY AND POLITICAL SCIENCE

No. 1. PERSONNEL OF THE CONVENTION OF 1861. By John Gilchrist McCormick }
LEGISLATION OF THE CONVENTION OF 1861. By Kemp P. Battle. } (Out of print.)

No. 2. THE CONGRESSIONAL CAREER OF NATHANIEL MACON. By Edwin Mood Wilson. (Out of print.)

No. 3. THE LETTERS OF NATHANIEL MACON, JOHN STEELE, AND WILLIAM BARRY GROVE, WITH NOTES By Kemp P. Battle. (Out of print.)

No. 4. LETTERS AND DOCUMENTS RELATING TO THE EARLY HISTORY OF THE LOWER CAPE FEAR, WITH INTRODUCTION AND NOTES. By Kemp P. Battle. (Out of print.)

No. 5. MINUTES OF THE KEHUKEY ASSOCIATION, WITH INTRODUCTION AND NOTES. By Kemp P. Battle. (Out of print.)

No. 6. DIARY OF A GEOLOGICAL TOUR BY ELISHA MITCHELL IN 1827 AND 1828, WITH INTRODUCTION AND NOTES. By Kemp P. Battle. (Out of print.)

No. 7. WILLIAM RICHARDSON DAVIE: A MEMOIR. By J. G. de Roulhac Hamilton.
LETTERS OF WILLIAM RICHARDSON DAVIE, WITH NOTES. By Kemp P. Battle.

No. 8. THE PROVINCIAL COUNCIL AND COMMITTEES OF SAFETY IN NORTH CAROLINA. By Bessie Lewis Whitaker.

VOL. 9, No. 1. THE SOCIETY FOR THE PROPAGATION OF THE GOSPEL IN THE PROVINCE OF NORTH CAROLINA. By D. D. Oliver.
CORRESPONDENCE OF JOHN RUST EATON. Edited by J. G. de Roulhac Hamilton.

VOL. 9, No. 2. FEDERALISM IN NORTH CAROLINA. By Henry M. Wagstaff.
LETTERS OF WILLIAM BARRY GROVE. Edited by Henry M. Wagstaff

VOL. 10, No. 1. BENJAMIN SHERWOOD HEDRICK. By J. G. de Roulhac Hamilton.

VOL. 10, No. 2. BARTLETT YANCEY. By George A. Anderson.
THE POLITICAL AND PROFESSIONAL CAREER OF BARTLETT YANCEY. By J. G. de Roulhac Hamilton.
LETTERS TO BARTLETT YANCEY.

VOL. 11, No. 1. COUNTY GOVERNMENT IN COLONIAL NORTH CAROLINA. By W. C. Guess.

VOL. 11, No. 2. THE NORTH CAROLINA CONSTITUTION OF 1776, AND ITS MAKERS. By Frank Nash.
THE GERMAN SETTLERS OF LINCOLN COUNTY AND WESTERN NORTH CAROLINA. By Joseph R. Nixon.

VOL. 12, No. 1. THE GOVERNOR, COUNCIL, AND ASSEMBLY IN ROYAL NORTH CAROLINA. By C. S. Cooke.
LAND TENURE IN PROPRIETARY NORTH CAROLINA. By L. N. Morgan.

VOL. 12, No. 2. THE NORTH CAROLINA INDIANS. By James Hall Rand.

VOL. 13, No. 1. THE GRANVILLE DISTRICT. By E. Merton Coulter.
THE NORTH CAROLINA COLONIAL BAR. By E. H. Alderman.

VOL. 13, No. 2. THE HARRINGTON LETTERS. Edited by Henry M. Wagstaff.

VOL. 14, No. 1. THE HARRIS LETTERS. Edited by Henry M. Wagstaff.

VOL. 14, No. 2. SOME COLONIAL HISTORY OF BEAUFORT COUNTY. By Francis H. Cooper.

VOL. 15, Nos. 1 and 2. PARTY POLITICS IN NORTH CAROLINA, 1835-1860. By J. G. de Roulhac Hamilton.

VOL. 16, No. 1. A COLONIAL HISTORY OF ROWAN COUNTY, NORTH CAROLINA. By S. J. Ervin. (Out of print.)

VOL. 16, No. 2. THE DIARY OF BARTLETT YANCEY MALONE. Edited by Wm. Whatley Pierson, Jr.
THE PROVINCIAL AGENTS OF NORTH CAROLINA. By Samuel James Ervin, Jr. (Out of print.)

VOL. 17, No. 1. THE FREE NEGRO IN NORTH CAROLINA. By Rosser Howard Taylor.
SOME COLONIAL HISTORY OF CRAVEN COUNTY, NORTH CAROLINA. By Francis H. Cooper.

VOL. 17, No. 2. JOURNAL OF A TOUR OF NORTH CAROLINA BY WILLIAM ATTMORE, 1787. Edited by Lida Tunstall Rodman. (Out of print.)

VOL. 18, Nos. 1 and 2. SLAVEHOLDING IN NORTH CAROLINA: AN ECONOMIC VIEW. By Rosser Howard Taylor. (Out of print.)

VOL. 19, No. 1. PRESENT STATUS OF MODERN EUROPEAN HISTORY IN THE UNITED STATES. By Chester Penn Higby.

VOL. 19, No. 2. STUDIES IN HISPANIC-AMERICAN HISTORY. Edited by William Whatley Pierson, Jr.

VOL. 20, No. 1. NORTH CAROLINA NEWSPAPERS BEFORE 1790. By Charles Christopher Crittenden.

THE JAMES SPRUNT STUDIES IN HISTORY AND POLITICAL SCIENCE

Vol. 20, No. 2. THE JAMES A. GRAHAM PAPERS, 1861-1884. Edited by Henry M. Wagstaff.

Vol. 21, Nos. 1 and 2. THE DEMOCRATIC PARTY IN ANTE-BELLUM NORTH CAROLINA, 1835-1861. By Clarence Clifford Norton.

Vol. 22, Nos. 1 and 2. MINUTES OF THE NORTH CAROLINA MANUMISSION SOCIETY 1816-1834. Edited by Henry M. Wagstaff.

Vol. 23, No. 1. THE PRESIDENTIAL ELECTION OF 1824 IN NORTH CAROLINA. By Albert Ray Newsome.

Vol. 23, No. 2. THE SECESSION MOVEMENT IN NORTH CAROLINA. By Joseph Carlyle Sitterson.

Vol. 24, No. 1. JEFFERSONIAN DEMOCRACY IN SOUTH CAROLINA. By John Harold Wolfe.

Vol. 24, No. 2. GUIDE TO THE MANUSCRIPTS IN THE SOUTHERN HISTORICAL COLLECTION OF THE UNIVERSITY OF NORTH CAROLINA.

Vol. 25, No. 1. NORTH CAROLINA BOUNDARY DISPUTES INVOLVING HER SOUTHERN LINE. By Marvin L. Skaggs.

Vol. 25, No. 2. ANTE-BELLUM SOUTH CAROLINA: A SOCIAL AND CULTURAL HISTORY. By Rosser H. Taylor.

Vol. 26, No. 1. THE PROHIBITION MOVEMENT IN ALABAMA, 1702 TO 1943. By James Benson Sellers.

VOLUME 27. PROHIBITION IN NORTH CAROLINA, 1715-1945. By Daniel Jay Whitener.

VOLUME 28. THE NEGRO IN MISSISSIPPI, 1865-1890. By Vernon Lane Wharton. (Out of print.

VOLUME 29. THE WHIG PARTY IN GEORGIA, 1825-1853. By Paul Murray.

VOLUME 30. THE SOUTH IN ACTION: A SECTIONAL CRUSADE AGAINST FREIGHT RATE DISCRIMINATION. By Robert A. Lively.

VOLUME 31. ESSAYS IN SOUTHERN HISTORY. Edited by Fletcher Melvin Green.

VOLUME 32. SOUTH CAROLINA GOES TO WAR. By Charles Edward Cauthen. (Out of print.)

VOLUME 33. REVOLUTIONARY JUSTICE: A STUDY OF THE ORGANIZATION, PERSONNEL, AND PROCEDURE OF THE PARIS TRIBUNAL, 1793-1795. By James Logan Godfrey.

VOLUME 34. THE POLITICAL LIBERALISM OF THE NEW YORK *Nation*, 1865-1932. By Alan Pendleton Grimes.

VOLUME 35. WAR LABOR BOARDS IN THE FIELD. By Allan R. Richards.

VOLUME 36. THE RALEIGH REGISTER, 1799-1863. By Robert Neal Elliott, Jr.

VOLUME 37. CONSTITUTIONAL DEVELOPMENT IN ALABAMA, 1798-1901: A STUDY IN POLITICS, THE NEGRO AND SECTIONALISM. By Malcolm Cook McMillan. (Out of print.)

VOLUME 38. AGRICULTURAL DEVELOPMENTS IN NORTH CAROLINA, 1783-1860. By Cornelius Oliver Cathey.

VOLUME 39. STUDIES IN SOUTHERN HISTORY. Edited by J. Carlyle Sitterson.

VOLUME 40. ANDREW JACKSON AND NORTH CAROLINA POLITICS. By William S. Hoffmann.

VOLUME 41. PHARAONIC POLICIES AND ADMINISTRATION. By Mary Francis Gyles.

VOLUME 42. JACKSONIAN DEMOCRACY IN MISSISSIPPI. By Edwin Arthur Miles.

VOLUME 43. FERRY HILL PLANTATION JOURNAL, JANUARY 4, 1838-JANUARY 15, 1839. Edited by Fletcher Melvin Green.

VOLUME 44. DEMOCRATIC PARTY DISSENSION IN NORTH CAROLINA, 1928-1936. By Elmer L. Puryear.

VOLUME 45. POLITICAL FACTIONS IN ALEPPO, 1760-1826. By Herbert L. Bodman, Jr.

VOLUME 46. LAUDATORES TEMPORIS ACTI: Studies in Memory of Wallace Everett Caldwell, Professor of History at the University of North Carolina, by His Friends and Students. Edited by Mary Francis Gyles and Eugene Wood Davis.

VOLUME 47. LEGAL ASPECTS OF CONSCRIPTION AND EXEMPTION IN NORTH CAROLINA, 1861-1865. By Memory F. Mitchell.

VOLUME 48. CLASS PRIVILEGE AND ECONOMIC DEVELOPMENT: THE CONSULADO DE COMERCIO OF GUATEMALA, 1793-1871. BY RALPH LEE WOODWARD, JR.

VOLUME 49. THE PEACE PROPHETS: AMERICAN PACIFIST THOUGHT, 1919-1941. BY JOHN K. NELSON.

VOLUME 50. THE RECRUITMENT OF CANDIDATES IN MENDOZA PROVINCE, ARGENTINA. By Richard Robert Strout.

www.ingramcontent.com/pod-product-compliance
Lightning Source LLC
Chambersburg PA
CBHW021406290426

44108CB00010B/417